What Were the Crusades?

What Were the Crusades?

JONATHAN RILEY-SMITH

MACMILLAN

First published 1977
Reprinted 1978, 1985, 1989

Published by
MACMILLAN EDUCATION LTD
Houndmills, Basingstoke, Hampshire RG21 2XS
and London
Companies and representatives
throughout the world

Printed in Hong Kong

ISBN 0-333-21373-4

The illustration on the cover depicts Christ leading crusader knights, from an early-fourteenth-century MS. (BM Royal 19 B 15, folio 37a). Reproduced by permission of the British Library Board.

Contents

Preface

In this book I have put down thoughts that have developed in over a decade of lecturing to and supervising students at the universities of St Andrews and Cambridge, so my first expression of thanks must be to them, especially Dr Bruce Beebe, whose unpublished thesis on King Edward I of England and the crusades is a good study of an aspect of the movement in the late thirteenth century. I am glad to have the chance of stating again how much I appreciate the wise advice of Dr R. C. Smail, my *magister*, who read the book in typescript, as did my wife, whose reactions as a 'general reader' have been of great value to me. I am, as always, grateful to her and to my children for providing the kind of environment in which I find it easy to work.

Cambridge   J. S. C. R.-S.

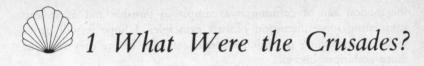# 1 *What Were the Crusades?*

THE crusading movement was one of the great forces in our history. Fought on a vast scale, in terms of both geography and the numbers of men involved, the crusades dominated the thoughts and feelings of western Europeans between 1095 and 1400 so profoundly that there was scarcely a writer on contemporary affairs who did not at some point refer to one of them or to the fate of the states established in their wake on the eastern shores of the Mediterranean, in Spain and along the Baltic coast. They still had some appeal as late as the eighteenth century. Even today it is hard to be indifferent to their history: they were launched in support of a cause which can be portrayed with equal force as the most noble and the most ignoble, and over the centuries men have turned to them for inspiration or as an object lesson in human corruptibility. In modern times the French have seen them as the first of their nation's colonial enterprises; in Palestine the British in 1917 and the Israelis in the last few decades have felt themselves to be the inheritors of their traditions; and a movement in the modern Christian Churches, consisting of the theologians of Liberation and the activists of the new Left, expresses, without seeming to realise the fact, some of the ideas of the crusading apologists. For good or ill the crusades introduced new forces into the politics of the eastern Mediterranean region which were to last for over 600 years and they helped to foster elements in Latin Christianity which are now seen as integral to it.

Yet, after nearly a millenium of interest and centuries of academic study, very few people have any clear idea of what a crusade was. A recent historian, Professor H. E. Mayer, has drawn attention to the extraordinary way in which a great deal of research is going on into the subject without there being any commonly agreed starting-point and he has appealed for 'an unambiguous, lucid and generally accepted definition of the term "crusade" '. In writing this little book I have had the modest aim of defining it as simply as possible and of at least stimulating some discussion of first principles. I hope it will prove useful as something to which students can turn before they read the more ambitious histories.

Definition is by no means easy. One cannot help wondering how to avoid gross over-simplification when trying to describe something which dominated Europe for so long. There are, moreover, very few clear descriptions to be found in medieval writings and it has been suggested recently that the fragmentary treatment given to the subject by canon lawyers and theologians is evidence for their reluctance to link the Church too positively to violence: it has never been easy for Christian writers to reconcile Christ's statements on force with the apparent necessity for order and stability in this world. There was no one term consistently used to describe the crusade or its participants. Besides the various vernacular words that appeared in the thirteenth century, like *croiserie* in French and English, it could be called a pilgrimage (*iter* or *peregrinatio*), a holy war (*bellum sacrum* or *guerre sainte*), a passage or general passage (*passagium generale*), an expedition of the Cross (*expeditio crucis*) or the business of Jesus Christ (*negotium Jhesu Christi*): it is worth noticing how many of these terms were euphemisms. Only in the late twelfth century did the technical word *crucesignati*, signed with the Cross, come to be used of crusaders. At first they had simply been referred to as pilgrims and so they continued for centuries to be called, especially if they were campaigning to the East. But it is some comfort to recall that historians of feudalism have faced up to similar problems. They have not been deterred from making serious attempts to define a very important political, economic and social system which was subject to regional variations, lasted a long time and for which there was no concise contemporary term. Not surprisingly it is possible to describe feudalism in all sorts of different ways, but the important thing is that the attempts have been made and many of them have added greatly to our understanding of the Middle Ages.

Contemporaries, of course, knew perfectly well what a crusade was. How did they recognise one? In the writings of chroniclers, apologists and canon lawyers and in the wording of the phrases used by those who drew up papal encyclicals we can perceive the signs that informed the faithful that a crusade was being preached. First the participants, or some of them, were called upon to take the Cross, which is to say that they were to make a vow to join a military expedition with defined aims. The vow itself was of a special kind, and I shall have something to say about it later, but for the moment what is relevant is that at some kind of formal, public ceremony, which varied from place to place, men and women, rich and poor, priests and laymen, made a voluntary promise to take part in the campaign. We must, however, never think of a crusade as containing only crusaders, for their numbers, especially in some of the thirteenth-century expeditions, were often quite small: there were always many hangers-on and camp followers attached to an army while it became common for large numbers of professional soldiers to be employed and even for crusaders to travel East with sums of money with which to buy mercenaries. By the thirteenth century, moreover, many who took the Cross never actually departed on campaign. Practising what was known as substitution or redemption, which I will describe later, they sent another in their place or contributed sums of money instead of going, thus helping to finance an expedition. It is also important to note that not all crusades were the large, elaborately organised affairs which have rather inaccurately been given numbers by historians. They could be very small or made up of scattered bands of men departing at different times over several years: in certain periods, the 1170s or the later thirteenth century, much crusading took this form. The second sign that a crusade was being prepared was that those taking the Cross were answering a call that could only be made by the pope. Thirdly, in consequence of their vows and the performance of the actions promised the crusaders gained certain well-known privileges. These were subject to development and new rights were added to those originally granted, but we may say that all crusaders were assured that their families, interests and assets would be protected in their absence and that in the Indulgence they enjoyed a major spiritual privilege. The Indulgence could only be granted by the pope or his agents and it was references to it in papal encyclicals that really informed people that a crusade was being promoted.

A striking feature of the Indulgences granted to the participants in some of the military campaigns that took place in western Europe was that they were specifically associated with those given to crusaders going to recover Jerusalem or defend the Holy Land.

> We concede to all fighting firmly in this expedition the same remission of sins which we have given to the defenders of the Eastern Church. (Pope Calixtus II in 1123 concerning Spain)

To all those who do not receive the same Cross of Jerusalem and determine to go against the Slavs and remain in that expedition we concede... that remission of sins which our predecessor Pope Urban of happy memory instituted for those going to Jerusalem.   (Pope Eugenius III in 1147 concerning Germany)

We wish that those men ... who take up arms to fight against the perfidious (the heretics) should enjoy that remission of sins which we have granted to those who labour in aid of the Holy Land.   (Pope Innocent III in 1207, concerning the war against the Albigensians)

We grant the Indulgence ... to all those who undertake this labour personally or at their expense, and to those who do not personally participate but send suitable warriors at their own expense, according to their means and quality, and also to those who personally assume this burden at another's expense, and we wish them to enjoy that privilege and immunity which were conceded in the general council to those aiding the Holy Land.   (Pope Innocent IV in 1246, proclaiming war against the Emperor Frederick II)

We have thought it worthy to concede those Indulgences which in similar cases were accustomed to be given by the Holy See to those going to the aid of the Holy Land.   (Pope John XXII in 1326, concerning Spain)

Reading these and other grants of the Indulgence, it is clear that to the papal *Curia* many of the expeditions in Spain, along the shores of the Baltic, against heretics and schismatics and even against lay powers in Western Europe were to be regarded as belonging to the same species as crusades to the East. This is confirmed in the writings of the great canon lawyer Hostiensis (d.1271) and in the thirteenth-century practice of commutation, by which a man could change the terms of a vow made, say, to help the Holy Land into participation in a European campaign. It is quite impossible to agree with those historians who have accepted as crusades only the expeditions destined for Jerusalem or sent to the aid of Latin Palestine: we cannot ignore the fact that medieval men had a broader view of what they were than that. But we also have to take into account a number of campaigns authorised by the popes but waged by men who, although they had taken the Cross and were assured protection, enjoyed Indulgences not specifically equated with those given to the defenders of the East. Hostiensis seems to have considered that these were not true crusades and we can do little else but follow him, even though it should be stressed that the absence of a reference to the Holy Land in a papal encyclical is not certain evidence that no equation with the crusades to Palestine was intended – the Livonian Crusade of 1199 was certainly linked in the minds of contemporaries to those in the East, even though this was not made clear in the surviving authorisation of Pope Innocent III. And even in cases in which a distinction was the papal *Curia's* intention, it is hard to know how to categorise such expeditions, since the participants had taken the Cross and enjoyed protection.

To contemporaries a crusade was an expedition authorised by the pope, the leading participants in which took vows and consequently enjoyed the privileges of protection at home and the Indulgence, which, when the campaign was not destined for the East, was expressly equated with that granted to crusaders to the Holy Land. This enables us to identify what was regarded as a crusade, but it cannot take us much further. We can only find out what qualified an expedition for papal authorisation of this particular kind, allowing the crusaders taking part to make vows and enjoy the privileges, by examining the features common to those we have recognised as crusades. They were, of course, primarily wars, even though they might be said to have transcended war in that at times they were seen by their apologists as instruments of peace in the West, while the expeditions to the East, and many of those in the West as well, were viewed as pilgrimages. But all crusades were expected to conform to the principles underlying and to a certain extent limiting the bearing of arms by Christians and a useful approach, therefore, is to look at them against the background of Christian ideas on war.

If there are occasions on which war is justifiable, and since the early fifth century many have believed that there are such occasions, then we must admit that in certain circumstances the Fifth Commandment, enshrining a divine prohibition against homicide, can be set aside. But what are those circumstances? Traditionally, there have been two distinct answers to this question among those Christians who are not pacifists. The first, the most commonly held and, curiously, the only one really discussed by moral theologians today, is usually called the theory of the Just War. Its premise is that violence is always sinful, but it recognises that, in intolerable conditions and provided that it is subject to stringent rules, war may be condoned by God. Early in the fifth century St Augustine of Hippo, the first and still possibly the most sophisticated Christian thinker on this matter, tried to define the criteria to which war must accord before it could be considered to be justifiable. These were later reduced, and greatly simplified, by theologians and canon lawyers to three. First, the war must have a just cause (*causa justa*) and normally such a cause could only be past or present aggression or injurious action by another. Secondly, it must rest on what was known as the authority of the prince (*auctoritas principis*). In other words it must be proclaimed by legitimate authority, usually, of course, secular, although we will see that it was an ecclesiastic with powers encompassing the authorisation of war who proclaimed a crusade. Five centuries before the crusades these first two criteria had been summed up by Isidore of Seville in a sentence which passed into the collections of canon law: 'That war is lawful and just which is waged upon command in order to recover property or to repel attack.' The third criterion was known as right intention (*intentio recta*). Each of the participants ought to have pure motives and war must be the only apparently practicable means of achieving the justifiable purpose for which it was to be fought.

The crusades, however, were expressions of another concept, that of Holy War, in which force of arms is regarded as being not merely justifiable and condoned by God, but positively sanctioned by him. The subject has not had the attention from theologians and historians that it deserves, but a starting point for discussion is that all Christian writers who accept the notion of violence, whether justifiable or sacred, recognise that it has not only a negative but also a positive side to it. The waging of war is a political act, necessitated by events in this world, and its positive aspect is therefore related to the needs of an imperfect natural order; it may, for instance, have the aim of restoring that order or the *status quo*. Arguments for Just War go no further than that. But the protagonists of Holy War, who invariably associate God intimately with some political structure or course of political events in this world, are led to believe that violence in support of that political structure advances his intentions for mankind. War becomes more than a necessary but unpleasant reaction to injustice or aggression; it is a positive step in accordance with God's wishes, since it is fought on behalf of a polity which itself is the product of his will. Holy Wars can only be waged, as the great theologian Jacques Maritain recognised

forty years ago, when the temporal order and God's intentions become
inextricably bound up with one another.

But a Holy War remains a Christian war and the conviction that it is
holy does not exempt it from the limitations placed by traditional
Christian thought on the use of violence. In particular, it must conform
to the criteria of the just cause, the authority of the prince and right intention. Of course it would be absurd to suppose that all crusades had
causes that reputable theologians would consider to be just or that all
crusaders had pure motives, but aberrations do not invalidate what a
crusade ought to have been, although studies of such matters certainly
cast light on the practical application of the crusading ideal. Apologists
were careful to write of the Indulgence being enjoyed only by those
whose motives could not be impugned and went to great lengths to
show how campaigns were justly caused, important above all because
the crusaders were volunteers, not conscripts, and, like most men,
would not generally participate in something obviously unjustifiable.
This book is concerned with definition, not with judgements on the
motives of individual crusaders or the worth of individual campaigns.

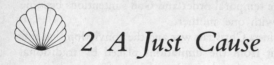 ## 2 A Just Cause

A Just Cause for War

By the middle of the thirteenth century Christian writers were generally in agreement that the just cause for a war must be defensive and their views prevail today. It is just to defend one's country, laws and traditional way of life, just to try to recover property unlawfully taken by another, perhaps even just to enforce by physical means a properly delivered judicial sentence. It is not just to wage a war of aggrandisement or of conversion. This principle, we shall see, applied to the crusade no less than to any war, but in the first century of the movement, when the just cause was still a subject of discussion, other justifications for crusading were being put forward. St Augustine's definition of a Just War, that it avenged injuries, presupposed a much less passive attitude on the part of the just than was later to be acceptable, especially in the notion of vengeance, which haunted canon lawyers until c. 1200, after which it seems gradually to have been dropped, and in a wide interpretation of the injuries to be avenged, which could include any violation of righteousness, God's laws or Christian doctrine. As late as the middle of the thirteenth century Hostiensis seems to have believed that Christendom had an intrinsic right to extend its sovereignty over all those who did not recognise the rule of the Roman Church or Roman Empire. Early on, moreover, there seems to have been some confusion as to whether or not the crusade could be waged as a war of conversion and at the time of the First Crusade some came perilously near to promoting it as such. One chronicler, Robert the Monk, made Pope Urban II at Clermont remind his audience of Charlemagne and Louis the Pious and other Frankish kings 'who destroyed the kingdoms of the pagans and incorporated them within the boundaries of Holy Church'. And, in a letter sent to the pope in 1098, after they had taken Antioch in Syria, the leaders of the crusade wrote that they had fought against Turks and pagans but not against heretics and begged Urban to come himself to eradicate all heresies. The waging of a missionary war against the heathen, which had long been an element in German thought, was a prominent theme in 1147, during the preparations for a campaign against the pagans in north-eastern Europe. The papal encyclical *Divina dispensatione,* which authorised this German crusade, emphasised conversions, in this echoing St Bernard, responsible above all for the pope's support, who in his letters utterly forbade any truce with the pagans 'until such time as, with God's help, they shall be either converted or wiped out'. It should be stressed that nowhere in *Divina dispensatione* did Pope Eugenius III explicitly justify the crusade as a war of conversion and that St Bernard's approach was not as simple as the quotation given above would suggest: to him the pagans directly threatened Christendom and it was only because there was no alternative to the use of physical force that they must be crushed if they would not be converted. But a close association between missions and war was always a feature of the north European crusades and it was in connection with one of them that a pope made the most outspoken reference of all. In 1209 Innocent III encouraged the King of Denmark to take the Cross and share in the Indulgence granted to German crusaders 'to extirpate the error of paganism and spread the frontiers of the Christian faith'. This was an extraordinary statement, coming as it did from one of the greatest canon lawyers and the leading apologist for the crusading movement among the medieval popes, even though the letter did contain a reference to the persecution of Christian preachers by the heathen and one historian has considered that it was in accord with more conventional ideas. It may have been a momentary aberration on Innocent's part or on that of some clerk in his *Curia,* but it is not the only curious pronouncement that he made on the crusades. In 1201 he decreed that such was the need of the Holy Land that a man could take the Cross without his wife's assent. This ran counter to the traditional principles of canon law on the binding and enduring consequences of the marriage contract: that no one could unilaterally refuse his partner marital rights without that partner's consent. It was an elementary mistake and later canon lawyers were careful to limit the exception to the sole case of the interests of the Holy Land. Innocent's statements to the King of Denmark and on a crusader's wife can perhaps only be understood in terms of his obsession with the crusading movement, an obsession unequalled in any pope save Gregory X, which led him to preach or authorise no fewer than six crusades. It is not surprising that he overstepped the mark at times.

The opinions that vengeance for such injuries as the mere denial of the Christian faith or the refusal to accept Christian government, and the opportunity for conversion by force constituted just causes, were those of minorities and were never held by most reputable Christian thinkers, among whom it was generally agreed that non-Christians could not be made to accept baptism nor could they be physically attacked simply because they were of a different faith – although a distinction was drawn between Jews and Muslims, against the last of whom force might be used only because they were already persecuting Christians. The undercurrent of belief in the missionary crusade seems to have weakened when the climate of opinion began to change around 1200: the Church was now entering the Thomist age, with its emphasis on the rights of the unconverted and on persuasion by means of reason. In the middle of the thirteenth century Pope Innocent IV authoritatively restated the conventional views. He asserted that infidels had rights in natural law and that a war of conversion was illegitimate; but he also argued that the Holy Land was rightfully Christian property, for it had been consecrated by the presence of Christ and conquered by the Roman, later to be the Christian, Empire in a Just War. As representative of Christ and heir of the emperors, the pope could reassert Christian jurisdiction in Palestine and the crusades to the East were merely recovering territory that rightfully belonged to Christians. A Just War, moreover, could be launched to repel unjust damage and as a punishment for sins; so the pope could proclaim a crusade against a pagan ruler, not because he was pagan but because he posed a threat to Christians or had sinned by, for instance, refusing to allow Christian missionaries to operate in his territories. Innocent's influence can be seen working particularly clearly in the writings of Hostiensis and in a treatise written by Humbert of Romans for Pope Gregory X in the early 1270s. Humbert set out to answer those who said that Christians should never take the initiative but were justified only in defending themselves when the Muslims launched an attack upon them. He replied that the Muslims were dangerous and sought whenever they could to harm Christianity; they had seized lands once in the possession of Christians and, moreover, they so openly consented to iniquity that no Christian could ever be at peace with them without incurring blame. The invasion of their lands was therefore justified and he argued for attacks upon them to weaken their power, to reintroduce the Christian faith in those lands from which it had been driven out and to express intolerance of sin. But he stressed that the crusade was not a war of aggression because its aim was the recovery of what had been Christian territory.

It has been suggested recently that it was only with Pope Innocent IV that the crusades, as Holy Wars, were truly made subject to the laws governing Just Wars. But in fact the traditional criteria for Just Wars, even if under discussion, had weighed heavily with apologists from the start. It is striking how consistently propaganda on behalf of the crusades — whether to the East or in Spain, along the shores of the Baltic, against heretics or Christian lay powers — justified them, and always had justified them, in terms of the recovery of property or of defence against aggression.

Crusades to the Near East

The just cause was in the mind of Pope Urban II when he preached the First Crusade. In the first week of March 1095 a council of bishops from France, Italy and Germany was in session at Piacenza. To it came an embassy from the Byzantine emperor Alexius I Comnenus appealing to the pope to encourage westerners to help defend the eastern Church against the Turks, who had swept through Asia Minor and had almost reached Constantinople. Urban replied with a sermon in which he urged men to help the emperor. His itinerary after Piacenza suggests that he was thinking of raising a small army to be sent to the East, perhaps under the captaincy of Count Raymond of Toulouse who had already been thought of by Pope Gregory VII for an expedition overseas, and certainly under the spiritual leadership of Adhémar of Monteil, Bishop of Le Puy, who may once have pilgrimaged to Jerusalem. After about a month at Piacenza Urban passed through northern Italy and on to France, whence he had come, accompanied by an impressive entourage which included four cardinals, two archbishops, several bishops and the great papal chancellor John of Gaeta, to favour the monastery of Cluny, where he had been prior, and to supervise the reform of the French Church. At Le Puy, the centre of Adhémar of Monteil's diocese, he issued a call to a council to be held at Clermont. By the end of August he was at S. Gilles, a favourite residence of Count Raymond of Toulouse, whom he may have met, for it seems that immediately after Urban had preached the crusade at

Clermont and far too soon for the news to have travelled south the count's envoys arrived to commit their master to the Cross. From S. Gilles the pope travelled slowly up the Rhône valley to Cluny, which he reached on about 18 October, staying at the monastery until the end of the month. On 14 November he was at Clermont and on the 18th the council opened. On the 27th, after the ecclesiastical business was finished, Urban preached the First Crusade to great crowds gathered outside the city in the open air and in a dramatic and obviously prearranged gesture Adhémar came forward first to take the Cross and to be appointed the pope's own representative in the army. Urban spent the eight months after Clermont preaching the Cross in western and southern France, but it soon became clear that the response to his call was very great, greater perhaps than he had anticipated. Late in December he wrote to Flanders, inviting its inhabitants to join. Early in February 1096 he commissioned two men to preach on his behalf in the Loire valley and in Normandy and England. From Pavia in September he wrote to those taking the Cross in Bologna and from Cremona in October he forbade the monks of Vallombrosa to participate.

It is hard now to fathom his mind. There survive reports of his sermon and his addresses to the clergy at Clermont written by four men who were probably present, but none was verbatim and all were written in the light of the success of the First Crusade. The surviving record of what the council of Clermont had to say on the crusade is based on notes taken by a bishop who was there. We have only three letters directly on the subject from Urban himself, the first written a month after the council. A slight inconsistency in these, a stress on the liberation of the eastern Churches and then a direct reference to the journey to Jerusalem, led to the suggestion, which has since become orthodox opinion, that, although the pope put forward Jerusalem as a goal to link the crusade with pilgrimages and to appeal to his listeners, his real purpose was the more limited one of fraternally answering the request of the Byzantine emperor for aid in the hope of bringing the Latin and Greek Churches closer to one another; it was his audience who took up the idea of the road to Jerusalem, originally a secondary, devotional aim, and fixed on it so that even before the crusade departed, the Holy City had become the primary objective. This interpretation has recently been challenged and it has been argued convincingly, on the evidence of chronicles and charters connected with the pope's preaching tour in France, that, although aid to the eastern

Christians and the union of the Churches were also aims, Jerusalem was uppermost in his mind from the start: the name of Jerusalem was far too potent to be used lightly, particularly by a reformer and ex-Cluniac like Urban. But whatever the uncertainty concerning the thoughts behind the preaching of the First Crusade there can be no doubts about its justification: there constantly recur in the sources the ideas of liberation (another word for recovery) and defence. The reports of Urban's sermons made him speak powerfully on the liberation of Jerusalem or the defence of the eastern Church; liberation is a theme of the canon of the council of Clermont on the crusade and of Urban's letters; and it is to be found in contemporary chronicles; an overwhelming weight of evidence suggests that the pope was proposing a war of reconquest, not of conquest.

With the taking of the Holy Land, of course, the justification for crusades to Palestine changed. The land consecrated by the presence of Christ was now in Christian hands and must be defended. Pope Eugenius III stressed this in 1145 and his words were echoed in later papal letters.

> By the grace of God and the zeal of your fathers, who strove to defend them over the years and to spread Christianity among the peoples in the area, these places have been held by Christians until now and other cities have courageously been taken from the infidel. . . .
>
> It will be seen as a great token of nobility and uprightness if those things which the efforts of your fathers acquired are vigorously defended by you, the sons. But if, God forbid, it comes to pass differently, then the bravery of the fathers will be shown to have diminished in the sons.

The city of Jerusalem was lost to Saladin in 1187 and was to be held by the Christians again only from 1229 to 1244. Of course its recapture came to be called for, although the burden of propaganda naturally rested on the need to defend what was left of the European settlement in the Holy Land. Even the invasion of Egypt, attempted in 1218 and 1249 and proposed at other times, was seen as contributing to the well-being of Latin Palestine. One chronicler made King John of Jerusalem in 1218 advise the invasion of Egypt to a council-of-war of the Fifth Crusade:

for if we could take one of these cities [of Alexandra and Damietta] it is my opinion that by the use of it we could recover all of this [Holy] land if we wanted to surrender it in exchange.

Since Egypt had been part of the Christian Roman Empire its conquest could also be justified as the recovery of a once Christian land.

Crusades in Spain

For a long time there had been wars against the Moors in Spain when Pope Urban II dissuaded Spaniards from joining the First Crusade and gave them the right to an Indulgence, establishing an analogy between the reconquests of the peninsula and Palestine. In 1100 and 1101 his successor Paschal II also forbade Spaniards to go to the Holy Land and granted an Indulgence to those who stayed behind to fight: he did not want military success against the Moors jeopardised by the desertion of warriors. From 1098 onwards the Indulgences given to Spaniards were often equated with those granted to crusaders to Jerusalem and in 1123 the bishops at the First Lateran Council found it possible to refer to those who took the Cross either for Jerusalem or for Spain, as though both oaths were of the same sort. By the time of the Second Crusade a contemporary could write of the Spanish army as being part of one great host fighting on several fronts of Christendom.

Spain had once been Christian land, but great parts of it were subject to infidels, who threatened the faithful in the North, and the Spanish crusades, like those to the East, were consistently portrayed as being defensive. In 1122 the foundation of the confraternity of Zaragoza was made 'for the defence of Christians and the oppression of Muslims and the liberty of Holy Church'.

Crusades in North-eastern Europe

In 1147, at the time when the Second Crusade was being prepared, some German crusaders, mainly Saxons, wanted to campaign not in the Orient but against the Slavs across the river Elbe. St Bernard, who was in charge of the preaching of the Cross, agreed, perhaps because he saw in Germany similarities to Spain. He seems to have acted on his own

initiative, only informing Pope Eugenius afterwards, but the pope con-
curred and a papal encyclical, *Divina dispensatione,* established the German crusade on the same lines as those in Spain and Palestine.
North-eastern Europe had never been part of the Christian Empire and
campaigning there could not be justified as the reconquest of Christian
land. And it is difficult nowadays to envisage much of a threat being
posed to Christendom by the backward Slav peoples: indeed at the
time relations with them were getting better. But although there was,
and always had been, an important missionary element in the German
expeditions against their neighbours, care was also taken to justify them
as defensive: *dilatio* and *defensio,* expansion and defence, went hand in
hand. A good example of this can be found in a letter in which Pope
Innocent III authorised the Livonian Crusade in 1199. To Innocent
there had been persecution of Christian converts in Livonia by their
pagan neighbours. An army must therefore be raised 'in defence of the
Christians in those parts' and protection was promised to all who went
'to defend the Church of Livonia'.

Crusades against Schismatics and Heretics

Since very early times, the use of force against heretics had been considered justified. The canonist Gratian in *c.* 1140 had laid the foundations that were to enable the Church itself, rather than secular
powers, to authorise such violence, but it was the Third Lateran Council in 1179 which first came near to proposing the launching of a
crusade against heretics. The decrees of the council enjoined all the
faithful for the remission of their sins to fight heresy and defend
Christendom against it. It referred to such a war as a just labour, and
stated that those taking part were to receive an Indulgence (although
not automatically the plenary Indulgence) and were to be protected
'just like those who visit the Holy Sepulchre'. One result of the new
decree was an extraordinary little expedition against the Albigensians
under a papal legate early in the 1180s. But the crusade can be seen
operating more certainly, with reference to schismatics, during the ill-
fated Fourth Crusade which, originally aimed at either Palestine or
Egypt, ended by taking the Christian city of Constantinople. Already
in 1203, as the expedition veered inexorably off course, there was a section of the army which was arguing for an invasion of the Greek Empire 'because it is not subject to the Holy See and because the emperor

of Constantinople usurped the imperial throne, having deposed and even blinded his brother'.

These justifications were again put forward in April 1204 when, after the emperors placed on the Byzantine throne by the western leaders had been murdered in a *coup d'état* inside Constantinople, the army was preparing for its final assault on the city. The Latin clergy preached sermons justifying the attack, and the burden of what they had to say was reported in almost identical passages by two of the eye-witnesses whose accounts have come down to us, Geoffrey of Villehardouin and Robert of Clari. The clergy

> showed to the barons and the pilgrims that he who was guilty of such a murder [of the emperors] had no right to hold land and all those who had consented were abettors of the murder; and beyond all this that they had withdrawn themselves from obedience to Rome. 'For which reasons we tell you,' said the clergy, 'that this war is lawful and just and that if you have a right intention to conquer this land and bring it into obedience to Rome all those who die after confession shall enjoy the Indulgence granted by the pope'.

It is interesting to find here an explicit reference to the crusade conforming to the criteria for a Just War. One of the arguments, it will be noted, was that political events in Constantinople constituted a sin, an offence which the crusade could punish – in 1203 Pope Innocent had commented that such things might be so but it was not for the crusaders to judge them nor had they assumed the Cross to vindicate this injury. The other argument was, as we should expect, that the Greeks were in schism, although the defensive nature of the operation was implicit rather than explicit. The same sort of reasoning can be perceived in Innocent's proclamation of the Albigensian Crusade. The date at which this crusade came into being is the subject of argument – perhaps it was as late as October 1208 – but already in 1204 the pope had written to the King of France encouraging him to take up arms in defence of the Church against the heretics and offering the same Indulgence as that granted to those who aided the Holy Land. In November 1207 he referred to the horrors of and threat from heresy which, he averred, must be dealt with as a doctor knifes a wound and, writing after the assassination of the papal legate, Peter of Castelnau, on 14 January 1208, he called on Philip of France to take up the shield of protection of the Church. In 1215 the Fourth Lateran Council repeated that the crusaders had the right to enjoy the same Indulgence as that given to defenders of the Holy Land. Similar justifications can be found on other occasions, for instance in the 1230s, when a crusade was launched in north Germany against the Stedinga peasants, who were regarded as heretics, and in the 1290s, when Pope Boniface VIII preached the Cross against the Colonnas, whom he portrayed as schismatics. However unattractive such reasoning may now appear to us, the crusades against heretics and schismatics were believed to be defensive. To Pope Innocent III in 1208 heretics were as bad as Muslims: they were a threat to Christendom, a threat, as Hostiensis put it, to catholic unity which was in fact more dangerous than that to the Holy Land.

Crusades against Lay Powers in the West

It has often been argued, and indeed was said by some in the thirteenth century, that the least justifiable crusades were those launched against secular opponents of the papacy in western Europe. But, again, they were justified in the traditional way; Hostiensis, indeed, was to suggest that there were no differences between the 'disobedient' and schismatics and heretics. To some historians the original 'political crusade' was that led in 1106 by Bohemond of Antioch against the Greeks, but as far as we can tell it was preached in terms of an expedition to Jerusalem, and it is more likely that the first true crusade against a Christian layman was that proclaimed by Innocent III against Markward of Anweiler. Markward was one of the lieutenants of the Emperor Henry VI, who, after the emperor's death, tried to keep control of the March of Ancona and later to seize the regency of the Kingdom of Sicily, harassing that set up by the pope for Henry's young son Frederick II. Innocent, who was preparing the Fourth Crusade, responded by preaching the Cross against Markward whom he claimed was in practice allied to the Muslims.

> We concede to all who fight the violence of Markward and his men the same remission of sins that we concede to all who go against the perfidy of the Muslims in defence of the eastern provinces, because through him aid to the Holy Land is impeded.

The pope was, in fact, proclaiming one crusade in support of another that was being prepared: Markward's actions were menacing the help that was to be sent to the Holy Land and in this way he posed the same threat as did the Muslims. The organisation of the campaign was very indecisive — it has recently been shown that it was a measure of desperation when all else had failed — and in 1203 Markward deprived it of reason by dying, but the same train of thought can be seen in the *Ad Liberandum* constitution of the Fourth Lateran Council in 1215, according to which those who broke the peace in Europe during the crusade, holding

> ecclesiastical censure in little esteem, can fear, not without reason, lest by the authority of the Church secular power be brought in against them, as those disturbing the business of the Crucified One, . . .

and probably in Clement IV's authorisation of a crusade in 1265 against the rebellious English nobles.

The next move was made by Pope Gregory IX, not in 1228–30 when his campaign against the Emperor Frederick II was certainly not a crusade and should be compared more with the steps taken to defend the papacy in the eleventh century, but in 1240. War had broken out again and Frederick was now threatening the city of Rome itself. In Rome Gregory publicly exhibited the holiest relics, the heads of SS Peter and Paul, distributed crosses and called on the populace to defend the liberty of the Church. The papal legate in Milan was permitted to preach the Cross in order to raise an army in Lombardy and crusade preaching was also authorised in Germany. A letter sent to Hungary in February 1241 listed the benefits to be granted to those taking the Cross: they were to enjoy the same Indulgence as that given to crusaders to the Holy Land; redemptions of vows were allowed and so were commutations to the campaign against Frederick of vows originally made for defence of Palestine. The defensive nature of the war was emphasised: Gregory pointed out that Christianity was 'in such peril' that military action had become necessary and he referred to the 'vows of the crusaders in defence of the Church against Frederick'. Justification in terms of defence, indeed, characterised all the appeals for the crusades against lay powers in the West: for instance in 1246 a new crusade against Frederick II was proclaimed for the defence of the catholic faith and the liberty of the Church and the crusade against King Peter of Aragon in 1284 was preached 'in defence of the catholic faith and also the Holy Land'.

A Cause for a Crusade

A crusade, whenever and against whomsoever it was aimed, was regarded as being essentially defensive and thus conformed to the basic principle of the just cause. Of course it has never been beyond the wit of man plausibly to excuse his actions, presenting them in the best possible light by calling attention to a threat that does not really exist, but it is undeniable that the just cause had important effects on the movement. A pope might proclaim a crusade, but success depended, as many popes found to their cost, not only on the papal call but also on the answer of the faithful to it. Men took the Cross for all kinds of motive, bad as well as good, but the doubts of ordinary people worried apologists and theoreticians like Hostiensis and in an idealistic age there could be no lasting appeal that did not have some clear justification. A just cause, therefore, was needed and it was bound to be a limiting factor, for a crusade had to be presented as a reaction to what others had done. The initiative had to lie with the enemy and a crusade was often merely a ponderously slow response to what he did.

As far as the cause for them was concerned the crusades did more than conform to the traditional criterion for a Just War; as Holy Wars they also had special features. The recovery of property or defence was related not to a particular country or empire but to Christendom at large, to the Church or to Christ himself. It was not the property of the Byzantine Empire or of the Kingdom of Jerusalem that was liberated or defended by the crusades to the East, but territory belonging by right to Christendom or to Christ. It was not Spaniards or Germans, but Christians, who were imperilled by the Moors and Slavs. The Albigensians menaced not so much France, nor Frederick II the papal patrimony, as they threatened the Church.

To understand this attitude we must take into account the political philosophy which dominated western European thought at the time. Christendom had many meanings, but in political terms it was seen not merely as a society of Christians but as a universal state, the Christian Republic, transcendental in that it existed at the same time in heaven and on earth. Providing the political context in which man could fully develop his potential for loving God and his neighbour, it was the only true sovereign state. Earthly kingdoms had no real political validity, being at best temporal conveniences which could be treated as its provinces. It had its possessions and its citizens. Any asset – such as territory once governed by Christians but now in the hands of outsiders – could be restored to its rule; any threat to its subjects, whether from without or within, must be resisted. A crusade was its army, fighting in its defence or for the recovery of property lost by it. The leaders of the First Crusade could write of the spreading of 'the kingdom of Christ and the Church'; and St Bernard could argue that the cause of King Louis VII of France, setting out for the East, was of importance not only to him 'but to the whole Church of God, because now your cause is one with that of all the world'. A century later Odo of Châteauroux made the same point in one of his sermons.

> But someone says, 'The Muslims have not hurt me at all. Why should I take the Cross against them?' But if he thought well about it he would understand that the Muslims do great injury to every Christian.

And in the late 1140s, when crusades were being fought at the same time on several fronts, they were seen as regiments in one Christian army.

> To the initiators of the expedition [wrote a German chronicler] it seemed that one part of the army should be sent to the eastern regions, another into Spain and a third against the Slavs who live next to us.

The universal Christian state was a monarchy, founded and ruled over by Christ, for whom in this world popes, bishops and kings acted as agents. Enemies of the commonwealth were the enemies of its king. Writers at the time of the First Crusade referred to the Muslims in the East as the 'enemies of God' and in one report of his sermon Urban II was made to say: 'It is not I who encourages you, it is the Lord. . . . To those present I say, to those absent I command, but Christ rules.' He hailed the crusaders as 'soldiers of Christ', while they wrote of themselves as 'the army of the Lord'. To Innocent III the crusade was an enterprise which was particularly Christ's own and those who aided the Muslims were acting against the 'interests of Christ himself and the Christian people'.

It was because of the special nature of its cause and its association with a political order established for the good of mankind by Christ that the crusade was not merely justifiable but was holy. Participation in it was especially meritorious. Of course it is the case that participation in a Just War can be in a way an act of merit, in the performance, for instance, of a patriotic service. But it can never be anything but inherently sinful, whereas the taking of the Cross was demanded as a religious duty, and one for which the layman was particularly qualified. The great preacher James of Vitry spoke of the crusade as being incumbent on the Christian as military service was upon a vassal.

When a lord is afflicted by the loss of his patrimony he wishes to prove his friends and find out if his vassals are faithful. Whoever holds a fief of a liege lord is worthily deprived of it if he deserts him when he is engaged in battle and loses his inheritance. You hold your body and soul and whatever you have from the Supreme Emperor and today he has had you called upon to help him in battle; and though you are not bound by feudal law, he offers you so many and such good things, the remission of all sins, whatever the penalty or guilt, and above all eternal life, that you ought at once to hurry to him.

From the ninth century a new path to martyrdom, dying in the war against the infidel, had been officially spoken of and in the eleventh century there had come the concept of the remission of the sins of warriors in a good cause and the idea of the soldier of Christ at the special disposal of the papacy. With Pope Urban II the crusade was proposed as a positive act of virtue, a means of Grace, an expression of love both of God, for whom one fought, and of one's neighbours in the eastern Churches, whom one was striving to liberate. And, because he saw it as linked to the Truces of God by which the Church was trying to impose some sort of peace in France, Urban stressed – references appear in all the reports of his sermons – the difference between the old unregenerate knight, who quarrelled with his neighbours, and the new knight, who fought for such a worthy cause.

Now become soldiers of Christ [he was reported as saying] you who a little while ago were robbers. Now legally fight against barbarians, you who once fought against brothers and blood-relatives. . . . Those who were the enemies of the Lord, now these will be his friends.

The idea expressed here was not new, but its impact on audiences is borne out by the way it was reiterated by preachers for a century. St

Bernard, in particular, concentrated on it. To him the old knight committed homicide, whether he lived or died, prevailed or was conquered; the new knight killed not man, but evil.

For how long will your men continue to shed Christian blood; for how long will they continue to fight amongst themselves? You attack one another, you slay one another and by one another you are slain. What is this savage craving of yours? Put a stop to it now, for it is not fighting but foolery. So to risk both soul and body is not brave but shocking, is not strength but folly. But now O mighty soldiers, O men of war, you have a cause for which you can fight without danger to your souls; a cause in which to conquer is glorious and for which to die is gain.

The knights of Christ fought in expiation of their sins and as a means to their salvation. They were, in the Old Testament imagery constantly used of them, the elect, the Israelites crossing the Red Sea. They were expected to conform to such standards of behaviour and dress as were suitable for members of the Lord's host. From 1145 onwards papal and lay decrees for crusaders contained what are known as sumptuary clauses demanding simplicity of dress and temperance in daily life.

And if at any time the crusaders should lapse into sin, may they soon rise again through true penitence, having humility in heart and body, following moderation both in clothing and in food, shunning altogether quarrels and envy, banishing inward rancour and anger, so that, fortified with spiritual and material weapons, they may do battle with the enemy, more secure in faith, not presuming on their own power but trusting in Divine strength.

And death, they were told over and over again in sermons, tracts and chronicles, was martyrdom. The prospect of immediate entry into paradise was constantly held before them by propagandists like St Bernard.

Go forward then in security, knights, and drive off without fear the enemies of the Cross of Christ, certain that neither death nor life can separate you from the love of God which is in Jesus Christ. . . . How glorious are those who return victorious from the battle! How happy are those who die as martyrs in the battle! Rejoice, courageous athlete, if you survive and are victor in the Lord; but rejoice and glory the more if you die and are joined to the Lord. For your life is fruitful and your victory glorious. But death. . . is more fruitful and more glorious. For if those who die in the Lord are blessed, how much more so are those who die for the Lord!

The crusade, therefore, conformed to the principle of the Just War in that it was concerned above all with the recovery of lost lands and with defence. But as a Holy War its cause related to the Church, to Christendom, seen as a political entity, and to Christ, the monarch of the universal Christian state. It is not surprising that it was regarded as a means of salvation for those taking part, who were doing their duty by Christ as they might by their temporal lord or king.

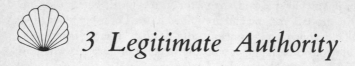 *3 Legitimate Authority*

Papal Authorisation

CHRISTIANS are faced with the problem of reconciling the demands on the individual of love with the apparent need in a sinful world to use force. St Augustine's answer has proved itself to be generally acceptable. In a private capacity no man ought ever to kill, even in his own defence; but he may be justified in doing so as a public duty. Public warfare, as opposed to personal acts of violence, must be legitimised by public authority. It follows that a Just or Holy War must be authorised by a ruler whose powers are normally considered to include the right to proclaim it. A difference between crusades and other Holy Wars was that the ruler who legitimised them was not an emperor or king, but the pope; and resulting from the papal initiative were the characteristic privileges enjoyed by crusaders, particularly the Indulgence, which could be granted only by him.

The way in which popes came to proclaim crusades was established by two of them: Urban II, who set the precedent when he preached the First Crusade in 1095; and Eugenius III, who issued for the Second Crusade *Quantum predecessores,* the first true crusade encyclical. Whatever the contribution of Pope Gregory VII to crusading ideas – and I shall touch on that question later – the initiative following the appeal of the Byzantine embassy to the Council of Piacenza was Urban's own. Many of the elements to be found in the writings connected with his visit to France – the criteria for war, and especially Holy War, the pilgrimage and the pilgrim's vow, the Truce of God, the concept of the Christian Republic – were old, but it was he who synthesised them into what was recognisably a crusade, giving the expedition a theoretical basis which was to prove itself to be extraordinarily long-lasting. He was, as one of the chroniclers put it, the 'chief author of the expedition' and he regarded it as his own. 'We have constituted our most beloved son Adhémar, Bishop of Le Puy, leader in our place of this pilgrimage and labour.' The acceptance of papal headship was expressed especially clearly in a letter written to Urban by the captains of the crusade in September 1098. They informed him of the death of Adhémar, 'whom you gave us as your vicar,' and they went on:

> Now we ask you, our spiritual father, who started this journey and caused us all by your sermons to leave our lands . . . to come to us and summon whomsoever you can to come with you. . .

What could be better than that

> you who are the father and head of the Christian religion should come to the chief and capital city of the name of Christ and yourself finish off the war *which is your own* . . . . If indeed you come to us and with us complete the journey begun through you all the world will be obedient to you.

The half century that divided the First and Second Crusades was a period in which histories and chronicles told the story of the success of Urban's enterprise; men pilgrimaged, or at least looked with pride and devotion, towards Jerusalem now that it was in Latin hands; Urban's successors tried to help the new Latin colony in the Holy Land; and St Bernard began to develop in his preaching and writing the theory of crusading. But on Christmas Eve 1144 the Muslims broke into the city of Edessa in northern Mesopotamia, the capital of the first Latin Christian county to be established in the wake of the First Crusade. The news of the disaster, the first real setback for the Latins in the East, caused a great stir in the West, but what then happened is still rather mysterious. On 1 December 1145 Pope Eugenius III issued the encyclical *Quantum predecessores,* but although this was addressed to King Louis VII and the nobility of France there is no evidence that it was published there. Meanwhile Louis was already planning to lead a French expedition to the Holy Land: it may be that the pope issued *Quantum predecessores* because he had heard of this, for Louis does not seem to have envisaged seeking papal authorisation when he announced his idea to the Christmas court held at Bourges. His proposal met with little response and his chief adviser Suger of S. Denis was against it. Louis postponed a final decision until the following Easter and called for an opinion from St Bernard, who declared that he would not consider anything without consulting the pope. The result was that on 1 March 1146 *Quantum predecessores* was reissued, with a very slight change in the text which does not concern us here.

The story of the publication of *Quantum predecessores* demonstrates two things. The first is that initiative did not always lie with the papacy. Louis VII was one of several leaders of major and minor expeditions (perhaps the most famous being his great-grandson Louis IX) who themselves took the Cross without prompting from Rome. The second is that, whoever was responsible for the first move, papal authorisation was considered to be essential at some stage: not only great passages but also the tiny enterprises that were, increasingly after 1250, to depart backed by papal appeals and fortified by papal privileges were authorised by papal letters. At first sight an exception might be found in some canonists' treatment of crusades against heretics. They argued that a general authority to princes had already been given by the Fourth Lateran Council and that therefore no special papal edict was required before the waging of war against them. But this, one must stress, was only because it was considered that papal authorisation had already been granted. *Quantum predecessores* itself recounted how Urban,

> sounding forth as a heavenly trumpet, summoned sons of the Holy Roman Church from several parts of the world to free the eastern Church.

It went on:

> And so in the Lord we impress upon, ask and order all of you, and we enjoin it for the remission of sins, that those who are on God's side, and especially the more powerful and the nobles, vigorously equip themselves to go against the multitude of the infidels.

The encyclical also established the form in which crusades would thenceforward be proclaimed. The way the papal letters were written developed over the years, their style became more flowery and more dense and they are a good guide to the progress of crusading ideas, but they kept to the pattern laid down by *Quantum predecessores,* consisting of sections in which the circumstances that made a new crusade necessary were described, the appeal for crusaders was made and the privileges to be granted to participants and supporters were listed. The greatest of them were the bulls of Innocent III's pontificate, *Post miserabile* (1198), *Ne nos ejus* (1208) and *Quia major* (1213), which together with the great constitution *Ad Liberandum* of the Fourth Lateran Council (1215) contain the most marvellous language and imagery. And in practically every word papal authority is made clear.

> But to those declining to take part, if indeed there be by chance such men ungrateful to the Lord our God, we firmly state on behalf of the Apostle that they should know that they will have to reply to us ˹on this matter in the presence of the Dreadful Judge on the Last Day of Severe Judgement.

We will see how unreal these pretensions were when it actually came to directing the course of a crusade.

A feature of Christianity is that, although it teaches that all man's actions are answerable to God and subject to the objective scale of values embodied in his laws, it divides governmental functions in this world into two distinct fields, the spiritual and the temporal. This separation of functions is to be found very early, even though there have been periods in which the boundary between them was indistinct or in which some institution – Late Roman emperorship, the thirteenth-century papacy, Anglican kingship – has been thought to transcend that boundary. In spite of, and paradoxically also because of, papal claims, at no period was the distinction between temporal and spiritual spheres of activity stressed more than during the central Middle Ages.

If ever there was a secular activity it is war and it is natural that in Christian history its prosecution or the physical repression of heresy should have been regarded as the duties of temporal rulers, emperors and kings. How then could a churchman like the pope authorise so secular an enterprise? We shall never understand the papal role in the crusading movement without first grasping the paradox that the popes were at the same time maintaining that the Church must run her own affairs freed from the control of lay rulers and that they, as the most responsible ministers of Christ in the earthly part of the Christian Republic, had some measure of authority on his behalf in temporal matters.

These contradictory claims had been made with great force during the Investiture Contest, which had begun as a dispute over church order and reform but had rapidly escalated so that in 1076 and 1080

Pope Gregory VII had provisionally and then definitively deposed King Henry IV of Germany. In trying to remove a man from an indisputably secular office the pope had stepped across the frontier that divided spiritual from temporal jurisdiction. In the past, it is true, popes had claimed superiority to emperors, but the origin of the imperial office in the West lay in a coronation performed by a pope on Christmas Day 800 and the emperors had duties which could be interpreted as making them merely agents of the Church. It was another matter with western kingship, which had grown up out of the fragmentation of the Roman Empire, owing little to the papacy, and had always been seen as a separate ministry for God. There were, moreover, no real precedents for papal intervention in the exercise of royal government other than the doubtful authorisation by Pope Zacharias of the removal from office of King Childeric of the Franks in the middle of the eighth century. Gregory VII's deposition of Henry IV was an extreme act which might be said to have been in advance of the development of papal theory – too advanced to be properly understood or appreciated by contemporaries – and at the time it was a failure in that Gregory was driven from Rome by Henry's forces and in 1085 died in exile. He was succeeded by Victor III and then in 1088 by Urban II, himself a strong Gregorian.

The great quarrel with the King of Germany went on and when Urban began his pontificate few German bishops recognised him and much of Germany and north and central Italy, including Rome, were controlled by Henry's anti-pope, Clement III. Urban set out to build up support for himself in the West and from Byzantium. By 1094 Rome was in his hands and the German king was losing ground in Italy; and in 1095, as the pope journeyed to France after the Council of Piacenza, Henry's son Conrad, who had rebelled against his father, became his vassal at Cremona. Against this background his preaching of the First Crusade had a political significance. It was an important move in the Investiture Contest, for when he called on the army of Christ to recover Christian land Urban was in fact assuming for himself the imperial function of directing the defence of the Christian Republic at a time when he did not recognise Henry as emperor: Gregory VII had deposed a king; Urban II took over the prime duty of a temporal ruler. With these actions the popes began to take a special place for themselves at the summit of both jurisdictions.

Although it took some time for political thinkers and canon lawyers to catch up with the ideas expressed in the deposition of Henry IV and the preaching of the First Crusade these foreshadowed what is known as the Papal Monarchy. By the early thirteenth century the pope was claimed to be Christ's Vicar, a special representative unlike any other earthly ruler, the Ordinary Judge of all things with a plenitude of power, standing in an intermediate position between God and the two hierarchies of ecclesiastical and temporal ministers. But even with the full development of the theory the popes' powers were less than absolute. In the first place the co-operative nature of the relationship between papal and temporal authority was still recognised: kings had their own share of government, holding a ministry for God in the exercise of which the pope would not normally interfere, for his court remained that of final appeal with an authority that could be invoked only in the last resort. Secondly, secular rulers could always act in ways in which popes would, perhaps could, not. The processes of papal jurisdiction, which were of course ecclesiastical, were not suited – and it was never pretended that they were – to the settlement of cases in temporal law. Thirdly, the popes really had no means of enforcing secular judgements even had they wanted to, for they had no effective means of imposing secular sentences. This can be seen clearly if one compares the reality of their government of the Church with the shadow of their government of the world. If there is one outstanding feature of the papacy in the central Middle Ages it is the way it gained direct control of and elaborated the administrative apparatus of the Church. The period saw great development of the whole machinery of government: of officials, courts and canon law, and the subordination of all, though never in practice quite as completely as a glance at structure would suggest, to Rome's will. But turning to the popes' relationship with the world, we find no such machinery. A pope like Innocent IV could solemnly depose a recalcitrant ruler like Frederick II, but he could only enforce his decision by resorting to the ecclesiastical apparatus, perhaps by threatening all Frederick's supporters with an ecclesiastical sanction like excommunication. Or he could launch a crusade.

It is not surprising that the papacy should look for means by which the temporal world, so alien to itself, could be adapted to its own processes of government. An example of this can be seen in Innocent III's decretal *Novit,* which justified papal interference in temporal matters *ratione peccati,* by reason of the sin involved in them. It has often been pointed out that since sin is potentially present in almost every human act this more or less gave the pope a blank cheque to intervene whenever and in whatever case he liked. But far more important than that – indeed it was to lead to problems of interpretation later – were the legal consequences of the transfer of a case *ratione peccati* to papal jurisdiction. Now a moral question, it became subject to the ordinary processes of ecclesiastical law and jurisdiction: in other words a temporal matter had become legally spiritual and had passed into a field in which the pope could properly operate. The crusade was another example of the same approach. A crusader was a soldier, but of a special kind, for he had taken a vow, *ipso facto* a spiritual matter, which resulted in his having the status of a pilgrim and consequently becoming, like a pilgrim, a temporary ecclesiastic, subject to church courts. The crusade vow, therefore, had a significance which was certainly clear by the middle of the twelfth century when the right of crusaders to answer cases in ecclesiastical courts was referred to. Of course secular courts were reluctant to agree to a reduction in their rights of jurisdiction and it came to be accepted that crusaders should answer to them on feudal tenures, inheritance and major crimes; but the principle was accepted and the crusader, although engaged in a secular activity, was incorporated into the system in which papal power freely worked. By the introduction of the vow and the granting of pilgrim status Urban II had created the conditions in which the pope could have authority over a crusade and use with regard to it the existing machinery of church government.

There was another side to this, for everything, including subjection in this matter to the control of the ecclesiastical apparatus, depended on vows being taken. When a pope proclaimed a crusade, this was no more than an appeal to the faithful to take the vow, which was essentially voluntary. He might threaten them with hell-fire but he could not make them take it or punish them if they did not. Without their fervour he could do nothing. It took, therefore, more than a pope to make a crusade. In the absence of a lay ruler's initiative, there had to be an adequate response to a papal appeal, and there were periods, particularly from 1150 to 1187, before the annihilation of the Christian army at the Battle of Hattin and the loss of the city of Jerusalem at last awoke the West, during which the papacy and Christian leaders in the East tried again and again with very little success to raise help for Palestine. In fact the difficulties encountered by popes in getting crusades off the ground were daunting. In order to maximise the benefits of whatever response there might be, peace had to be made to prevail in Europe; agents had to be appointed to publicise the appeal

and organise recruitment; and finance, increasingly important as time
went on, had to be raised.

Peace in Christendom

Long tradition associated the Christian Republic with peace. To St
Augustine, on whose writings the idea of the universal Christian state
was rather inaccurately based, peace was a distinguishing feature of the
true state, the City of God. The crusade itself was from the first seen as
an instrument of peace, closely associated with the movement for
Truces of God: it is clear that Urban II hoped to direct the bellicosity
of French knights overseas, bringing a measure of calm to the coun-
tryside. In the twelfth and thirteenth centuries it was believed that
peace in Europe and the unity of Christendom were essential precon-
ditions for the success of a crusade; and calls, often with reason, for
truces and unity are to be found again and again in papal letters: persis-
tent rivalry between the kings of France and England certainly
hindered the raising of a crusade in the 1170s and 1180s. The appeals
reached a climax with Pope Innocent III. To him the disunity of
Christendom was a shameful scandal and after 1204 he believed that on
the reform of a Church now united by the capture of Constantinople
depended the reconquest of Jerusalem. He felt as deeply about political
disputes in western Europe, even, as we have seen, preaching the Cross
against Markward of Anweiler for impeding a crusade and threatening
others with the same fate. In the preamble to the encyclical of 1198
which proclaimed the Fourth Crusade he seethed with powerful indignation, in a voice not heard since that of St Bernard.

> Now indeed . . . while our princes pursue one another with inex-
> orable hatred, while each strives to vindicate his injuries, suffered at
> the hands of another, there is no one who is moved at the injury suf-
> fered by the Crucified One . . . .Already our enemies insult us, say-
> ing, 'Where is your God, who cannot free himself or you from our
> hands?'

The calls of the popes for peace and unity were never very successful
and indeed the eventual failure of the crusades to hold the Holy Land
has been attributed partly to the growing disinclination in the later
thirteenth century of western powers, deeply involved in their own

rivalries, to participate. This is an exaggeration of the true situation, but it is clear that by the 1270s the papacy was beginning to realise the futility of trying to organise a great expedition at a time when kings had their minds on other matters.

Preaching

No papal proclamation after the first was itself enough to move Europe. Encyclicals had to be followed up by personal visits and constant publicity, a process known as the preaching of the Cross. It was obviously important that the popes should have control over this and therefore over recruitment. It might be supposed that they would have been only too happy with an enthusiastic response – or sometimes indeed with any reaction at all – and it is true that Innocent III and his successors tried to make their preachers' tasks easier by granting Indulgences even to those who merely listened to their sermons; it is a measure of the difficulties faced by the propagandists that the amount of Indulgence given to the audiences at crusade sermons was steadily increased as the thirteenth century wore on. But in fact there were occasions on which almost as bad for Rome as indifference in the West was the overenthusiasm of men whom the popes wanted to remain at home. Urban II may not have envisaged the uncontrollably large numbers who responded to his sermon at Clermont and he and his successors tried, sometimes unsuccessfully, to dissuade Spaniards from leaving the struggle in Spain and going East. Eugenius III did not want Conrad of Germany to take part in the Second Crusade but could do little to prevent him. In 1198 Innocent III seems to have had no desire for the participation in the Fourth Crusade of European monarchs, after the quarrelling and rivalries displayed on the Third and what may have been an effort by the Staufen emperors to seize control of the movement; he was lucky in that no king felt constrained to join. The matter was delicate in that it can be shown that often the response of ordinary knights to the preaching depended on the enthusiasm or indifference of the king or great magnates in a particular area.

In fact preaching was never completely controlled by the papacy. The central Middle Ages had many popular evangelisers and these have an important place in the history of the crusades. The most famous of them, Peter the Hermit, was active in central France and the Rhineland in 1095–6 and was followed East by an army of the poor, travelling independently of the other bands of crusaders, which was decimated by the Turks in western Asia Minor although Peter himself and the remnants of his followers were still to play a significant part at Antioch in northern Syria in 1098. Among his successors were Rudolph, a Cistercian monk whose influence in the Rhineland worried St Bernard at the time of the Second Crusade; Nicholas, the boy who launched the pathetic and misnamed Children's Crusade in 1212; and the Master of Hungary, the preacher of the Crusade of the Shepherds in 1251. The sermons of these men dwelt on those messianic, visionary themes with the emphasis on the rewards of the poor that characterised the populist movement which underlay the crusades and occasionally erupted in migrations towards the Promised Land, which was believed to be a paradise only the underprivileged could acquire.

A far greater part, however, was played by the official propagandists among whom were, of course, the popes themselves. We have already seen Urban II following up his call at Clermont by touring western and southern France. In 1215 Innocent III opened the Fourth Lateran Council with a sermon which partly concerned the crusade and in 1216 he preached the Cross in central Italy; at Orvieto, as at Clermont 120 years before, the crowds were so great that he addressed them in the open air, in spite of the heavy rain. In 1274 Gregory X referred to the crusade in at least three sermons at the Second Council of Lyons. But the popes could not, with their responsibilities and commitments, engage in many personal appearances and they had to rely on agents, most commonly, of course, local bishops. At Clermont Urban II urged the bishops to preach the Cross and in December 1099 Paschal II asked the French bishops to encourage knights to go to the Holy Land and especially to compel those who had already taken the Cross: there survives a letter, written by the Archbishop of Rheims to a suffragan, announcing the fall of Jerusalem to the crusaders and ordering that in all parishes there should be prayers for victory, fasting and the collection of alms. Throughout the period of the crusades a stream of letters flowed from the papal *Curia*, ordering bishops to preach the Cross themselves or help those sent by the popes to do so; and it seems that by the 1180s, at least in Britain, the prelates had with the assistance of the lesser clergy developed a fairly systematic procedure for crusade preaching.

The papacy also employed special agents. In February 1096 Urban II gave Robert of Arbrissel, who was later to found Fontevrault, commission to preach the Cross in the Loire valley and he ordered Gerento,

Abbot of S. Bénigne of Dijon, to publicise the crusade in Normandy and England. In 1100 Paschal II sent to France two cardinals who held a council at Poitiers and encouraged the faithful to join a crusade to the East. The best known of the early agents was St Bernard, who was employed by Pope Eugenius III to preach the Second Crusade in France and was forced, because of Rudolph's success, to extend his activities to Germany. The terms of Bernard's commission are not clear: he was certainly not a papal legate, and so could not have been given powers to act in this matter as if he were the pope himself, although the success of his preaching, the force of his personality and influence he had with Eugenius clearly gave him a very great authority. The first use of legates in the preaching of the Cross appears to have been in 1173–4 and from then on they were often employed.

A new development came with Innocent III's pontificate. He combined the use of special agents and provincial clergy by appointing local churchmen as his representatives. In 1198, when he proclaimed the Fourth Crusade, a legate was sent to France and free-lancers like the famous preacher Fulk of Neuilly were allowed to operate, but also two men in each province were chosen from among the higher clergy to preach the Cross together with a Templar and a Hospitaller. In 1208, when he tried, at least in France and Lombardy, unsuccessfully to promote a new crusade, he proposed to use much the same system, but in 1213 he introduced a more elaborate one. He himself kept an eye on the preaching in Italy, but for nearly every province in Christendom he also appointed small groups of men – the numbers varied slightly – many of whom were bishops. Innocent referred to them as executors, with the powers of legates in this matter, and he laid down that they should live modestly, being accompanied by only a few servants; they should preach, receive vows and, if given any donation for the Holy Land, store it in a religious house; they could appoint deputies in each diocese: in Liège and Cologne four of these were chosen – and the pope advised the Bishop of Ratisbon to appoint deputies who could assemble the populace of two or three parishes to address them where they could not deal with them individually. Perhaps the most successful of the executors was Oliver, the *scholasticus* of Cologne, whose preaching in that province, sometimes accompanied, it was said, by miracles, aroused great enthusiasm. Outside the scheme lay Hungary, where every bishop was to preach the Cross; Latin Syria and Palestine, where James of Vitry, the new Bishop of Acre and the greatest preacher of the day, was to raise crusaders; Denmark and Sweden, where the legate, the Archbishop of Lund, was to be assisted by the Archbishop of Uppsala; and France, to which papal legates, first Robert of Courçon and later Archbishop Simon of Tyre, were sent. This elaborate, perhaps overelaborate, structure does not seem to have been used again with regard to all Christendom, although, as in 1234, its details might be repeated in individual provinces. On other occasions prelates might be asked to preach themselves or to choose men to do so, or groups of clergy, like the Franciscans and Dominicans in the 1230s, might be directly appointed to publicise the crusades. There was, however, a tendency to give individual preachers the legation and wide powers. Examples are Conrad of Porto in Germany and Italy in the 1220s, Odo of Châteauroux in France and Germany in the 1240s and Ottobuono Fieschi over Norway, Flanders, Gascony, Britain and Ireland in 1265. Ottobuono had authority to appoint subordinate preachers, notaries and collectors; he preached some sermons himself, but generally delegated powers to whomsoever he thought fit, especially local friars.

Finance

Crusades were expensive and tended to become more so as the mercenary element in them increased. The costs of equipment, supplies and above all transport – most went by sea – were often too heavy for the participants; in 1202 the crusaders in Venice found themselves quite unable to pay for shipping that had been arranged for many more men than had actually arrived at the port of embarkation. It was quite usual for kings or the greater lords to pay inducements to or a part of the expenses of those of their followers who took the Cross. The total cost of the crusade of 1248–54 to King Louis IX of France was estimated at 1,537,570 *livres* or more than six times his annual income; and this was certainly an underestimate as it can been shown that he spent over 1,000,000 *livres* in Palestine after his disastrous campaign in Egypt was over. Quite early on it became clear that sources of finance other than crusaders' pockets would have to be tapped.

Rulers soon came to demand subsidies from their subjects. In 1146 Louis VII imposed on France a general census to raise money for the Second Crusade: it is not clear what form this took, but it was charged on the Church as well as the laity and may have been a forced feudal levy. In 1166 a tax for the Holy Land, based on the value of movable property and income, was collected by Louis and Henry II of England. In 1185 Henry of England and Philip of France levied a graduated tax on income and movables and demanded a tenth of the alms left by those who died in the ten years following 24 June 1184. In 1188 Henry imposed the famous Saladin Tithe for one year on the income and movables of those, clerks and laymen, who did not take the Cross, and in June 1201 the papal legate Octavian persuaded John of England and Philip of France to contribute a fortieth of a year's income from their lands and to raise the same from the estates of their vassals. These occasional taxes are to be found throughout the thirteenth century: for instance Louis IX of France pressed towns to give him money for his crusade in the 1240s and in 1270 the English parliament granted the Lord Edward a crusade twentieth. In 1274 Pope Gregory X demanded, with what success is not known, that every temporal ruler levy from each subject one silver penny.

The value of the alms and legacies of the faithful, given from the first and particularly in the outburst of popular enthusiasm which had followed the conquest of Palestine, was appreciated by the popes, who ordered that chests be placed in churches for their collection, from the middle of the twelfth century granted Indulgences, though not plenary Indulgences, to those who contributed to the movement in this way, and encouraged the faithful to make bequests to the Holy Land in their wills.

The popes themselves naturally played the most important part in the financing of crusades. They exploited the normal judicial processes of the Church — under Gregory IX and Gregory X the proceeds of fines imposed on blasphemers were sent to the Holy Land — but they also took new measures. They began to allow the redemption of crusade vows for money payments. Several different trains of thought led to this important development. First, the belief that all should contribute in some way to the movement was reflected in the growing practice of granting Indulgences in return for donations rather than participation. Secondly, the Church was faced by large numbers who were in fact incapable of fighting but had taken the Cross, in spite of the general feeling that they should not participate in the crusades. One of the reports of Urban's sermon at Clermont made him state that no old men or women without husbands or suitable companions or priests without licence should take part, and in his letters to Bologna and Vallombrosa he forbade some religious to go under any circumstances, other clerks without permission, young married men without the consent of their wives and parishioners without first seeking advice. In 1188 Henry II of England laid down that most of his crusaders were not to take women and at about the same time the writer Ralph Niger inveighed against those clerics, monks, women, paupers and old men who went on crusades. In 1208 Innocent III wrote to the faithful in Lombardy and the March, proposing that those who were not capable of fighting should send soldiers in their place at their own expense. Thirdly, churchmen and canon lawyers had to deal with those who had taken the Cross in the first flush of enthusiasm and then wanted to be dispensed from their vows. As early as the tenth century it had been considered possible to send someone in one's place on pilgrimage and in the twelfth century, while it was difficult to get relaxation from the obligations of a crusade vow, it was not impossible – indeed it seems to have become quite common by the time of the Third Crusade.

From the pontificate of Alexander III onwards popes in decretals and canon lawyers in their commentaries began to consider dispensation, substitution (the sending of another in place of the crusader), redemption (dispensation in return for a money payment) and commutation (the performance of another penitential act in place of the one originally vowed). In the early years of his pontificate Innocent III laid down some general rules. These were exceptionally severe in that they confirmed the Roman law concept of the hereditability of vows – a son must perform a vow undertaken and not fulfilled by his father – but they also stated that the pope, though only he, could grant delay in the performance of a crusade vow or its commutation or redemption; the amount to be paid in redemption should equal the sum that would have been spent had the crusader actually gone with the expedition. The influence of these rulings can be seen working from 1213 onwards in papal letters and the conciliar decree concerning the preaching of the Fifth Crusade, which referred to commutation, redemption and deferment, and in the actions of Robert of Courçon and Archbishop Simon of Tyre, the papal legates in France, who encouraged everyone, whatever his health and state, to take the Cross, causing great scandal but clearly in order that moneys could be raised from the subsequent redemptions. From 1240 onwards, in spite of papal admonitions, redemptions were being granted almost as a matter of course to anyone who asked for them or paid for them, although for a short period, following the loss of Palestine in 1291, they became much harder to obtain. Finance from them became very important as the thirteenth century progressed, but the system was open to great abuse and came in for much criticism – and it was only made worse by the half-hearted attempts of some popes to reform it.

The greatest financial contribution came from the direct taxation of the Church by the popes: a substantial part of Louis IX's expenses must have been paid for by the French clergy. The first hint of new ideas on the contribution of the Church to the crusades is to be found in letters of 1188 from Pope Clement III to the clergy of Canterbury and Genoa encouraging them to direct some of their wealth to the support of the crusade. Ten years later Innocent III ordered the prelates of Christendom to send men and money to the Fourth Crusade and he repeated this injunction in *Quia major* of 1213, but meanwhile, in December 1199, he had taken a momentous step. He had come to the conclusion that there was nothing for it but to impose a tax upon the whole Church, although, obviously worried about the possible reaction from the bishops, he assured them that this was not to become custom or law or establish a precedent and he informed them that he himself would send a tenth of his revenues to the aid of the East. He ordered the clergy to pay a fortieth of all their revenues, after deducting anything owed in unavoidable usurious contracts; a very few religious were allowed to pay a fiftieth. Provincial councils were to discuss the matter and within three months a council in each diocese was to organise collection with the aid of a Templar and a Hospitaller. With the advice of the same two brothers and leading local figures each prelate was to hire soldiers and provide poor crusaders with subsidies. The levy proved to be extremely difficult to raise: by 1201 it had been gathered neither in England nor in France and in 1208 it had not been collected even in parts of Italy. Although in 1209 Innocent III laid a tax on the churches in the domains of the crusaders against the Albigensians, it must have been the failure of the measure of 1199 that persuaded him not to ask for another levy in 1213. But two years later a twentieth for three years was demanded of the Church by the Fourth Lateran Council, although again emphasis was placed on the pope's own contribution. From this time onwards income taxes were built up into a regular system of taxation, the most extensive of them being promulgated in 1274 at the Second Council of Lyons, a sexennial tenth from which none was to be exempt. Usually apportioned at a tenth, these taxes were demanded of the universal Church or of the clergy in a single country for periods varying from one to six years. Settlement was normally sought in two equal instalments each year, although resistance was common and the payments were nearly always in arrears. At first the proceeds were paid to local crusaders or sent directly to the Holy Land, while the popes simply received accounts, but in 1220 Pope Honorius III was already overseeing the transmission of the moneys. By the middle of the thirteenth century it had become customary for the popes to grant the yield of the taxes to kings or lords who had promised to go on crusade; if the king did not then depart, the money, which had been deposited for him in monasteries, was delivered to papal merchants for sending to Rome. But such was the resistance of the temporal authorities to this practice that the popes seldom received all they should.

Enormous sums were raised from alms, bequests, redemptions and taxes and there was a need for some efficient machinery for their collection. In 1188 Pope Clement III had ordered bishops to appoint clerks to collect money and spend it on troops, but in 1198 Innocent III himself chose collectors from among the churchmen in each province; it was typical of his methods that although these were local men they were instituted directly by him. In the following year he left the organisation of his new tax on the clergy to the bishops, perhaps to assuage local feelings, but the lack of co-operation very soon led to officials being sent from Rome to oversee collection and Innocent returned to central control in 1213: his preachers in the provinces were also to be involved in the raising of money. Papal commissioners were put in charge of the new twentieth levied on the Church in 1215 and the whole system was carried further by Innocent's successor Honorius III. Papal collectors are to be found operating throughout the thirteenth century; and in 1274 all Christendom was divided into twenty-six districts administered by collectors and sub-collectors. The taxes of 1199 and 1215 were assessed by the clergy themselves, but in 1228 Pope Gregory IX ordered the papal collectors to choose for this task special deputies who were to compel local churchmen under oath to value clerical incomes in a district.

Preaching and finance were two fields in which the popes could make use of the highly developed bureaucracy of the Church and we can trace the emergence of a characteristically elaborate machinery to act on their behalf. But their problems did not end with the recruitment of crusaders and the raising of money to subsidise them. Where was a crusade to go? And how was it to be controlled on the way?

Strategy

Crusading strategy was a moral matter, for the Holy War, being also Just, had to be fought in a way that would achieve its ends most painlessly. Of course in the conditions of the time and given the impossibility of co-ordinating the movements of contingents from different parts of Europe so that they would all come to the same place on the same date, long-term planning could present crusaders with nothing more than some general guide-lines. Events would always overtake plans made in the West and the final decisions had to be left to councils-of-war held on the spot. In 1238 the Christian leaders in Palestine suggested to Thibaut of Champagne that the fleet bringing his crusade ought to apply to Limassol in Cyprus, where it could refit and revictual. Here a council-of-war would discuss whether it was best to proceed to Syria or to Egypt; Limassol, they pointed out, was equally distant from Acre, Alexandria and Damietta. Although in the 1240s King Louis IX of France had clearly made plans to invade Egypt from the start, he did not give the final orders until his arrival in Cyprus. Some general planning, however, was made in the West. Pope Innocent III began the practice of receiving frequent reports from local Christians on political conditions in the East – he certainly took advice from them when making plans for the Fifth Crusade – and from the 1270s onwards there survive many memoirs written for the popes, most of which were composed in the early fourteenth century when the Christians had lost the Holy Land and a major effort was needed to recover it. Perhaps the most revealing insight into discussions on strategy can be found in King James I of Aragon's description of a debate at the Second Council of Lyons in 1274 in which both he and Pope Gregory X took part. Present were leaders of the Military Orders and experienced crusaders, among whom there seems to have been general agreement that large, elaborately organised crusades were expensive, often difficult to provision and support and did little long-term good. In fact a new strategic approach had been dominant since the 1250s, with an emphasis on the build-up of permanent garrisons in the Holy Land and the encouragement of small, manageable expeditions which could periodically succeed one another in the East. This was to remain the chief strategic thinking until the loss of all the Palestinian mainland in 1291. One often reads of a decline in crusading fervour after the middle of the thirteenth century, but this can be exaggerated: historians have been misled by the disenchantment with large international expeditions and the change in strategy in favour of small locally organised crusades.

Control

The crusades were papal instruments, the most spectacular expressions of the Papal Monarchy, the armies of the Christian Republic marching in response to calls from the men who on earth represented its monarch. We have seen that popes faced great difficulties in promoting and financing them and indeed the organisation needed was almost beyond the abilities of men of the time. But once an army had been collected together, the logistic problems solved and a goal set, the troops had to be controlled at a distance and this was the most difficult task of all. From the First Crusade onwards popes were represented in the armies by legates. A legate would be appointed to supervise the whole crusading army, but there could also be subordinate legates chosen to oversee national or regional contingents, though their relationship with their superiors was not always easy: on the Second Crusade Arnulf of Lisieux and Godfrey of Langres, each assisted by a man from his diocese, were papal representatives with the Anglo-Norman and French crusaders, but did not get on happily with Theodwin and Guy, the legates to the whole expedition. Legates were always churchmen and herein lay an insuperable problem. The popes and their representatives were priests and as such were forbidden by canon law to take up arms and fight. Conduct and temporal direction of the crusades, therefore, could not belong to them. This was expressed particularly clearly in c. 1150 by St Bernard, who wrote to Pope Eugenius III after being approached to lead a new crusade. How could he command military forces? It was now time, he wrote, to draw the two swords, spiritual and temporal, at the pope's disposal. Both St Peter's swords must be drawn, one by his hand, but the other at his command, for it seems that Peter himself was not personally to wield the temporal weapon, as he had been ordered by Christ on the eve of the crucifixion to put up his sword into his scabbard.

One legate whose powers have been studied closely is Adhémar of Le Puy, appointed 'leader' of the First Crusade. The general conclusion seems to be that, to Pope Urban, Adhémar's leadership was to be understood not as captaincy but in the context of spiritual duties, expressed through advice, arbitration and exhortation. The limitations on

Adhémar's powers of command are paralleled over and over again in the history of the crusades, and it is not surprising that the Fourth Lateran Council was irritatingly vague on the responsibilities of priests in the Christian army, who

> should diligently devote themselves to prayers and exhortations, teaching the crusaders both by word and example, so that they may always have before their eyes Divine Fear and Love and do not say or do anything that offends the Divine Majesty.

Pope Innocent III wrote with regard to another legate: 'As Joshua fights he ascends with Aaron the Mount of Contemplation and prays.' An exception, it has been suggested, was Pelagius of Albano on the Fifth Crusade and certainly Pelagius's very active role on campaign was criticised at the time. But the papal letter that set out his duties was perfectly in accord with tradition and at no time was his military leadership officially sanctioned: it was rather that on an expedition with no universally accepted captain Pelagius, who had great strength of personality, was able to dominate the councils-of-war. He did not command: he advised and tried to get general consent to his proposals; and his advice was not always taken.

Canon law, in fact, made the pope and his legate dependent on the goodwill of secular leaders, who alone could exercise military command. Over the most potent expression of his temporal claims a pope had very little control once an army was on the move and he could only watch helplessly if it was carried off course. This point has not been stressed enough with regard to the most tragic travesty of all, the assault by the Fourth Crusade upon the Byzantine Empire. There has been much debate on this diversion and all sorts of theories have been put forward to explain it. The least acceptable is that which makes Innocent III a party to a plot in the West to divert the crusade to Constantinople, for it credits the pope with far more power than he actually possessed. One must not confuse what he did after the expedition was over with his attitude before and during it. There is no doubt that a very short time after the capture of Constantinople he was engaged in an all-out effort to subordinate the Greek Church to Rome. In his demands for conformity he was doing something new – such a rigorous attitude towards the eastern Churches was not hitherto to be found in the Latin states in the East – but his acceptance and exploitation of a novel situation, however unattractive this might appear to be to us, should not be taken as evidence that from the start he was involved in plans to conquer Greece. We have seen that he was obsessed by the crusades and by the need to help the Holy Land. In the years 1202 to 1204 he was also comparatively young and inexperienced. Faced by a group of ruthless politicians, who actually prevented the legate Peter Capuano from joining the crusade at Venice, and by a leviathan that went lumbering away out of control, his compliance and long silences, which have aroused suspicion, can surely best be interpreted as hesitation, an inability to decide how to put his precious instrument back on its right path.

We have seen that the authority which legitimised this form of the Holy War was the papacy; that the crusaders' vows enabled a temporal activity to be brought under some ecclesiastical authority; that the popes could act with effect in the proclamation, preaching and financing of a crusade; but that once the army was on the march their powers were more theoretical than real. No spiritual leader, however exalted, could really exercise control over so secular an affair as war.

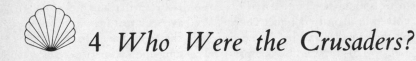 4 *Who Were the Crusaders?*

The Vow

THERE could be no crusade without crusaders and what made a man a
crusader was the taking of a vow. This vow was introduced by Pope
Urban II when at Clermont he asked his audience to make promises
and told those who answered his call to sew crosses on their clothes as a
public sign of their commitment. This was a new element in the Christian Holy War, although it was the product of a train of thought already
in his mind before November 1095: at Piacenza in the previous March
he had replied to the appeal from the Greeks by urging men to take an
oath to help God and the Byzantine emperor against the pagans. Of
course Christian vows had had a long history and for a long time had
been viewed as creating legally binding obligations, but over the next
century and a half they were to be treated exhaustively by canon
lawyers. They came to be defined as deliberate commitments made to
God to do or not to do certain acts. They could be simple, made with
no formalities and therefore not enforceable as far as the Church was
concerned, or solemn, publicly taken, expressed in the present tense and
legally binding; .general, obligatory on all Christians, or special,
resulting in individual, voluntary acts; necessary, in that they were
needed for salvation, or voluntary, undertaken out of personal devotion; pure, being absolute commitments, or conditional. A man would
go through several stages — termed *deliberatio, propositum* and *votum* —
before he was definitely committed, but once he had taken a *votum* this,
if unfulfilled, was binding on his heirs, although in certain circumstances he could be dispensed from it or could commute it. The
definition just given was the product of a long period of development,
but it is a useful starting-point from which to describe the vow to
crusade. This was usually solemn, always special and voluntary and
often conditional. It resulted in a temporary commitment which in

terms of the expeditions to the East seems generally to have been to visit the Holy Sepulchre in Jerusalem with the qualification that the pilgrimage must be made in the ranks of an organised armed expedition authorised by the pope. Surviving evidence for the Albigensian Crusade suggests that in that case the vow was made to war against the heretics and enemies of the faith in Languedoc. There was a very close relationship between the vows of crusaders and pilgrims. Canon lawyers made little differentiation between them and it was only around the year 1200 that they mentioned the crusaders' vows independently; the obligation of a crusader was to make what was regarded as a kind of pilgrimage and many of his privileges had previously been enjoyed by pilgrims; the rites for the taking of the Cross (of which, incidentally, none survives before the later twelfth century: they may not have developed independently before that time) appear to have been variants of those for making pilgrimages and it is probable that they derived from them: crusaders could even be invested with the scrip and staff of pilgrims as well as with the cross that marked their special promise.

Privileges

The taking of the vow and participation in a crusade had consequences for the status and rights of the man involved. He became, as we have seen, a kind of temporary ecclesiastic, subject to the courts of the Church. The vow he had made was a means by which his immediate enthusiasm could be turned into a legal obligation, enforceable by the judges to whom he was now answerable, and as early as the First Crusade the papacy was prepared to excommunicate those who failed to carry out what they had promised. The church courts would impose, or threaten to impose, the ecclesiastical sanctions of excommunication, interdict and suspension on reluctant crusaders, though canon lawyers went so far as to propose the disinheritance of heirs who did not carry out the unfulfilled vows of their dead fathers. But crusaders also gained the right to enjoy certain privileges as soon as they had taken the Cross or at least had begun to fulfil their obligations. It must be stressed that the Indulgence was not necessarily one of those that came into effect immediately, for it could not be decided whether it became effective on the taking of the vow or after the performance of the act for which the vow had been made. It will therefore be discussed separately.

The other privileges are often listed under the headings of spiritual rights, those contributing to the good of a crusader's soul, and temporal, those pertaining to his physical well-being. But all of them, apart from the right to benefit from the prayers offered for crusaders by the universal Church, which was not technically a privilege at all, were in fact legal exemptions from the operation of the courts or invitations to the courts to act on the crusader's behalf. They are perhaps better divided into those which eased the life of a crusader in a world of legal niceties and technicalities and those which were descended from or were elaborations of the original privileges enjoyed by pilgrims.

The first group can be quickly dealt with. One of them, the licence to clerics who joined the crusade to enjoy their benefices for a time, even though non-resident, and to pledge them to raise money for the journey, is to be found in the twelfth century, although it was not fully confirmed by the papacy until the thirteenth. The rest were granted from the pontificate of Innocent III onwards and by the middle of the thirteenth century may be summarised as: release from excommunication by virtue of taking the Cross; the licence to have dealings with excommunicates while on crusade without incurring censure; the right not to be cited for legal proceedings outside one's native diocese; freedom from the consequences of an interdict; the privilege of having a personal confessor, who was often allowed to dispense his patron from irregularities and to grant pardon for sins, like homicide, which were usually reserved for papal jurisdiction; and the right to count a crusade vow as an adequate substitute for another vow made previously but not yet carried out.

The privileges of the second group are more important. At the time of the First Crusade pilgrims were subject in the same way as clerics to church courts; their persons were protected from attack, a security that was reinforced as the Peace Movement gained ground; they were assured that lands and possessions seized by others during their absence would be returned to them; they could demand hospitality from the Church; they were in theory exempted from tolls and taxes and immune from arrest; and they may already have had the right to a suspension of legal proceedings in which they were involved until their return. Crusaders enjoyed the same rights from the first. As temporary churchmen they were subject in all but a few exceptional matters to ecclesiastical law and were exempt from secular jurisdiction in cases that arose after they had taken the Cross. At Clermont Urban II accorded them the protection of the Truce of God and throughout the papacy stressed that their persons should be secure. In their absence their families and properties were protected by the Church, which assumed this duty during or very soon after the First Crusade. Cases on the question were already being examined by ecclesiastical judges very early in the twelfth century and the principles were stated at the First Lateran Council and in *Quantum predecessores,* to be constantly repeated thereafter.

> And we decree that their wives and children, goods and possessions should remain under the protection of Holy Church; under our protection and that of the archbishops, bishops and other prelates of the Church of God. And by apostolic authority we forbid any legal suit to be brought thereafter concerning any of the possessions they held peacefully when they took the Cross until there is absolutely certain knowledge of their return or death.

> Since [wrote Pope Gregory VIII to the crusader Hinco of Serotin in 1187] you. . . having assumed the sign of the living Cross, propose to go to the aid of the Holy Land, we. . . take under the protection of St Peter and ourselves your person, with your dependants and those goods which you reasonably possess at present, . . . stating that they all should be kept undiminished and together from the time of your departure on pilgrimage overseas until your return or death is most certainly known.

The Church itself, through the agency of the bishops or, in the cases of some important crusaders, of special officials called *conservatores crucesignatorum,* oversaw the protection of the lands. It was common, particularly in England where the crown often acted as the guardian of their property, for crusaders also to appoint attorneys to defend their interests in their absence. Crusaders also came to be entitled to *essoin,* a delay in the performance of services and in judicial proceedings to which they were a party until their return; to a quick settlement of outstanding court cases if they so willed; to permission to count the crusade as restitution of some article stolen; to the right to dispose of or mortgage fiefs or other property which was ordinarily inalienable; to a moratorium on debts and exemption from interest payments while on crusade; and to a freedom from tolls and taxes.

Then, of course, there was the Indulgence. A question that much concerned canon lawyers in the thirteenth century was whether this was effective from the moment the Cross was taken or only once the crusade had been accomplished: in other words, was it consequent upon the making of the vow or the performance of the act for which the vow was made? This was important since upon a ruling hung the hopes of heavenly reward for crusaders who died before completely fulfilling their vows or even before they had begun to carry them out. St Thomas Aquinas was of the opinion that the wording of the papal grants of Indulgence was vital here: if an Indulgence had been conceded to those who took the Cross for the aid of the Holy Land, then the condition of the Indulgence was merely the making of the vow and not the journey; if, on the other hand, an Indulgence had been given specifically to those who went overseas, then the condition, the crusade itself, must be fulfilled before it could be effective. But it is clear that there was not universal agreement on the matter, which was complicated by the fact that Indulgences could also be granted to those who participated in crusades but took no vows at all. All one can be certain of is that, unlike other privileges, the Indulgence was not an automatic consequence of the taking of the vow.

But what was the Indulgence? Official teaching is that, after confession, absolution and the performance of the works that earn it, a sinner is granted by the Church on God's behalf remission of all or part of the penalties that are the inevitable consequence of sin. This remission applies not only to the canonical punishment imposed by the Church itself, usually by a priest in the confessional, but also to the temporal punishment imposed by God either in this world or in the next. The doctrine is influenced by the distinction between the guilt of and the punishment due for sin, known to Hugh of St Victor and Gratian in the early twelfth century, and by the concept, only fully formulated in the thirteenth century but present in an embryonic form much earlier, of the Treasury of Merits, an inexhaustible credit-balance of merit stored up by Christ and the saints on which the Church can draw on behalf of a repentant sinner. The first Indulgence is only to be found in the middle of the eleventh century, the theory of Indulgences developed with the crusades, and the early grants display a deplorable vagueness of purpose and confusion of terminology. It is, therefore, generally agreed that the Indulgence as we know it cannot have been fully accepted, at an official level, until the thirteenth century, although, whatever the popes and their advisers may have thought, ordinary Christians assumed from the first that it meant a remission of all punishment due for sin, an assurance of direct entry into heaven. It is, however, possible that the developed view of the Indulgence began to be accepted in Rome rather earlier than is nowadays supposed.

In 1063 what was arguably the first recognisable Indulgence was granted by Pope Alexander II to warriors in Spain: 'We, by the authority of the holy apostles Peter and Paul, both raise their penance from them and make remission of their sins.' It is clear that two ideas were present in this formulation. First, penance, the penalty enjoined by the Church, was waived, but secondly, sins were remitted. It was the expression *remissio peccatorum*, remission of sins, which came closest to the developed Indulgence, since it referred to the extinction of the sins involved, and therefore presumably of their consequences, without distinction between penance and divine punishment. Urban II used the term twice, in his letter to Flanders in 1095 and in 1098–9, when he granted to those defending Tarragona in Spain the same Indulgence as was given to crusaders, but he was not consistent, for he also drew upon the other strand of thought to be found in Alexander's letter. Canon 2 of the Council of Clermont declared:

> Whoever for devotion only, not for honour or financial gain, joins the expedition for the freeing of the Church of God in Jerusalem, can count that journey as a substitute for all penance.

Here we have simply the dispensation from the penance enjoined for a sin in return for the performance of another penitential act. The conciliar canons as they have come down to us are not entirely trustworthy, but in this matter they are echoed in Urban's letter to Bologna, in which, with a reference to Clermont, he assured those who went

> only for the salvation of their souls and the liberation of the Church, by the mercy of God and the prayers of the Catholic Church and by our authority and that of nearly all the archbishops and bishops in Gaul, we remit all penance for those sins for which they will have made true and perfect confession.

We may conclude that Urban himself had not fixed on a definite terminology for the Indulgence and was probably unclear in his own mind about it. The same was true of his successor, Paschal II, who in 1099 wrote of the remission of sins, but in 1101 of the remission of penance.

Uncertainty persisted during the next half-century, although there can be discerned a tendency towards the idea of the remission of sins rather than penance. There are statements on the remission or pardon of sins in the decrees of the First Lateran Council in 1123 and in an encyclical of Pope Adrian IV in 1157, and the idea was especially prominent in the preaching of the Second Crusade. St Bernard wrote of 'the Indulgence of sins and eternal glory' and told his correspondents:

> Receive the sign of the Cross and the supreme pontiff, the vicar of him to whom it was said, 'Whatever you loose on earth will be loosed in heaven', offers you that full Indulgence of all sins of which you have made confession with a contrite heart.

Pope Eugenius III's letter *Quantum predecessores* of 1145, in spite of looking back to the precedent set by Urban II, went quite a long way towards the developed view of the Indulgence, perhaps under St Bernard's influence.

> By the authority of omnipotent God and Blessed Peter the Prince of the Apostles, conceded to us by God, we grant remission of and absolution from sins, as instituted by our aforesaid predecessor, in such a way that whosoever devoutly begins and completes such a holy journey or dies on it will obtain absolution from all his sins concerning which he has made confession with a contrite and humble heart; and he will receive the fruit of everlasting recompense from the rewarder of all.

But the most important step was taken by Pope Alexander III. In 1165, when he published his first call to crusade, he simply issued a version of *Quantum predecessores,* including, of course, the reference to the Indulgence quoted above. And in *In quantis pressuris* of the following year he granted 'that remission of sins which Pope Urban of pious memory and our predecessor Eugenius instituted' and wrote of 'absolution from all sins', related to the merits of SS Peter and Paul, and 'remission of all sins'. The significance of these phrases becomes clearer when they are compared to a careful reference to the remission of enjoined penance elsewhere in the letter and we may conclude that to whoever drafted it the remission of sins was not meant to apply only to the penalties imposed in confession. This was rash and one can perhaps detect anxiety at the papal *Curia,* for by 1169, when the next crusade encyclical, *Inter omnia*, was published, there had been a change of heart. *Inter omnia* made reference to the remission of sins, but it also contained a remarkably cautious statement on the Indulgence, referring to it as 'that *remission of penance imposed by the priestly ministry* which Urban and Eugenius are known to have established'. There could be no doubt what kind of Indulgence was being granted here, for the term *remission of penance* was strengthened by the additional reference to the priest in the confessional and Alexander stressed this in a letter of the same day to the Archbishop of Rheims, in which he wrote of 'Indulgence of penances'. But over the next twelve years the papal *Curia* changed its mind again, and this time finally. This change may have taken place in the early 1170s, when there was, in a bull for the crusade against the Slavs, a reference to the remission of sins. But it had definitely occurred by 16 January 1181 when Alexander issued a new crusade encyclical, *Cor nostrum*. Parts of it were modelled on *Inter omnia*, so any differences are significant. In it, for those who fought for two years in the Holy Land

> by the authority confided in us on behalf of the piety of Jesus Christ and the blessed apostles Peter and Paul we grant them absolution from all their crimes concerning which they have made confession with contrite and humble hearts.

This was, of course, far from being a really precise statement of the fully developed doctrine of Indulgences, but in comparison with the vacillation that had gone before its firmness is very striking and it is worth mentioning that thenceforward all papal letters, save one of Celestine III which contained muddled drafting, referred to the remission of sins rather than of penance, adding, from Innocent III's pontificate when the formula reached its definitive form, the phrase 'and we promise them a greater share of eternal salvation as the reward of the just'. It is as if we can see the papal *Curia* making up its mind and deciding to follow the course that would lead, if it had not done so already, to the idea of the Indulgence as we know it. And by the early thirteenth century even the higher clergy had our idea of Indulgences, as we can see from one of James of Vitry's sermons.

> Crusaders who, truly contrite and confessed, are girded in the service of God and then die in Christ's service are counted truly as martyrs, freed from both venial and mortal sins and from all enjoin-

ed penance, absolved from the penalties for sin in this world, from the penalties of purgatory in the next, secure from the torments of Gehenna, crowned with glory and honour in eternal beatitude . . ..
Do not in any way doubt that this pilgrimage will not only earn you remission of sins and the reward of eternal life, but it will also offer much to wives, sons, parents, living or dead: whatever good you do in this life for them. This is the full and entire Indulgence which the supreme pontiff, according to the keys committed to him by God, concedes to you.

Who Were the Crusaders?

Two features of the vow were that it could be taken by anyone, of whatever sex or walk of life, and that the action promised was essentially temporary: a layman or a priest would put his normal occupation aside for a short time to go crusading. Historians of the crusades refer often to kings, magnates and knights and also describe the movements among the peasantry, but it is important to remember that the appeal of the crusades was confined to no class and a significant part was played by artisans, merchants, burgesses of all kinds, and even criminals whose sentences could be commuted in return for participation or settlement in the Holy Land. In the late twelfth century attempts were being made in England to list the crusaders living in certain areas: in Lincolnshire they were nearly all poor and included a clerk, a smith, a skinner, a potter, a butcher and a vintner; 43 crusaders were to be found in the archdeaconry of Cornwall, including a tailor, a smith, a shoemaker, 2 chaplains, a merchant, a miller, 2 tanners and 2 women. In 1250 the ship *St Victor*, bound from France to the East, was carrying 453 crusaders, of whom 14 were knights and leaders of groups, 90 retainers and 7 clerics; the remaining 342 passengers were commoners and the surnames of several of them suggest burgess origins; 42 were women, 15 of whom accompanied their husbands. 1 travelled with her father and 2 with their brothers.

Taking part in a crusade, therefore, would be men and women of all classes, even in the thirteenth century when redemption would have enabled many to have released themselves by making money payments. It would be interesting to know how these heterogeneous bands of people were organised, but the subject has never been studied and one can only make some tentative suggestions. When a king like Louis VII or Philip II or Richard I, or a very important magnate like Thibaut of Champagne or the Lord Edward, took part it was natural that he should be in unquestioned command, although if two kings were on the same expedition they would never allow themselves to be subject to one another: the French troops on the Third Crusade remained obstinately independent of Richard of England even after the departure of Philip of France. Secondly, a knight like Geoffrey of Sergines, about whom more below, would organise his own band of followers and then of course lead them on campaign. Thirdly, groups of crusaders, thrown together by circumstances or drawn from the same region, would elect their own leaders. Such captains might be appointed temporarily – immediately after the arrival in Egypt of the first contingent of the Fifth Crusade the crusaders chose someone to command them until the rest of the army arrived – but full-time leaders were also elected and this procedure must have been very common: the thirteenth-century translator of the History of William of Tyre assumed that it was what had happened on the First Crusade. It can be seen in operation during the planning for the Fourth Crusade when Boniface of Montferrat was chosen as leader and also during the Fifth, for when they gathered for departure the participants from the Rhineland and the Low Countries elected William of Holland as captain and George of Wied as second-in-command; once in Egypt the crusaders appear to have been divided into nations and the Germans seem to have chosen Adolph of Berg to command them; after his death in 1218 George of Wied was elected to succeed him. It was no doubt essential for a noble to be chosen for such an office. Fourthly, authorities in the West might pick officers to command the contingents from their districts: at the time of the Fifth Crusade Italian towns like Asti and perhaps Sienna may have chosen commanders before the departure of their forces. Fifthly, at the initiative of a local magnate or a high ecclesiastic or town burgesses in the West, citizens might organise themselves into a confraternity, a common form of religious association, though here committed to the defence of Christendom. As early as 1122 a confraternity in Spain was playing a part in the reconquest and another in Toulouse was established by the bishop to participate in the Albigensian Crusade. Confraternities from Spain, Pisa, Lombardy and Tuscany, England and Châteaudun in France maintained bands of crusaders in the East, and their importance is shown by the significant part their leaders played in politics of the Kingdom of Jerusalem.

Crusaders drawn from so many walks of life must naturally have had a great many reasons for taking the Cross. Of course not all of them were moved by high ideals and at one time it was fashionable to explain the appeal of the crusades, especially the First, almost entirely in economic terms. There was economic misery in parts of France in the later eleventh century and recent studies have shown how complex social developments in the knightly class contributed greatly to the response from certain areas. The desire for a new life in a new land or even a sense of duty to one's family, which one could help by removing oneself from the scene, found expression in the reconquests of Spain and Sicily and in the colonisation movement east of the Elbe. They may also be revealed in the Latin conquest of Palestine and later of Greece. There can also be little doubt that the chance of leaving the country for a time with the privilege of having their lands, including recent gains, protected in their absence and a delay in any court proceedings that might be pending appealed to many who were in political or legal difficulties and there is often to be found a correlation between political disturbance and the popularity of the Cross in a district. It has recently been shown how the response in the late 1260s to crusade appeals in England was linked to the consequences of the civil war of a few years earlier: many of those whose acquisitions or behaviour during the war would have been subject to court investigation went on crusade with the Lord Edward, thus putting off any decision on their gains or actions for a few years.

But too much can be made of mundane motives at the expense of ideals. Economic and social pressures may have conditioned some men psychologically to answer Urban II's call in 1095, but it is important not to confuse the colonising movement which grew up once Palestine and Syria had been conquered with reactions at the time of the departure of the First Crusade. It is far-fetched to suppose that those in search of land, already available in Spain and Germany, clearly saw colonial gain at the end of a march of thousands of miles with unknown dangers on the way. One often finds, moreover, that the response to the appeals was to some extent conditioned by the attitudes of the great men in particular neighbourhoods: if these chose to go, others would follow. But if the magnates had strong economic motives they were surely in favour of staying at home. The ideals of the crusades must genuinely have attracted many. Participation in them expressed the most profound feelings of popular spirituality, and there can be little doubt that their spell lasted a very long time. Ordinary men were deeply moved by the concept of the new knight and by the desire to serve

Christ by taking up his Cross, by defending the Church and by physically occupying and holding the land sanctified by his presence. And the idea that here at last was a fruitful field of action for the layman – one that he was especially qualified to undertake – had a powerful appeal in an age when the priesthood was privileged and of great prestige, and the life of the laity was regarded very much as second best to that of the religious. Crusade sermons dwelt on these themes, and one cannot believe that the preachers would have persisted with them had they made no impression on those they were addressing.

Geoffrey of Sergines

The crusades were at their most popular between 1187 and 1250 and thereafter enthusiasm began to wane in an atmosphere of growing cynicism and indifference. We must not, however, exaggerate the decline, for the call to crusade would continue to inspire men for centuries. It would not be out of place to spend a few pages on the career of one of the leading crusaders of the mid-thirteenth century, although he is now almost forgotten. Geoffrey of Sergines (c. 1205–69) came from a village north of Sens and not far from Paris. His family had close links with the Church: a brother was abbot of S. Jacques-de-Provins; Peter of Sergines, the Archbishop of Tyre who was captured by the Muslims at the Battle of Gaza in 1244, may have been a relative; and so may have been Margaret of Sergines who was abbess of Montivilliers.

Geoffrey is mentioned by chroniclers in connection with military engagements in Palestine in 1242 and 1244. The most likely date for his arrival in the East would be 1 September 1239, with an inglorious crusade under Count Thibaut of Champagne and Duke Hugh of Burgundy which contained a number of officials and servants of the French crown. He returned to France in 1244 and then in 1248 travelled East with King Louis, to whom he had been closely attached as early as 1236, when he was permitted by his previous liege-lord, Count Hugh of Blois, to become the king's liegeman, the most effective means of formalising a close relationship, since one was bound to one's liege-lord before all other men. An intimacy between the two men is confirmed in John of Joinville's account of Louis's crusade. John wrote of Geoffrey as of one who, like himself, was among the king's closest confidants. He was one of a select band of eight companions who stood guard over the king at Damietta and throughout the crusade he was to be found in the king's council and entrusted with important duties. On 5 April 1250, as the crusade retired in disorder from Mansurah, he alone stood by and protected the king: Louis was later to say that Geoffrey had defended him against the Egyptians as a good valet swats the flies around his lord. Louis set out for home in April 1254 but before going he arranged to leave behind Geoffrey, who was made Seneschal of Jerusalem and given command of a special contingent of 100 knights, with money to employ additional crossbowmen and sergeants. The granting of these two different posts needs some explanation. The seneschalcy was the most prestigious and demanding of the great offices of the crown of Jerusalem and Geoffrey was to hold it until his death. In the absence of the king or regent, and provided the ruler had not appointed a lieutenant to represent him, the seneschal presided over meetings of the High Court, the most important of the royal courts in which all liege-vassals of the crown had the right to sit and speak. He was, therefore, *ex officio* the second man in the judicial hierarchy. He also supervised the *secrete*, the royal financial office and treasury, which worked according to Muslim practice. With this post Geoffrey became a fief-holder of Jerusalem and ranked among the political leaders of the kingdom. His long period of office must have given him an unrivalled experience of the working of the courts and royal administration, but one should not automatically infer from this that he had administrative abilities, because with his appointment can perhaps be seen a change in the way seneschals were chosen. Two of his successors, Robert of Crésèques in 1269 and John of Grailly from 1272 to 1278, were, like him, crusaders in command of regiments supported by the French crown and it may be that the King of France had demanded the seneschalcy for his captains as part of the deal by which he financed a permanent garrison in the Holy Land.

In time Geoffrey came to be appointed to offices within the kingdom that carried even greater responsibilities. From 1259 to September 1261 and from 1264 to 1267 he governed Palestine on behalf of absent regents and from September 1261 to 1263 and perhaps for a few months in 1264 he was regent himself. With only a few breaks, therefore, he ruled the Kingdom of Jerusalem from 1259 to 1267 and he did so well: alone of the governors of the period his reputation for severe though impartial justice was recognised by the chroniclers. 'He held the land well and the country at peace', wrote one, 'and he was a good justiciar'. Another wrote that

he was a very strong justiciar and in his time hanged many thieves
and murderers, nor was he willing to spare anyone because of his
birth or the gifts he could give, nor on account of friendship or any
other matter.

A particularly scandalous case resolved by him concerned a knight who
had killed a Cypriot bishop and had taken refuge with the Pisans in
Acre, the chief city of the kingdom. Geoffrey invaded the Pisan quarter
with men-at-arms – a sign of a strong ruler was his attitude towards the
powerful and highly privileged Italian merchants – and forced the
Pisans to surrender the murderer to him.

In 1254 King Louis had also made Geoffrey captain of a French contingent left behind in the Holy Land and it was Geoffrey's activities as
a military leader that brought him fame in the West. With his establishment of this force the King of France began a practice that he
and his successors were to follow for several decades. Under captains
like Geoffrey, Oliver of Termes, Erard of Valéry and Robert of
Crésèques, this company was one of the most formidable fighting
forces in the Holy Land. Geoffrey, who also led his own private regiment in the 1260s, remained in over-all command of the French troops
until his death. These were supposed to be financed by the French
crown, but a rather ironical remark by the poet Rutebeuf suggests that
they were already short of cash in the mid-1250s. In October 1265 the
Patriarch of Jerusalem, the Masters of the Temple and the Hospital,
Geoffrey and Oliver of Termes wrote to Louis on behalf of some
merchants from whom they had borrowed 1500 *livres*. The merchants
could not recover the money from the king because in a shipwreck on
the way home they had lost the receipts with which they had been
issued. Geoffrey and Oliver added that on Louis's authority they had
borrowed another 2500 *livres* of Tours. In 1267 the patriarch wrote a
long letter to the Commander of the Templars in France, with detailed
instructions on the various diplomatic moves he was to make to help
the cause of the Holy Land in the courts of western Europe. He pointed
out that Geoffrey needed 10,000 *livres* of Tours a year to keep his
forces, presumably both his own and those of France, in being: this
may have been because in a military disaster the year before his troops
had been badly knocked about. Some of his knights, the patriarch
reported, were wanting to leave and so to pay them the patriarch
himself and the Masters of the Temple and the Hospital had asked for
3000 *livres* of Tours from the crusade hundredth that was being levied

on the French Church. But already in 1266 Louis had sent letters of credit to Geoffrey and to Erard of Valéry 'to retain knight pilgrims in the Holy land' and in June 1267 Geoffrey and Erard were issuing receipts and having the letters certified in Acre by the patriarch and the Masters.

Geoffrey returned briefly to the West in the early 1260s. At this time he took the Cross once more and planned to travel East with a large company of knights. On 13 February 1262 Pope Urban IV gave him licence, as a crusader, to have a portable altar at which Mass could be celebrated; his chaplain was permitted to administer the sacraments to his knights and companions; and he was exempted from any decree of excommunication or interdict issued by a papal agent or, interestingly, by the Bishop of Acre, unless his name was specifically mentioned in a papal decree. The next few years revealed his devotion to the crusading cause, which was to keep him in the East until his death and nearly bankrupted him. He was now commanding his own company as well as the troops paid for by Louis and in February 1263 Urban IV asked the King of France and the King of Navarre, who as Count of Champagne was a French landowner, to send the proceeds of a market tax, called the *denarius Dei* and normally used for charitable purposes, to Geoffrey himself, who had taken on his shoulders practically the whole weight of the guard of Palestine and whose livelihood was threatened by the burden: the pope granted Indulgences to those who paid the *denarius Dei* and those who administered it. Some time probably between February and June 1265 Urban's successor, Clement IV, was himself giving attention to Geoffrey's needs. In letters to Louis and to the Archbishop of Tyre, the collector of crusade taxes in France, he emphasised, as Urban had done, how completely Geoffrey had committed himself to the well-being of the Holy Land. But although aided financially by the French crown Geoffrey was now oppressed by poverty, was threatening to leave and had asked for a subsidy from the crusade hundredth in France. The pope had agreed to this and he wrote to Geoffrey, informing him that financial help was on its way and adding, by way of encouragement, that he recognised how much the Holy Land depended on him. 500 *livres* were paid over in June, but more was needed and in mid-1267 the patriarch reported that Geoffrey would have to leave Palestine to sell his fiefs in France unless cash arrived.

Geoffrey died on 11 April 1269. Although an active man and certainly not a failure as captain, seneschal, regent and lieutenant of regents, he was no intellectual: there is no evidence for this in the writings associated with the feudal nobility in Palestine, a society which was always ready to praise brain-power. And although he was brave and a good warrior we have evidence for one act of stupidity as a military commander. In August 1266 he was in command of an important part of the vanguard of a Christian army raiding into Galilee which was ambushed and badly mauled by Muslim troops because in the search for loot it had carelessly allowed too great a distance to separate it from the main body of Christians. Geoffrey's qualities were conventional – John of Joinville called him a 'good knight and prud'homme' – and they were summed up in a remarkable poem, *La complainte de Monseigneur Geoffrei de Sergines*, written in 1255–6 by the great French poet Rutebeuf, who knew the area of France from which Geoffrey came. To Rutebeuf Geoffrey was the finest of all knights, valiant and bounteous of soul. When he lived in France he was known as a gentle, courteous and debonair man with much love for God and Holy Church. He never deceived anyone, feeble or strong, and he was generous to poor neighbours.

> He loved his liege-lord so much
> That he went with him to avenge
> The shame of God over the seas.
> One ought to love such a prud'homme.
> With the king he moved and went,
> With the king he there remained,
> With the king he bore good and ill.
> There has never been such a man.

Geoffrey was severely honest and impartial as a judge. He was deeply loyal to St Louis, risking his life in defence of his king in the retreat from Mansurah in 1250. Earlier in the crusade, when hopes were still bright and the Christians were negotiating with the infidel the return of the city of Jerusalem in exchange for their conquests in Egypt, the Muslims had demanded Louis himself as a hostage. Geoffrey had fiercely opposed this in a council held in the Christian camp, saying that he would prefer them all to be killed or captured to the reproach of leaving their king a hostage with the enemy. He was very pious, which would explain why he got on so well with St Louis and also his devotion to the crusades. The popes of the 1260s wrote of him as one who was totally committed, to the extent of exercising a ministry: 'devoting himself wholly in the ministry for the Crucified One. . . the one and only minister in the defence of the Holy Land'. In fact he might be compared, though a layman, to a brother of one of the Military Orders and he must have had a strong influence on his son, who also took the Cross and fought with Charles of Anjou in southern Italy.

This devotion to the crusades must not be seen in isolation. Geoffrey was not the only man to identify himself with them. Careers like his were to be found not only in the Military Orders, but also among laymen like Erard of Valéry, John of Grailly and Oliver of Termes, whose remarkable life reveals almost as much commitment as does Geoffrey's. These free-lance crusaders, not necessarily attached to a major expedition, were heirs to a tradition of crusading that went back to the twelfth century. But in the 1250s and 1260s their kind of war against the infidel was coming to be accepted as the right one for the times, as there evolved the new strategy of the maintenance by western powers of permanent garrisons in the Holy Land, backed up by many small expeditions which could be put together quickly and would provide immediate aid. Geoffrey of Sergines, as a crusader, captain of the French forces in the East and commander of his own company, played a large part in the application of these ideas at a time when they were developing. His career shows how important a role one of these garrison captains could play in the affairs of the Holy Land and his commitment, paralleled in other lives, should make us think twice before suggesting that the crusading movement was losing momentum. An ideal that could inspire such men was still very much alive.

The Military Orders

It is questionable whether one ought to consider the brothers of the Military Orders at all in a chapter on crusaders. It is true that the Military Orders were founded as or developed into institutions closely associated with the crusading movement and inspired by its ideals, and it was because of this that some of them became very well-endowed. They were committed to the reconquest of Christian territory or to the defence of Christendom and they operated alongside the crusaders or in the same areas as they did. They were associated with the movement by its apologists, particularly St Bernard who, in his great defence of the Templars, the *De laude novae militiae*, developed with reference to them the theme of the new knighthood fighting on behalf of Christ. Some eight decades later James of Vitry defined their duties very much in terms of the crusades:

The brothers of the Military Orders are ordained to defend Christ's Church with the material sword, especially against those who are outside it; that is against the Muslims in Syria, against the Moors in Spain, against the pagans in Prussia, Livonia and Comania ... against schismatics in Greece and against heretics everywhere dispersed throughout the universal Church.

The Orders, he went on, differed in their habits and customs, 'but all are united in defence of the Church against infidels'. But however closely the Orders' aims were in accord with those of crusades, the brothers were not crusaders. Some, like the Templars, took vows which, at least in the actions to be performed, the reconquest of Jerusalem and the defence of the Holy Land, had similarities to those of crusaders, but others did not: the promises made by a brother of the Hospital of St John – to be obedient and chaste, to live in poverty as a serf and slave of the sick – made no reference whatever to the defence of Christendom. And even when a Military Order did impose a vow to defend Christendom upon its members, the form the promise took made it fundamentally different from that of a crusader. A brother of a Military Order was permanently committed to his duty; he was not a pilgrim, whose condition was essentially temporary, and so the concept of pilgrimage did not enter into his vow at all. This difference between the crusader and the brother of a Military Order was well brought out in one of James of Vitry's sermons, in which he told the story of a crusader who had been captured along with some Templars by the Muslims. On being asked if he was a Templar he replied, 'I am a secular knight and a pilgrim.'

It is not easy to generalise about the Military Orders because there were many of them and among them there was great variation. They followed different rules. Some, like the Orders of the Temple, the Hospital of St John and St Lazarus, drew recruits from all parts of Latin Christendom; others, like the Orders of St Mary of the Germans (the Order of the Teutonic Knights), Santiago, Alcantara, Calatrava and St Thomas, were nationally based. Some, like the Temple and the Hospital, were immensely rich; others were tiny and poor. Some were highly privileged, exempt from the authority of diocesan bishops and answerable only to Rome, prototypes of the great international Orders that grew up in the later Middle Ages – indeed the Orders of the Friars owed a great debt to the Templars and Hospitallers; others were in terms of privileges quite insignificant. The whole *raison d'être* of some was the defence of the faith; but others, like the Hospital of St John, had originated as purely charitable institutions which had only slowly, and then with the disapproval of the popes, turned themselves into Military Orders, and in them charitable activities remained their primary responsibility. Others still, like St Mary of the Germans, were founded both to fight and to care for the sick. But there were also some important and fundamental similarities. All were religious Orders, that is to say that they were religious institutes for which solemn vows were made and in which the brothers followed rules of life and the monastic *horarium* and submitted themselves to canonical discipline. Their essential characteristic was that a number of the professed lay brothers were themselves warriors. Any religious institution could have vassals owing military services or could employ mercenaries to garrison castles and protect territory, but these would not make it a Military Order. The Military Orders themselves made use of vassals and many mercenaries – in any engagement the number of brothers-at-arms in their forces was always comparatively small – but it was the class of fighting brothers that gave them their special features. And it was these lay brothers, rather than the priests as was normal in most religious Orders, who came to dominate them, being far more numerous and providing the great and lesser officers.

The Military Orders never had any difficulty in drawing in recruits, even as late as the eighteenth century, although their wealth, privileges and rivalries and a suspicion, very general in the West and rather unfair, that they were not pulling their weight made them increasingly unpopular with the clergy and with ordinary people in the thirteenth century. In fact their rules reflected the muscular qualities of the twelfth-century Latin Church; they showed none of the sympathy for alien ideas which after 1200 became a feature of the Christianity of St Thomas. Internationally run and highly privileged instruments of papal power, echoing contemporary notions of and ambitions for ecclesiastical organisation, the structures of the greater among them were if anything overelaborate and proved quite inadequate for their needs: organised on a vast scale, they were also massively incompetent. This led to the paradox that, although the spearheads of what were among the richest religious Orders of the time, the Convents in Palestine were always starved of money and often near bankruptcy.

The brothers in the East, standing to arms in a defensive war, marooned themselves in those magnificent fortresses which today still stand as mute monuments to the ideal of the just cause, the most beautiful and most depressing reminders of it. Yet by one of those quirks of history two of the Orders, the Hospitals of St John of Jerusalem and St Mary of the Germans, have survived. Both, especially the Hospital of St John on Rhodes until 1523 and on Malta until 1798, have played an important role into modern times and although today their tasks have greatly changed they are living relics of the age of the crusades.

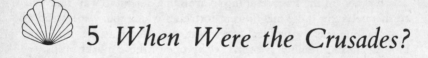

5 *When Were the Crusades?*

WE ARE now coming to the end of our enquiry and have reached the stage at which we can made a definition. A crusade was a manifestation of the Christian Holy War, fought against the infidels in the East, in Spain and in Germany and against heretics, schismatics and Christian lay opponents of the Church for the recovery of property or in defence. Its cause was just in the traditional sense, but it was related to the needs of all Christendom or the Church, rather than to those of a particular nation or region, and it was because it was Christ's own enterprise that it was not merely justifiable but was positively holy. Legitimate authorisation was given to it by the pope as head of Christendom and representative of Christ, rather than by a temporal ruler. At least some of the participants took a vow which subordinated them to the Church and assured some papal control over them in matters other than the actual waging of war. A crusade was regarded as a form of pilgrimage and pilgrimage terminology was often used of the crusaders and their campaigns; the vow the crusaders took was based on that of pilgrims and so were many of the privileges they enjoyed in consequence of it, particularly the protection of themselves, their families and properties. They were also granted Indulgences and when they were not engaged in war in the East these were specifically related to those given to crusaders in the Holy Land.

One ought now to try to give chronological bounds to the movement. When was the first and when the last crusade? Some answer to the first of these questions can be found if we look before 1095 at one campaign, which has often been seen as a crusade, and at the plans for another. In 1063–4 a French expedition, led by the Duke of Aquitaine and associated with Catalans and Aragonese, took Barbastro in Spain. At the same time a Truce of God was proclaimed in Catalonia so that there should be peace behind the lines and Pope Alexander II issued the first Indulgence for the combatants. Here was an international army fighting the Muslims for the recovery of once Christian property, linked, as was the First Crusade, to a Truce of God and supported by the pope, who granted the participants an Indulgence. But there was no formal papal authorisation, no concept of pilgrimage and above all no vow made by those taking part and therefore no protection for them. It cannot be called a true crusade.

Following the Battle of Manzikert in 1071 the Seljuk Turks overran Asia Minor and the young Byzantine Emperor Michael VII, disregarding the bad feelings between the Latin and Greek Churches, appealed to the new Pope Gregory VII for aid. Gregory, hoping to bring the Churches together, reacted vigorously and there survive five letters written by him to various correspondents between February and December 1074. He dwelt on the sufferings of the eastern Christians and the necessity of bringing them fraternal aid. He compared service in the army to service of the Church, calling on one man 'to defend the Christian faith and the heavenly king', and he stressed the heavenly rewards that would result: in one letter he wrote that 'by momentous labour you can acquire eternal mercy' and in another he exclaimed that while it was glorious to die for one's fatherland it was still more glorious to die for Christ. The expedition was his own and he might lead it himself: he reported to King Henry IV of Germany that over 50,000 men were ready to go if they could have the pope 'in the expedition as leader and high priest' and he even suggested that under his leadership the army might push on to the Holy Sepulchre. He was thinking, extraordinarily enough, of leaving Henry behind to keep and defend the Roman Church in his absence. Much of this, of course, was hyperbole and the plans were given up when Gregory and Henry became involved in the Investiture Contest. But one can see here the concept of the Holy War and papal authorisation of it, some idea of eternal reward and also a reference to Jerusalem. Gregory's ideas may have been more developed than these letters reveal – he was later regarded as the father of the crusades – while what we know of Pope Urban II would make it very possible that he was merely following in the footsteps of his master. But on the evidence before us we cannot go so far. Gregory's letters contain no clear link between the planned expedition and pilgrimages, no Indulgence and, again, no sign of the vow and resulting protection for crusaders. Until further evidence comes to light one is forced to conclude that the plans of 1074 were not really those for a crusade, that the traditional date of 1095 for the origins of the movement is correct and that it stemmed from an initiative taken by Urban II.

It is still not possible to decide when the crusades came to an end. Certain elements long survived. Papal authorisations of war against Islam and grants of crusade Indulgences were made regularly up to the last quarter of the eighteenth century. The Knights of St John continued to wage an increasingly ineffective war against the Turks up to 1798, when they were driven from Malta by Napoleon, and their Order is still in existence. The *Bula de la cruzada*, giving rights based on those of crusaders, and the *cruzada*, an ecclesiastical tax linked to grants of Indulgences and minor privileges, were still to be found in Spain and Latin America into very modern times. But when was the last time that the essential elements of papal authorisation, the Indulgence and the vow, came together? The existence of papal letters proclaiming the crusade and granting Indulgences is not enough. When were the last crusaders? At the moment this question cannot be answered. There were certainly men who had taken the Cross in the sixteenth century and there may have been some in the seventeenth and even possibly in the early eighteenth century, fighting in the armies of Venice or Austria or the Holy League against the Turks. But the nearer we get to the present day the more the mists swirl in, obscuring our vision. Frankly, until some enterprising historian decides to research the subject and evidence of vows to crusade in this period comes to light, the last crusade, in the true sense of the term, cannot be dated. But we are left with the tantalising possibility that it took place less than three centuries ago.

Select Bibliography

This bibliography does not include translated sources. I feel strongly that the reading of scattered narrative accounts has little value for students, other than in showing them what medieval chronicles are like. And it can be positively misleading, for creative historical research does not rest on the uncertain foundations provided by a single witness, but involves the careful comparison of many fragments of evidence, coming in different forms and from different directions. It would be much more useful for the student if his instructor were to assemble as much translated evidence as possible for one incident or series of events; and this can be profitably done for each of the first four major crusades. Those who want to get hold of reasonable translations of many of the narrative accounts of the expeditions to the East will find references to them included in Mayer's *Bibliographie* (about which more below), and several of the local European chronicles and histories have also been translated.

H. E. Mayer, in his *Bibliographie zur Geschichte der Kreuzzüge* (Hanover, 1960), has compiled a first-class bibliography of books and articles published before 1958–9, containing over 5 000 titles. Professor Mayer issued a supplement for the years 1958–67 as 'Literaturbericht über die Geschichte der Kreuzzüge', in *Historische Zeitschrift*, Sonderheft 3 (1969), and his regular short reviews for *Deutsches Archiv für Erforschung des Mittelalters* are a good guide to what is being brought out year by year.
  A competent and up-to-date short history of the crusades to the East is H. E. Mayer, *The Crusades* (Oxford, 1972). For the general reader the best of the large-scale works is S. Runciman, *A History of the Crusades*, 3 vols (Cambridge, 1951–4), which has the inner unity and interest which comes from the work of a single author, and for this reason is to be preferred to K. M. Setton (editor-in-chief), *A History of the Crusades*, 2nd. ed., 3 vols published so far (Madison, 1969–). This enterprise, often termed the 'Wisconsin History of the Crusades', suffers from the usual failings of collaborative projects and is far from being comprehensive, although some individual chapters are very good and others are on topics that are not easily read about elsewhere. J. Prawer, *Histoire du royaume latin de Jérusalem*, 2 vols (Paris, 1969–70) has some interesting things to say about the movement.
  The crusades of the fourteenth century have been described by A. Z. Atiya, in *The Crusade in the Later Middle Ages* (London, 1938) and in vol. III of Setton (ed.), *A History of the Crusades* (referred to above), and briefly by A. T. Luttrell, 'The Crusade in the Fourteenth Century', in J. R. Hale *et al.* (eds), *Europe in the Late Middle Ages* (London, 1965). But this is a field in which a good, detailed work is badly needed; for the moment it is true to say that in many ways the best studies are two written in the nineteenth century: J. Delaville Le Roulx, *La France en Orient au XIVe siècle: Expéditions du maréchal Boucicaut*, 2 vols (Paris, 1885–6), and N. Iorga, *Philippe de Mézières (1327–1405) et la croisade au XIVe siècle* (Paris, 1896). Very little has been written on the crusades after 1400.

The historical background to and the development of the concept of the crusade were described in a great work by C. Erdmann, *Die Entstehung des Kreuzzugsgedankens* (Stuttgart, 1935), although his views were to some extent challenged in two important studies: M. Villey, *La croisade: Essai sur la formation d'une théorie juridique* (Paris, 1942), which is perhaps the best book yet written on the concept of the crusade; and P. Rousset, *Les origines et les caractères de la première croisade* (Neuchâtel, 1945). And·Erdmann's interpretation of Urban II's thinking at the time of the First Crusade has been questioned convincingly by H. E. J. Cowdrey, 'Pope Urban II's Preaching of the First Crusade', in *History*, LV (1970). Cowdrey has also summarised the attitude of the monastery of Cluny to the crusading movement: see his 'Cluny and the First Crusade', in *Revue Bénédictine*, LXXXIII (1973).

A contribution to our knowledge of the papal attitude towards war in the eleventh century has been made by S. Robinson, 'Gregory VII and the Soldiers of Christ', in *History*, LVIII (1973). The Just War itself has been studied by F. H. Russell, *The Just War in the Middle Ages* (Cambridge, 1975), and there is an interesting article by R. H. Schmandt, 'The Fourth Crusade and the Just-War Theory', in *Catholic Historical Review*, LXI (1975).

Canon law was the first concern of M. Villey in *La croisade* (referred to above), and he turned again to the subject in his 'L'idée de croisade chez les juristes du moyen âge', in *Relazioni del X congresso internazionale di scienze storiche: III, Storia del medio evo* (Florence, 1955). A significant contribution to the study of canon law is made by J. A. Brundage, *Medieval Canon Law and the Crusader* (Madison, 1969), and Brundage has also produced many interesting articles, among which might be mentioned:

'Cruce signari: The Rite for Taking the Cross in England', in *Traditio*, XXII (1966);

'A Note on the Attestation of Crusaders' Vows', in *Catholic Historical Review*, LII (1966);

'The Crusader's Wife: A Canonistic Quandary', in *Studia Gratiana*, XII (1967);

'The Crusader's Wife Revisited', in *Studia Gratiana*, XIV (1967);

'The Army of the First Crusade and the Crusade Vow: Some Reflections on A Recent Book', in *Medieval Studies*, XXXIII (1971).

In the last-mentioned study, Brundage shows beyond doubt that Urban II did introduce the vow in 1095.

The Indulgence has been discussed by J. A. Brundage, *Medieval Canon Law* (referred to above) pp. 145–55, by H. E. Mayer, *The Crusades* (referred to above) pp. 25–40, and by M. Purcell, *Papal Crusading Policy 1244–1291* (Leiden, 1975) pp. 35–98; but the most comprehensive work is N. Paulus, *Geschichte des Ablasses* (Paderborn, 1922–3). A. Gottlob's discussion in his *Kreuzablass und Almosenablass* (Stuttgart, 1906) is still useful.

The crusade was an instrument of the Papal Monarchy. Papal bulls from Urban II to Innocent IV are studied in U. Schwerin, *Die Aufrufe der Päpste zur Befreiung des Heiligen Landes von der Anfängen bis zum Ausgang Innozenz IV* (Berlin, 1937), and papal participation in the movement in the second half of the thirteenth century is examined in M. Purcell, *Papal Crusading Policy* (referred to above). An important work, establishing what happened at Clermont, is R. Somerville, 'The Councils of Urban II: Decreta Claromontensia', in *Annuarium Historiae Conciliorum*, Supplementum 1 (1972). Useful studies of the policies of Innocent III are H. Roscher, *Papst Innocenz III. und die Kreuzzüge* (Göttingen, 1969), and M. Maccarone, 'Studi su Innocenzo III. Orvieto e la predicazione della crociata', in *Italia sacra*, XVII (1972). For the financing of the crusades and developments in papal taxation, see especially W. E. Lunt, *Papal Revenues in the Middle Ages*, 2 vols (New York, 1934) and *Financial Relations of the Papacy with England*, 2 vols (Cambridge, Mass., 1939, 1962); and P. Guidi (ed.), 'Rationes decimarum Italiae nei secoli XIII e XIV. Tuscia. I. La Decima degli anni 1274–1280', in *Studi e Testi*, LVIII (1932).

Challenging contributions to the study of individual crusades to the East or of periods of crusading history are the following:

J. H. and L. L. Hill, *Raymond IV de Saint-Gilles, 1041(ou 1042)–1105* (Toulouse, 1959). These authors expounded their important view of the role of the legate Adhémar on the First Crusade in 'Contemporary Accounts and the Later Reputation of Adhémar, Bishop of Puy', in *Medievalia et Humanistica*, IX (1955);

G. Constable, 'The Second Crusade as seen by Contemporaries', in *Traditio*, IX (1953);

R. C. Smail, 'Latin Syria and the West, 1149–1187', in *Transactions of the Royal Historical Society*, 5th ser., XIX (1969);

G. B. Flahiff, 'Deus Non Vult. A Critic of the Third Crusade', in *Medieval Studies*, IX (1947);

J. P. Donovan, *Pelagius and the Fifth Crusade* (Philadelphia, 1950);

B. Z. Kedar, 'The Passenger List of a Crusader Ship, 1250: Towards the History of the Popular Element on the Seventh Crusade', in *Studi medievali*, 3rd ser., XIII (1972);

B. Beebe, 'The English Baronage and the Crusade of 1270', in *Bulletin of the Institute of Historical Research*, XLVIII (1975).

The best introduction to the views held of the crusades in the thirteenth century is in P. A. Throop, *Criticism of the Crusade. A Study of Public Opinion and Crusade Propaganda* (Amsterdam, 1940).

On Spanish crusades, a competent introduction is to be found in J. G. Gaztambide, *Historia de la Bula de la Cruzada en España* (Vitoria, 1958). See also C. J. Bishko, 'The Spanish and Portuguese Reconquest', in Setton (ed.), *A History of the Crusades*, vol. III (referred to above) and two studies by R. I. Burns: *The Crusader Kingdom of Valencia*, 2 vols (Cambridge, Mass., 1967) and *Islam under the Crusaders* (Princeton, 1973).

On Baltic crusades, see the narrative account by E. N. Johnson, 'The German Crusade on the Baltic', in Setton (ed.), *A History of the Crusades*, vol. III. Some sensible things about them have been written by F. Benninghoven in his *Der Orden der Schwertbrüder* (Cologne, 1965).

On the Albigensian Crusade, the best treatment in English is in W. L. Wakefield, *Heresy, Crusade and Inquisition in Southern France, 1100–1250* (London, 1974). Among other works one would recommend J. Madaule, *The Albigensian Crusade* (London, 1967) and P. Bellperon, *La croisade contre les Albigeois* (Paris, 1942).

Crusades against the lay powers in the West were treated in H. Pissard, *La guerre sainte en pays chrétien* (Paris, 1912), but see also:

J. R. Strayer, 'The Political Crusades of the Thirteenth Century', in Setton (ed.), *A History of the Crusades*, vol. II;

E. Kennan, 'Innocent III and the First Political Crusade', in *Traditio*, XXVII (1971);

P. Toubert, 'Les déviations de la Croisade au milieu du XIIIe siècle: Alexandre IV contre Manfred', in *Le Moyen Age*, LXIX (1963).

Twelfth-century warfare is the subject of R. C. Smail's magisterial study, *Crusading Warfare (1097–1193)* (Cambridge, 1956).

The best general history of the Military Orders before 1312 is still H. Prutz, *Die geistlichen Ritterorden* (Berlin, 1908). For individual Orders, see:

J. S. C. Riley-Smith, *The Knights of St John in Jerusalem and Cyprus, c. 1050–1310* (London, 1967);

J. Delaville Le Roulx, *Les Hospitaliers à Rhodes jusqu'à la mort de Philibert de Naillac (1310–1420)* (Paris, 1913);

R. Cavaliero, *The Last of the Crusaders. The Knights of St John and Malta in the Eighteenth Century* (London, 1960);

M. L. Bulst-Thiele, 'Sacrae Domus Militiae Templi Hierosolymitani Magistri', in *Abhandlungen der Akademie der Wissenschaften in Göttingen*, LXXXVI (1974);

M. Melville, *La vie des Templiers* (Paris, 1951);

M. Tumler, *Der Deutsche Orden im Werden, Wachsen und Wirken bis 1400* (Vienna, 1955);

K. Forstreuter, *Der Deutsche Orden am Mittelmeer* (Bonn, 1967);

M.-L. Favreau, *Studien zur Frühgeschichte des Deutschen Ordens* (Stuttgart, 1974);

F. Benninghoven, *Der Orden der Schwertbrüder* (Cologne, 1965);

D. W. Lomax, *La Orden de Santiago, 1170–1275* (Madrid, 1965);

J. F. O'Callaghan, *The Spanish Military Order of Calatrava and its Affiliates* (London, 1975).

On the Latin confraternities in the East, see J. S. C. Riley-Smith, 'A Note on Confraternities in the Latin Kingdom of Jerusalem', in *Bulletin of the Institute of Historical Research*, XLIV (1971).

On Islamic history, recent works of especial interest are: E. Sivan, *L'Islam et la croisade* (Paris, 1968); C. Cahen, *Pre-Ottoman Turkey* (London, 1968); and D. Ayalon, 'Studies on the Structure of the Mamluk Army', in *Bulletin of the School of Oriental and African Studies*, XV–XVI (1953–4). There have been some good biographies of sultans, in particular N. Elisséeff , *Nūr-ad-Dīn*, 3 vols (Damascus, 1967), and H. L. Gottschalk, *Al-Malik al-Kamil von Egypten und seine Zeit* (Wiesbaden, 1958). A recent biography of Saladin is A. S. Ehrenkreutz, *Saladin* (New York, 1972), but the study in preparation by M. C. Lyons and D. Jackson promises to become the standard life of the crusaders' most famous opponent.

List of Original Sources

The following are original sources to which reference is made directly or indirectly in the text.

Abbreviations

A.O.L.   *Archives de l'Orient latin*
M.G.H.   *Monumenta Germaniae Historica*, ed. G. H. Pertz *et al.* (Hanover/
                Weimer/Berlin/Stuttgart/Cologne, 1826 ff.)
M.G.H.S.   *M.G.H. Scriptores* (in Folio et Quarto) 32 vols (1826–1934)
P.L.   *Patrologiae cursus completus. Series Latina*, publ. J. P. Migne, 217 vols and 4
                vols of indexes (Paris, 1844–64)
R.H.C. arm.   *Recueil des historiens des croisades. Documents arméniens*, 2 vols (Paris,
                1869–1906)
R.H.C. Oc.   *Recueil des historiens des croisades. Historiens occidentaux*, 5 vols (Paris,
                1844–95)
R.H.G.F.   *Recueil des historiens des Gaules et de la France*, ed. M. Bouquet *et al.*, 24
                vols (Paris, 1737–1904)

Acta imperii selecta, ed. J. H. Böhmer (Innsbruck, 1870)
Acta Pontificum Romanorum inedita, ed. J. von Pflugk-Harttung (Stuttgart,1888)
Adrian IV, Pope, 'Epistolae', *R.H.G.F.*, XV
Alexander III, Pope, 'Opera Omnia', *P.L.*, CC
'Annales Colonienses maximi', *M.G.II.S.*, XVII
'Annales de Terre Sainte', ed. R. Röhricht and G. Raynaud, *A.O.L.*, II (1884)
Annales ecclesiastici, ed. C. Baronius, O. Raynaldus, A. Pagi and A. Theiner, 37 vols
    (Bar-le-Duc/Paris, 1864–82)
'Annales Stadenses', *M.G.H.S.*, XVI
Aquinas: *see* Thomas
Baudri of Dol, 'Historia Jerosolimitana', *R.H.C. Oc.*, IV
Bernard of Clairvaux, 'De laude novae militiae ad milites Templi liber', *Sancti Bernardi
    Opera*, ed. J. Leclerq, C. H. Talbot and H. M. Rochais (Rome, 1963) vol. III
—, 'Epistolae', *P.L.*, CLXXXII; note also the translation of St Bernard's letters
    by B. S. James (London, 1953)
Bernold, 'Chronicon', *M.G.H.S.*, V
Boniface VIII, Pope, *Registre*, ed. G. Digard, M. Faucon, A. Thomas and R. Fawtier, 4
    vols (Paris, 1884–1939)
Calixtus II, Pope, *Bullaire*, ed. U. Robert, 2 vols (Paris, 1891)
Cartulaire général de l'ordre des Hospitaliers de St-Jean de Jérusalem (1100–1310), ed. J.
    Delaville Le Roulx, 4 vols (Paris, 1894–1906)

Chroniques des églises d'Anjou, ed. P. Marchegay and E. Mabille (Paris, 1869)
Clement IV, Pope, *Registre*, ed. E. Jordan (Paris, 1893–1945)
Codex diplomaticus et epistolaris Moraviae, ed. A. Boček *et al.*, 15 vols (Olmütz, 1836–1903)
'Continuation de Guillaume de Tyr de 1229 à 1261, dite du manuscrit de Rothelin', *R.H.C. Oc.*, II
Corpus Juris Canonici, ed. A. Friedberg, 2 vols (Leipzig, 1879–81)
Diplomatarium Norvegicum, ed. C. R. Unger *et al.*, still in progress (Christiana [Oslo], 1847–)
'Documents et mémoires servant de preuves à l'histoire de l'île de Chypre sous les Lusignans', ed. L. de Mas-Latrie, *Histoire de l'île de Chypre* (Paris, 1852–5) vols II and III
'Documents relatifs aux Plaisançais d'Orient', ed. A. G. Tononi, *A.O.L.*, II (1884)
'Emprunts de Saint Louis en Palestine et en Afrique', ed. G. Servois, *Bibliothèque de l'Ecole des Chartes*, 4th ser., IV (1858)
Epistolae Pontificum Romanorum ineditae, ed. S. Löwenfeld (Leipzig, 1885)
Epistolae saeculi XIII e regestis pontificum Romanorum selectae per G. H. Pertz, ed. C. Rodenberg, *M.G.H.*, 3 vols (Berlin, 1883–94)
Epistulae et chartae ad historiam primi belli sacri spectantes, ed. H. Hagenmeyer (Innsbruck, 1901)
'L'estoire de Eracles empereur et la conqueste de la Terre d'Outremer', *R.H.C. Oc.*, I–II
Eugenius III, Pope, 'Epistolae et Privilegia', *P.L.*, CLXXX
'Fragmentum Historiae ex veteri membrana de tributo Floriacensibus imposito', *R.H.G.F.*, XII
Fulcher of Chartres, *Historia Hierosolymitana*, ed. H. Hagenmeyer (Heidelberg, 1913)
Geoffrey of Villehardouin, *La conquête de Constantinople*, ed. E. Faral, 2 vols (Paris, 1961)
Gerald of Wales (Giraldus Cambrensis), *Opera*, ed. J. S. Brewer (Rolls Ser., 21) 8 vols (London, 1861–91)
Gervase of Canterbury, *The Historical Works*, ed. W. Stubbs (Rolls Ser., 73) 2 vols (London, 1879–80)
Gesta Francorum et aliorum Hierosolimitanorum, ed. R. Hill (London, 1962)
Gesta regis Henrici secundi et Ricardi primi, ed. W. Stubbs (Rolls Ser., 49) 2 vols (London, 1867)
'Les Gestes des Chiprois', *R.H.C. arm.*, II
Gregory VII, Pope, *Epistolae vagantes*, ed. H. E. J. Cowdrey (Oxford, 1972)
—, *Registrum*, ed. E. Caspar, *M.G.H.* (*Epistolae selectae*, 2) 2 vols (Berlin, 1920–3)
Gregory IX, Pope, *Registre*, ed. L. Auvray, 3 vols and tables (Paris, 1896–1955)
Gregory X, Pope, 'Constitutiones pro zelo fidei', ed. H. Finke, *Konzilienstudien zur Geschichte des 13 Jahrhunderts* (Münster, 1891) pp. 113–17
Guibert of Nogent, 'Historia quae dicitur Gesta Dei per Francos', *R.H.C. Oc.*, IV
Hamburgisches Urkundenbuch, ed. J. M. Lappenberg *et al.*, 4 vols so far (Hamburg, 1907–67)
Helmold of Bosau, 'Chronica Slavorum', *M.G.H.S.*, XXI
Henry of Livonia, 'Chronicon Lyvoniae', *M.G.H.S.*, XXIII
'Historia Compostellana', *España Sagrada*, ed. H. Flórez *et al.* (Madrid, 1765) vol. XX
Historical Manuscripts Commission, *Fifth Report* (London, 1876)
—, *Report on Manuscripts in Various Collections* (London, 1901) vol. I
Honorius III, Pope, *Regesta*, ed. P. Pressutti, 2 vols (Rome, 1888–95)
Hostiensis, *Summa Aurea* (Basel, 1573)
Humbert of Romans, 'Opus Tripartitum', ed. E. Brown, *Fasciculus rerum expetandarum et fugiendarum* (London, 1690) vol. II
Innocent III, Pope, 'Opera Omnia', *P.L.*, CCXIV–CCXVI

—, 'Quia major', ed. G. Tangl, *Studien zum Register Innocenz III* (Weimar, 1929) pp. 88–97

—, *Register*, ed. O. Hageneder and A. Haidacher (Graz, 1964) vol. I

Innocent IV, Pope, *Commentaria in Quinque Libros Decretalium* (Turin, 1581)

—, *Registre*, ed. E. Berger, 4 vols (Paris, 1884–1921)

James I, King of Aragon, *Chronica*, ed. M. Aguiló y Fuster (Barcelona, 1873)

James of Vitry, *Lettres*, ed. R. B. C. Huygens (Leiden, 1960)

—, 'Sermones vulgares', ed. J. B. Pitra, *Analecta novissima* (Paris, 1888) vol. II

John of Joinville, *Histoire de Saint Louis*, ed. N. de Wailly (Paris, 1874)

John of Salisbury, *Historia pontificalis*, ed. M. Chibnall (London, 1956)

Layettes du Trésor des Chartes, ed. A. Teulet *et al.*, 5 vols (Paris, 1863–1909)

Martin IV, Pope, *Registre*, ed. Ecole française de Rome (Paris, 1901–35)

'A New Eyewitness Account of the Fourth Lateran Council', ed. S. Kuttner and A. García y García, in *Traditio*, XX (1964)

Odo of Châteauroux, 'Epistola', ed. L. d'Achery, *Spicilegium* (Paris, 1723) vol. III, pp. 624–8

—, 'Sermones de tempore et sanctis' ed. J. B. Pitra, *Analecta novissima* (Paris, 1888) vol. II

Odo of Deuil, *De profectione Ludovici VII in Orientem*, ed. V. G. Berry (New York, 1948)

Oliver of Paderborn, *Schriften*, ed. H. Hoogeweg (Tübingen, 1894)

Orderic Vitalis, *Historia ecclesiastica*, ed. A. Le Prévost (Paris, 1855) vol. IV; new ed. by M. Chibnall in progress (Oxford, 1969–)

Otto of Freising, *Gesta Friderici I Imperatoris*, ed. B. von Simson, *M.G.H.S. in usum scholarum* (Hanover/Leipzig, 1912)

Papsturkunden für Templer und Johanniter, ed. R. Hiestand (Göttingen, 1972)

'Papsturkunden in Florenz', ed. W. Wiederhold, *Nachrichten von der Gesellschaft der Wissenschaften zu Göttingen*, Phil.-hist. Kl. (Göttingen, 1901)

Papsturkunden in Spanien. I. Katalonien, ed. P. Kehr (Berlin, 1926)

Peter the Venerable, *Letters*, ed. G. Constable, 2 vols (Cambridge, Mass., 1967)

Quinque compilationes antiquae, ed. A. Friedberg (Leipzig, 1882)

Quinti belli sacri scriptores minores, ed. R. Röhricht (Geneva, 1879)

Ralph of Diceto, *Opera historica*, ed. W. Stubbs (Rolls Ser., 68) 2 vols (London, 1876)

Ralph Niger, 'De re militari et triplici via peregrinationis Jerosolimitanae', part ed. G. B. Flahiff, 'Deus Non Vult. A Critic of the Third Crusade', in *Medieval Studies*, IX (1947)

'Rationes decimarum Italiae nei secoli XIII e XIV. Tuscia. I. La Decima degli anni 1274–1280', ed. P. Guidi, in *Studi e Testi*, LVIII (1932)

Regesta pontificum Romanorum, comp. A. Potthast, 2 vols (Berlin, 1874–5)

La Règle du Temple, ed. H. de Curzon (Paris, 1886)

Robert of Clari, *La conquête de Constantinople*, ed. P. Lauer (Paris, 1956)

Robert the Monk, 'Historia Iherosolimitana', *R.H.C. Oc.*, III

Roger of Howden, *Chronica*, ed. W. Stubbs (Rolls Ser., 51) 4 vols (London, 1868–71)

Rutebeuf, *Onze poèmes concernant la croisade*, ed. J. Bastin and E. Faral (Paris, 1946)

Sacrae antiquitatis monumenta historica, dogmatica, diplomatica, ed. C. L. Hugo, 2 vols (Estival, 1725–31)

Sacrorum conciliorum nova et amplissima collectio, ed. G. D. Mansi, 31 vols (Florence/Venice, 1759–98)

Suger of S. Denis, 'Epistolae', *R.H.G.F.*, XV

—, *Vie de Louis le Gros. Suivie de l'histoire du roi Louis VII*, ed. A. Molinier (Paris, 1887)

Testimonia minora de quinto bello sacro, ed. R. Röhricht (Geneva, 1882)

Thesaurus novus anecdotorum, ed. E. Martène and U. Durand, 5 vols (Paris, 1717)

Thomas Aquinas, *Opera Omnia*, 25 vols (Parma, 1852–73)

Urban IV, Pope, *Registre*, ed. J. Guiraud, 4 vols (Paris, 1901–58)

Vetera monumenta historica Hungariam sacram illustrantia, ed. A. Theiner, 2 vols (Rome, 1859–60)

William of Malmesbury, *De gestis regum Anglorum libri quinque,* ed. W. Stubbs (Rolls Ser., 90) 2 vols (London, 1887–9)

William of Tyre, 'Historia rerum in partibus transmarinis gestarum', *R.H.C. Oc.,* I

Index

Index

The following abbreviations are used:

A   Abbot (of)   E   Emperor
Archbp   Archbishop (of)   K   King (of)
B   Bishop (of)   p. leg.   Papal Legate
C   Count (of)

Women Who Dared

To Break All the Rules

Jeremy Scott

ONEWORLD

A Oneworld Book

First published by Oneworld Publications, 2019

ISBN 978-1-78607-193-4
eISBN 978-1-78607-194-1

Typeset by Palimpsest Book Production Limited,
Falkirk, Stirlingshire
Printed and bound in Great Britain by Clays Ltd, Elcograf S.p.A.

Oneworld Publications
10 Bloomsbury Street
London WC1B 3SR
England

To Sasha and Daisy, in admiration

CONTENTS

PREFACE

It probably seems strange that at this moment I have chosen to write about these independently minded women.

Since I got my first job in advertising in the 1960s, I've been surrounded by women who were quicker and smarter than their male counterparts, and I found them much more fun to be around.

I have always been attracted to rule-breakers, and in particular women with a streak of daring, and my book was always intended as a homage to and a celebration of these women who, despite everything, really did change the culture we live in.

1

MRS SATAN:
PRESIDENTIAL CANDIDATE

She was the best of womankind; she was the worst. She was a shameless adventuress, or a pioneer who broke the trail for her sex. Some denounced Victoria Woodhull as a prostitute, others claimed she had power from the Evil One to cast spells – particularly over men. She was reviled or exalted, either damned or applauded as an inspiration to every woman. Her opponents wanted to see Victoria burned at the stake, but her courage and will were undeniable. For the domesticated masses yearning at the kitchen sink of heartland America in the 1870s, she gave voice to a dream of liberty.

Victoria Woodhull and the lineage of bold women in this book form a rare species; they possessed a priceless gift – personal charisma. From infancy they displayed a power that made them utterly different to other people. Charisma is a quality elusive to pin down, but you recognise it instantly on meeting – and react to its effect It radiates a force that enables its owner to get away with actions that others cannot. As these women demonstrate, in a manner that seems at times almost supernatural.

Victoria was born one of thirteen children in a shack in the backwoods of Ohio. She received almost no schooling; yet at the age of thirty-four she stood for the Presidency of the USA. Due to one egregious impediment, she failed to fulfil the American Dream.

She launched her campaign with defiance: 'All this talk of women's rights is moonshine. Women have every right. They have only to exercise them. That's what we're doing...'

For half the population of the country this was flagrant heresy — women should be brought up to know their place — and most of the other half agreed with this verdict, or found it expedient to say so. For the rest she lit a candle in the dark; she spoke the unsayable. But there was more to follow. Rejoicing in the outrage she incited, Victoria then went further, much further:

> *First Proclamation*
> *While others argued the equality of women with men, I proved it. While others sought to show that there was no valid reason why women should be treated as inferior to men, I boldly entered the arena. Having the means, courage, energy and strength necessary for the race...I now announce myself candidate for the Presidency of the United States of America.*

Such was Victoria's announcement of intent, which she ended with a postscript, *I expect criticism.*

Criticism is much too mild a word for what she did receive. She got abuse, ridicule, vilification and death threats. People spat at her in the street. The February 1872 edition of *Harper's Weekly* ran a cartoon of the deplorable Third Party candidate who had the barefaced cheek to run for the Presidency.

Victoria, portrayed with a scowl and Devil's wings, displays a poster preaching FREE LOVE. Along with her ambition to govern the country she'd taken up a cause very contrary to the moral climate of the time: everyone, married or not, had the right to engage in sex with any willing partner they

"GET THEE BEHIND ME, (MRS.) SATAN!"—[See Page 112.]
WIFE (with heavy burden). "I'd rather Travel the hardest Path of Matrimony than follow your Footsteps."

chose. Behind the diabolic image of Victoria in the poster, in the background, Mrs Everywoman can be seen toiling up a steep, rocky path, an infant tied to her waist, carrying on her back an incapable drunken husband. The caption: *GET THEE BEHIND ME MRS SATAN. I'd rather travel the hardest path of matrimony than follow in your footsteps.*

★ ★ ★

In *Woodhull & Claflin's Weekly*, the five-cent magazine
Victoria had started with her sister Tennessee two years
earlier, Free Love had been the first of the many causes
she chose to promote. Free Love featured in her manifesto
and campaign speeches. Her other policies – women's
suffrage, equal pay for the sexes, workers' rights, trade unions,
nationwide healthcare, abolition of the death penalty and
an end to 'the slavery of marriage' – proved no less incen-
diary to a male electorate. She was armed to confront its
ranks. Along with looks and a charismatic 'presence',
Victoria possessed a further strength: she was a mesmeric
speaker. She connected instantly with her audience, it was
impossible to disregard her. She conveyed a passionate
sincerity, and evoked raw emotion in her hearers. Expressed
in adoration or odium, the crowd's response to her was
tangible. Many of her meetings ended in such uproar that
it required police to disperse the warring factions.

Among young disaffected women in America – and at
the time there was a great deal for young women to be
disaffected about – she won the hearts and minds of many
delirious supporters. Older, married women abhorred her
views. Except for a few independent-minded males, men
universally condemned her; the mayor of Boston banned
her from speaking in the city. For newspapers, the only form
of media in that period, she was a gift. She provided the
stories they most valued: scandal and infamy. The press united
in damning her, together with every plank of her election
campaign and aspect of her character.

All publicity is good publicity; it breathes life into its
offspring. *Woodhull & Claflin's Weekly* had been the first
magazine in the USA to publish Karl Marx's *Communist
Manifesto*. Victoria introduced to America the bogeyman
that would haunt the country ever after with his pernicious

doctrine. Now in her campaign speeches she told her audience, 'If the very next Congress refuses women all the legitimate results of citizenship, we…shall erect a new government… We mean treason; we mean secession, and on a thousand times grander scale than that that of the South. We are plotting revolution; we will overthrow this bogus republic and plant a government of righteousness in its stead.'

This was sedition. What to do with such a woman?

On election day, Victoria's rackety supporters invaded the polling stations to vote for her. Police had to subdue the mob. Then an official in a frock coat read his brief text from a scrap of paper: these women could not vote for Mrs Woodhull because women did not possess a vote. The handful of males who attempted to do likewise were also told this was impossible, but for a different reason. The Presidential candidate and her sister Tennessee were currently locked up in a cell in Folsom Street Jail on a criminal charge.

The Great American Dream that anyone can make it to become President, like all stories, requires a dramatic arc. And for the arc fully to illustrate that ascending curve, it must begin at the baseline. Victoria Claflin Woodhull's start to life could not have been more mean, squalid, or less auspicious than it was.

In 1838 when she was born, Homer, Ohio was a nothing frontier settlement with a post office and general store on a dirt road going nowhere, surrounded by a scatter of outlying farms on the prairie. It housed an agricultural, churchgoing community governed by hard work, homespun values and strait-laced probity.

The family Claflin with thirteen children — three died in

infancy – inhabited a shack by the gristmill, run by their
father Buck, and the slum was swollen further by his twin
brother with wife and squalling kids. Over the years the
stable and a timber outbuilding had been used to accommodate the extended family with their growing brood. There
was no running water, except for the stream powering the
mill, and no sanitation. The place was a shantytown, and
considered a disgrace that brought shame upon the township.

Victoria's mother Roxanna was German-Jewish by extrac-
tion, illiterate, small, plain, always dressed in black and
invariably pregnant. The impression she gave was not helped
by her characteristic shuffling gait. As a mother she was
wholly unreliable. The disarray the family lived in, the
sleeping pallets and bedding littering every floor, the dirty
dishes and unwashed children bothered her not at all. She
lived more in the spirit world than the real, earning small
sums as a medium, fortune teller and healer.

Roxanna was a follower of the German mystic and doctor
Franz Mesmer, who propagated the theory that an invisible
fluid in the human body ruled its health. Illness was the
result of blockages to its free circulation through the system.
However, these could be cured by the skilled practitioner
putting the patient into a state of trance, then using suggestion to remove the obstacle causing the condition. Mesmerism
– later renamed hypnotism – baffled and enraged the medical
establishment, who denounced the practice for its lack of
any scientific basis. Yet, with some patients, it appeared to
work. Qualified doctors showed rare in heartland America
in the period, their knowledge limited, and the medicines
they prescribed cost money. In these most fundamental and
down-to-earth communities like Homer, Ohio, the seemingly miraculous cures offered by Roxanna held irrational
appeal for some.

Most of the townsfolk had no truck with such specious waffle. They regarded Roxanna with dismay, doing their best to avoid her. Not always possible, for the spirit had the habit of seizing her in public spaces, obliging her to broadcast its message to everyone around. Respectability and appearance figured high in hometown America. A decent orthodoxy held the community close. A madwoman incontinently sharing her religious visions at midday on Main Street was out of order.

Victoria and her siblings' relationship with their mother varied to extremes of instability. Roxanna's mood swung between bursts of ecstatic affection, during which she would clasp them to her, thanking God for their birth, and deliberate sadism when she whipped them with a cane until she drove them to tears – when she threw down the switch, clapped her hands and laughed in glee at their humiliation.

Nor was Buck their father a comforting presence in the family. Lengths of cane stood in a barrel of rainwater on the porch to keep them flexible for use by both parents. His appearance and manner did nothing to reassure the solid citizens of Homer; his shifty look was aggravated by having only one eye. In childhood he had been blinded in the other by an arrow while playing at Indians. He and Roxanna were each so distinctively ugly it was remarkable their children resulted so good-looking. Victoria and Tennessee – eight years younger and the last of their children – were particularly striking, though not at all alike. Victoria had long auburn hair, large luminous blue eyes and delicate features. An innate calm distinguished her from other members of the family. Her temper remained even, her voice soft and manner gentle in the tumult. She possessed a natural gracefulness, even as a child. Where that grace stemmed from, other than within, is impossible to imagine, for nothing in her family or circumstances displayed grace.

By contrast, Tennie – as she came to be called – radiated animation, an infectious vitality. She smiled and laughed easily. There was a gaiety about her, an alertness and quickness in gesture and movement quite unlike her older sister's serenity. Her face appeared more sensual, her expression often mischievous. As she grew older she wore her dark hair in a cropped mop of tangled curls; she looked what she was, a daring tomboy.

With Roxanna as ruling matriarch at the mill, spirits were a daily and nightly presence in the home. When Victoria was three, she witnessed the death of the elderly housekeeper who had been with them for years, and saw her body lifted up to heaven by angels. She played regularly with her two spirit sisters, who had died as babies, and later received visits from an old man in a white robe she came to look upon as her 'guide'.

Dressed poorly in hand-me-down clothes stitched by their mother, the numerous children intermittently attended school in Homer, but were not welcomed into the homes of other pupils. Victoria's formal education lasted only for three years. She was eleven when her father Buck created the final scandal that caused the whole lot of them to be evicted from the town.

The gristmill earned little. Buck had offended many of those he dealt with, and was obliged to travel wide to find new customers. He and his clan were itinerant as gypsies in their upbringing, and he developed an itch to move on and reinvent himself in greater prosperity someplace else.

For a cunning man, the scheme he hatched seems astonishingly naïve. He insured the mill, then too soon afterwards set off on foot on a Saturday to visit other towns in the area in search of outlets for his business. That evening, he rented a room for the night in a settlement some fifteen miles distant. As he told it later, he was woken by a dream his wooden gristmill was in flames. Rousing the landlord to borrow a horse, he hurried home to find the place had inexplicably burned down during the night. Next day he claimed on the insurance.

Few in Homer had reason to like Buck, and no one trusted him. His alibi was seen as all too convenient. This was a criminal act and a breach of the trust that held the community together. An impromptu group of townsfolk and farmers marched on the family encampment in righteous fury, with the intent to hang him from a nearby tree. Only on the intervention of the church minister was he given the option to leave town, *now*.

With the lynch mob still battling his outnumbered clan, Buck scurried off fast, headed for the prairie with nothing but the clothes on his back and small change in his pocket. A week later a church bazaar raised sufficient funds to send his disorderly family after him, wheresoever he had fled, and to the satisfaction of everyone the town was finally cleansed of the deplorable Claflins.

Reunited, the tribe roamed Ohio, picking up a living of sorts when they encamped. Buck once had been somewhat trained as a surveyor, and the skill came of use in new territory. He knew enough about horses to buy and sell them. Roxanna's familiarity with the occult found a limited market wherever they stopped. Her two eldest daughters obtained work locally on their various stopovers and, in time, local husbands. Not that marriage meant leaving home. The Claflins were inseparably bound as a family, because they were regarded with such suspicion wherever they landed; the constant rumpus and sheer number of them made them the worst of neighbours. The clan absorbed the two new members, who moved in to contribute to its upkeep and become part of the whole.

Buck was a rogue who adapted readily to opportunity. Roxanna a survivor plus, and endlessly resourceful. She concocted a beauty remedy, cooked up in a cauldron in the yard. The children bottled and labelled it Life Elixir for the Complexion, with a woodcut of the blossoming Tennie. Loading up a wagon they took the stock on tour. Wherever they stopped, Buck used a bullhorn to summon a crowd and puff the product, while Roxanna provided an add-on by telling fortunes on the side.

The family came to roost finally at Mount Gilead, Ohio, a larger and more prosperous town than Homer, on a dirt highway leading west. Here, when Victoria was fifteen, Roxanna married her off to a doctor, the most eligible son-in-law within reach.

Canning Woodhull came from a distinguished family in Rochester, NY, where his future career lay assured, but the mania of the gold rush of 1849 infected him as it did so many and he set off on the arduous crossing to California. He fell ill in Mount Gilead, and on recovery prolonged his stay to start a practice there. An Easterner educated at Boston University, he stood out as something of a rarity in the town, respected though looked upon as a bit of a dandy in the way he dressed.

For Roxanna, the doctor typified an ideal of security, stability and respectability. Victoria's marriage to him represented a notable step up on the social ladder, but he soon revealed himself to be flawed and feckless as her own brood.

According to Victoria's biographer Theodore Tilton:

Her captor, once possessed of his treasure, ceased to
value it. On the third night after taking his child
wife to his lodgings, he broke her heart by remaining
away all night at a house of ill-repute. Then for the
first time she learned, to her dismay, that he was
habitually unchaste, and given to long fits of intoxi-
cation… Six weeks after her marriage…she discovered
a letter addressed to him in a lady's elegant penman-
ship, saying, 'Did you marry that child because she
too was *en famille?*'… The fact was her husband, on
the day of his marriage, had sent away into the
country a mistress who a few months later gave birth
to a child.

Canning's drinking cost him patients. His practice lay in the
neighbourhood and rumour spread quickly. He and Victoria
were forced to relocate to the anonymity of a new city,
repeating the pattern she had known since infancy.

The couple were in Chicago when she gave birth to their
first child, Byron. Aged only sixteen, Victoria found herself
snared in the drudgery of motherhood, cooking and keeping
house. Her husband showed himself incapable of holding
down a job. They depended on a small allowance sent them
by Canning's parents in the East, who remained unaware of
the seriousness of their son's condition.

Housebound and without local friends, Victoria's lifeline
existed in contact with her robed guide, who sustained her
spirit. She knew her destiny to be greater than the mundanity
of now. In a dream he revealed the vision of a busy port and
harbour filled with ships…and his raised arm pointed west.
Funded by Canning's father, the couple with their baby Byron
joined a wagon train to make the long trek to San Francisco.

There the harbour was certainly full of ships, and the

streets teeming with people. Due to the gold rush, the city's population had swelled from 100,000 to more than a quarter-million over the last five years. Jerry-built wooden houses, shanties, huts and hovels cluttered the steep surrounding hills. Dirt streets formed a warren of hotels, saloons, storefronts and one-room offices for gold assayers, surveyors and lawyers. The boardwalk was packed with an unruly mob of winners, losers, traders, card sharps, thieves, clamorous and roiling in the uncouth manners of an unfettered boom.

Victoria, who had known only provincial life, could have found the place overwhelming, particularly with baby and sodden husband to support. But no. She never lacked in courage and had unwavering trust in her spirit guide and the destiny awaiting her. She answered an ad: CIGAR GIRL WANTED. The work was in a theatre. Her looks and bearing were so distinctive the job led to a part in a play, *New York by Gaslight*, paying $52 per week.

She had a talent for performance. Also the ability to learn fast – and much more than the words of her role. She knew already that she could *connect*, people warmed to her instinctively. Here she discovered she could get the same response from an audience: she could arouse its emotion. To personal charisma and the charm she'd been born with, she added the theatrical techniques of an actor. On stage, playing to a crowd, she came into her full self. The applause she received confirmed her.

She had to hire help to look after Byron while she worked, Canning could not be trusted to do so. Often, when she came home after a performance, he was not there. He had taken to using morphine – then readily available – while nowise cutting down on drink. His behaviour worsened. He lied, cheated, filched her earnings, and disappeared on prolonged binges... From the last of which he failed to return for several months. When finally he stumbled back, broken, vagrant, sick, it was to find his home occupied by strangers who shut the door on him.

Victoria had taken the baby and gone back to her Claflin family in Ohio. Despite her popular reception she'd quit the stage and, with her sister Tennie, launched upon a spectacular new career.

Buck Claflin was the one who had hit upon the idea.

In America in the 1850s mass media did not exist, nor did the telephone. News travelled at 8 mph, the pace of a trotting horse. A couple of days had already passed before Buck glanced through a copy of Cincinnati's principal newspaper and happened to see its report of the Fox sisters' public seance in that city – where their performance enthralled a full house, who had paid big money to see, hear and, if possible, touch these phenomenal children in the flesh.

To understand why requires their backstory. In 1848, Doctor Fox, his wife and their six children had moved into a farmhouse in Hydesville, NY. The previous owner had wisely concealed the rumour that the place was haunted, but it was not long before the new owners began to hear inexplicable sounds of movement together with loud rapping on their walls.

Two of the children started to clap their hands or snap their fingers in response. Over a period of weeks they set up a method of communication similar to that used by prisoners in adjoining cells. Word of this marvel spread, prompting an increasing number of thrill-seekers to visit the property. Authority, church ministers and self-defined experts investigated the manifestations, questioning the 'ghost' via the sisters. They concluded the effects were fraudulent, but this did little to diminish the girls' growing celebrity. The pair of them, aided by the ghost of a pedlar murdered and buried on the farm, cued the advent of Spiritualism in America.

The cult grew and spread. It gained its following mainly from the bottom of the social ladder; most of its adherents were women. So too were the first mediums, who soon sprang into being. Seances, staged for small gatherings – not all of them believers in the occult – developed into 'Inspirational Entertainment'. The Fox sisters grew in popular demand.

Learning of their reception in Cincinnati, Buck hurried home to read the account to his illiterate wife Roxanna. At that time they were still peddling patent medicines from the back of a travelling wagon, including a cure for cancer Roxanna brewed up on the kitchen stove. It was selling well, but in the newspaper report the couple spotted a far greater opportunity to make their fortune.

Soon after, the Claflins upped sticks and moved with their dependants to Cincinnati. Renting a house in a good neighbourhood, they hung out a shingle: TENNESSEE CLAFLIN AND VICTORIA WOODHULL, CLAIRVOYANTS. The front parlour was kept tidy for use as a consulting room where Roxanna provided a somewhat disconcerting reception, but clients were reassured by meeting their comely medium Victoria, now twenty-two, and her rosy-cheeked co-practitioner Tennie, fifteen. Victoria soon entered a state of trance, then started to transmit personal messages from the Other Side, together with counselling; Tennie specialised in hands-on psychic healing, transferring her youthful health and revitalising energy to the recipient. Seances were attended by groups of men, paying one dollar a head. Further services to hand included fortune telling and magnetic healing. Prices were steep but demand stood up.

No customers complained but inevitably this coming and

going in a quiet residential street attracted attention, accompanied by gossip and speculation. As in Homer, the Claflins' presence was thought to lower the tone of the neighbourhood. The police paid a visit to the house.

The family departed Cincinnati in a moonlight flit, their ranks now increased by Canning Woodhull, who had somehow found his way cross-country to rejoin them, broken, contrite and a hopeless morphine addict. Though Victoria had every reason to despise him, she'd accepted him back without reproach. She remained steadfast as Mother Courage in the way she took responsibility for the feckless brood surrounding her.

They took the act on tour in two covered wagons with Buck as advance man hyping their arrival in towns through Illinois, Kansas and Missouri. Victoria and Tennessee formed the stars, but it provided a living of sorts for all. Roxanna took the money, while Woodhull's job was to look after Byron but, even in this, he showed himself deficient. During one of their rare sojourns in a proper house their son fell out of a second-floor window and suffered brain damage. The boy remained incapable of functioning normally and never after could be left unsupervised.

The American Civil War accelerated the spread of Spiritualism in North and South on both sides of the conflict. Men enlisted to fight in its bloody battles, but their wives remained at home. These may have missed their husbands and worried for their safety; nevertheless their absence offered a degree of freedom previously unknown to them. Spiritualist gatherings provided a place for women to meet together, to talk and to share. These assemblies provided the cradle to a nascent sisterhood that never before had found an environment in which it might exist, let alone flourish as it did now. During the course of the war, the Spiritualist Movement gained more than three million followers throughout the country.

The Claflin roadshow continued to tour with success: its two stars were pulling in real money. For a while Tennie performed solo as the only medium when Victoria gave birth to a daughter, Zulu Maude, in 1861. Her husband Canning had become a hopeless drunk, incapable of work and culpably irresponsible, yet she had not ceased having sex with him. Before the infant was even weaned she went back to work.

When the war ended, the Claflins headed south in their horse-drawn wagons to tour Arkansas and Missouri, offering Spiritualist seances, hands-on healing and fortune telling, plus a range of Roxanna's home-brewed medicines – a cure for cancer still the biggest seller. Wherever they stopped, the pubescent Tennie attracted male admirers. One of the more prosperous of these young suitors proposed marriage, which she accepted blithely. A local minister performed the rite on demand but, afterward, the groom showed no desire to set up a marital home on their own, instead bedding down with his bride in one of the wagons. The marriage lasted only for a matter of days before he spotted a $10 bill in her purse and challenged her on its source. She refused to explain how she had obtained it, resulting in a violent row, which turned physical when he struck her. The family reacted as one. Subduing the overdressed interloper, they threw him off the wagon, dumping her ex face down in the road – end to the honeymoon and the last she saw of him.

In 1866 the roadshow arrived in St Louis. A Spiritualist society had grown up there during the war, despite opposition. Particularly from the Church, which denounced the pseudo-religion as fakery and female hysteria. Shortly after the Claflins' appearance, the society invited Victoria to speak for the Movement in a public debate with a church minister. The *St Louis Times* sent their occasional correspondent, James Blood, to cover the event.

Blood held down another and more secure job as City Auditor in St Louis. In his late thirties, he had distinguished himself as a colonel in the Confederate army during the war, sustaining five bullet wounds. With a wife, two children and a substantial house, he denoted a man of standing in the locale. But his true nature lay at odds with his reputable situation in life.

The Civil War effected a shift in the way many in the United States considered their values. Alternative, counter-cultural sects and cults came into being, along with opportunity for advocates to publish their views in print. Blood was a closet Free Thinker – though, he knew it both inappropriate and unwise to articulate such radical concepts to colleagues or even family. He had fallen out of step with the bourgeois orthodoxy of his career and status – outgrown what he regarded as the 'unnatural tie of marriage and monogamy'. As he had his job, though, he still maintained the façade expected of him at work and at home. Yet, buttoned up tight within the dutiful disguise of city functionary lay a visionary idealist ⸺⸺⸺⸺⸺⸺⸺ man and woman could live ⸺ in Eden before the Fall, naked, unashamed and innocent of sin. He believed in Free Love and in Utopia. Moreover, he knew where Utopia existed, in the Oneida Community in upstate New York near the Canadian border. He believed this was the place where he belonged…if ever he found the courage to burst his chains and remake himself.

From his seat near the front of the hall, in St Louis, Blood watched the debate's two principals mount the stage. The reverend minister wore a dog collar and clerical black, Victoria a gown daringly cut to the mid-calf. The MC introduced the speakers to the audience, and she opened the argument, presenting the case for Spiritualism.

As a speaker Victoria conveyed passionate sincerity, her conviction reached the dullest mind. And with this, beauty, wholesomeness, radiant health, lustrous hair and enthusiasm. On the stage – and even more so one-to-one – she could cast a spell.

In Blood, her presence and voice induced a revelation. Although he'd showed himself heroic on the field, it would seem that he was one of those individuals who go through life seeking a character larger than their own in which to submerge their identity. For such a man, Victoria personalised the ideal. He had been staring at her for no more than ten minutes before his initial astonishment morphed to infatuation.

At the end of the debate – which she carried – very many wanted to meet Victoria. She was mobbed by fans, all of them young women striving to touch her as if she were a saint capable of miracles. Blood hesitated on the fringe of the excited crowd. He had sound cause to approach her, but was in too great a turmoil. Instead he chose the shy lover's stratagem, booking an appointment for spiritual healing as a patient. The single account we have of their meeting is Theodore Tilton. 'A handsome, side-whiskered young man with an erect military bearing came to consult her one day. Victoria saw him walking across the darkened room toward her, watched him sit down in the chair provided. Then, before he could even tell her his problem, she went into a trance. "I see our futures linked," she told the stranger. "Our destinies bound together by the ties of marriage."'

These ties of marriage were exactly what Blood wanted

to abolish; he believed in Communism and Free Love. Now, one of those principles adapted on the instant to embrace this radiant being as his future wife. Tilton's description is scant on detail but whatever it was that did occur in that first encounter, it resulted in Blood losing his reason. He had fallen in love, and here was the cue to recreate himself as the man he must be.

There existed a couple of problems impeding the destiny Victoria foresaw, in that both of them were currently married and living with their spouses. Yet love conquered all. Blood precipitately threw up his respectable job and quit home, promising to provide well for wife and family. At the same time Victoria confided her two children to her unreliable kin, who took the new situation in their stride, resolving to keep the Spiritualist show going with Tennessee solo in the starring role.

Blood reinvented himself almost overnight, transforming into another character entirely. Appearance, dress, attitude, manner…all changed including his name: James Harvey. Victoria assumed the identity of Madame Harvey, and together the couple took off in a covered wagon to work the backwood roads of Missouri and the Ozark Mountains. She knew she could earn wherever they stopped, she could provide an experience many yearned for. She represented a moveable resource for both of them. Blood's role was promoter and publicist – as had been Buck Claflin's. From city auditor in frock coat to showman busker of a travelling roadshow made for a stark career switch, but the reborn James Harvey embodied an altogether different man from the former Colonel Blood.

Victoria had sat through less than three years in school. She could read – and did so avidly, everything Blood put before her – but barely write. Even her signature varied. But she presented preternaturally intelligent, alert and curious – the perfect student. He became her tutor and besotted lover. Seated together on the high driving bench as their wagon rolled through the lush heartland of the Midwest, Blood talked and Victoria listened.

He entrusted her with his radical social theories, which rejected the concept of private property and were proto-Marxist in essence. He told her of the Utopia in upstate New York promising the ultimate destination of their travels. There they would make their home in the commune to live by these same principles in love and harmony, secluded from the avaricious, possessive and self-seeking materialist world.

Blissfully united beneath a clear blue sky, the lovers journeyed toward the paradise they believed awaited them...

2

MONOGAMY IS
UNACCEPTABLE BEHAVIOUR

Victoria and Blood headed toward Eden in no urgency to reach the place. Their current idyll, clopping through a sunlit landscape to camp each night beneath the stars, was too perfect to foreclose, and too rich-making. At the larger settlements along the route they halted to put on a show. Blood, her pitchman, never failed to muster a crowd of locals including eager clients. Theirs was a winning gig with all the elements of a prairie musical except the songs.

Western musicals offer feel-good entertainment and reliably provide a happy ending...but on finally reaching their destination the couple discovered Eden not as they expected.

Monogamy is selfishness and unacceptable behaviour. Such was the premier doctrine of the Oneida Community, established in 1848 by John Noyes, who graduated from Yale Divinity School with the intention of taking Holy Orders. But his novel interpretation of Christian theology that sin did not exist so disconcerted his spiritual directors that they refused him entry to the ministry.

Thus liberated, he set up his own remote parish near to the Canadian border on forty-plus acres of partially cleared land and forest, accessible by only a single track. There its members built a large house that soon accommodated thirty-seven people who lived communally, sharing their possessions, under the rule of their founder. Men and women enjoyed complete equality. With the property came a sawmill and a farm. The first they ran as a timber business, while the farmland was worked by both male and female members, all of whom dressed in trousers, which women wore over their bulky skirts as 'bloomers'. To dress attractively or to pay undue attention to personal appearance was seen as vanity and reprimanded.

If a female and male member wished to get together to conceive a baby, they were interrogated by a committee who determined whether they made a suitable match. If they were judged not to do so, the couple were separated and kept apart. To defy the committee's ruling meant expulsion. This programme of selective breeding proved rather successful – especially for the founder, Noyes. Of the fifty-three children born there, he fathered nine himself. Soon after infants were weaned they were separated from their birth mother and raised communally. A continuing bond with the birth mother was discouraged.

So far, so Chairman Mao: Communism subject to the whimsical rule of an all-powerful dictator. Other doctrines conformed to the same rigid political system, one of these being public denunciation of each other's failings, followed by 'a shameful humiliating experience'. Only Noyes was exempt; he believed it prejudicial to his leadership.

Governance of this Utopia necessitated twenty-one standing committees and forty-eight administrative departments controlling every activity. However, in its daily routine the community was surprisingly free and easy. Its members could get up in the morning at any hour they wanted, and stay in bed all day if they chose. No job was obligatory, and if you didn't feel like going to work that was perfectly acceptable. And then of course there was free sex, lots and lots of it. You could enjoy as much sex as you wanted with any partner, provided he or she agreed. To be possessive of another could get you expelled. Jealousy was condemned as sin.

When Victoria and Blood enrolled in the community, they found every form of sex actively promoted, indeed taught. Noyes utilised narrowly selected passages on love from the New Testament for his gospel, but Oneida's teaching manual and curriculum drew upon a very different classic text, the *Kama Sutra*. The primary lesson was in male continence. The student must learn to prolong the act as long as required to provide full satisfaction to his partner; to release semen was a no-no. Training began at a tender age. From puberty, youths were encouraged to engage with post-menopausal women. In the hands of an experienced teacher the novice gained the ability to withhold his own selfish orgasm, to the benefit of both. Girls were taught to discover their own sexual tastes – along with a full range of imaginative techniques depicted in the Hindu primer.

Victoria welcomed new concepts and experiences. Blood too, in theory and the radical philosophy he'd espoused. But *in the flesh*? When they involved his beloved wife? He found himself to be less of a Free Thinker than he thought. Despite all his reconstructed principles, sexual jealousy persisted innate in him. Now the serpent uncoiled, reared its head and struck. Its venom stung through his veins; he suffered acute distress, he couldn't handle it. Along with the sting, he realised he had swapped his former St Louis orthodoxy only for another offering far less freedom. Noyes' authoritarian regime was intolerable. Disillusioned and depressed, Blood absconded from Eden with Victoria.

They returned to the family fold, now located in a rented house in Chicago. There she comforted and revived his spirit, urging him to shape up and act. He did so, legally divorcing his wife with a handsome settlement. Likewise, Victoria divorced Woodhull to marry him. They lived with the family, while her ex remained in situ beneath the same roof. The only sign of friction came from Roxanna, who at times showed herself resentful at his taking over Victoria's management. However, at other moments she flung herself in his lap to call him the best son-in-law she ever had and smother him with unwanted emotion.

Why did the couple choose to return to the bosom of the family when they'd enjoyed so profitable and satisfying a relationship on the road? However useless and demanding, Victoria loved her kin. She was not complete unless at their core, caring for the tumultuous brood. Tennie, her collaborator in all things, described her own similar situation pragmatically: 'Since I was fourteen years old, I have kept thirty-five or forty dead-heads.'

In Chicago Victoria and Tennie worked as 'oracles', and something more as the occasion offered. Trouble followed within weeks. They were prosecuted for fraudulent fortune telling and evicted. They set up in Philadelphia only for the same difficulty to reappear, whereupon they moved to Indianapolis. Here the sisters were no longer mediums and fortune tellers, but had become spiritual healers. Blood advertised their practice in the paper and the children distributed flyers throughout the neighbourhood.

Orthodox medicine was a crude business in the 1860s, lacking anaesthetics, antibiotics and other drugs. A physician's capability was limited; often he could diagnose the cause of a patient's suffering but lacked the wherewithal to treat, let alone cure, their affliction. The only pain relief was morphine, an opioid that many became dependent upon. Then, and how much more widely in our present day. Surgery was barbaric, and performed in non-sterile conditions. Those subjected to such butchery very often contracted sepsis and died.

Doctors could not be relied upon to heal. People were driven to search more widely for a cure for their ills. Victoria and Tennie's therapeutic skills were pre-hyped by Blood; his ads and flyers quoted testimony to the success of their methods. New patients who came to consult them often had failed to find relief in conventional medicine, and did so in last hope. The persona of the two practitioners was encouraging. The pair personified health, vigour and positivity. They listened attentively to the patient's medical history, prompting them to detail. After he or she had unburdened themselves of the past, Victoria would go into a trance, seeking to detect the psychic imbalance at the root of their ailment, then direct spiritual energy to realign it within the system. Following this procedure, the patient was referred to Tennie, who provided massages that included pressing her bared flesh to theirs. This transferred her vibrant life force to invigorate their own, stimulating their pulse rate to rise, circulation to improve and despondency lift. Many reported amelioration of their condition, though often this did not endure for long – requiring further appointments to maintain. Only rarely did the lame discard their crutches and walk, though on occasion they did and were seen to do so. The Claflin sisters' practice in Indianapolis grew highly successful.

According to Tilton:

people flocked to her from a distance. Her rooms
were crowded and her purse grew fat. She reaped a
golden harvest... First at Indianapolis, and afterward
at Terre Haute, she wrought some apparently miraculous cures... She received in one day, simply as fees
for cures which she had wrought, five thousand
dollars. The sum total of the receipts of her practice...
up to the time of its discontinuance by direction of
the spirits in 1869, was $700,000.

Money flowed more freely in the US during the era of
post-war reconstruction. Industry expanded into the Midwest,
serviced by new railways competing to lay their track across
the continent. The railroad companies colonised the food
basket of the country, controlling distribution of its produce
to the eastern city markets. The railroad barons, Cornelius
Vanderbilt, Leland Stanford, James J. Hill, invented 'Big
Business' in America; along with John D. Rockefeller in oil,
and Andrew Carnegie, steel. These men were unscrupulous
chancers in a high-stakes game. Their rivalry was intense and
rewards vast. They were a new breed: moguls, driven by
ambition and greed, prepared to cheat as necessary to win
the hand.

Indianapolis prospered and grew following the city's
connection to the eastern seaboard. Thanks to Victoria and
Tennie's success, the Claflin tribe enjoyed a notably higher
standard of living than ever before. Roxanna was restrained
from telling fortunes or proclaiming her religious visions on
the street, and mostly was kept out of sight. One of her
daughters had stepped in to fill her role as medical recep-
tionist, brushed up and dressed in nurse's uniform. A
previously unknown stability had come to underpin the
family's existence. There was every reason for them to remain

where they were and continue the practice; it seemed the Claflins had finally settled to roost. But in 1869 the spirits intervened to direct Victoria elsewhere.

Victoria had always maintained that she was guided by a spirit mentor, an older man wearing a white robe. He had first appeared to her in early adolescence but had never spoken. Now he chose to do so for the first time, identifying himself as the Athenian statesman Demosthenes, and instructing her to close the practice in Indianapolis and move to New York City where destiny awaited her.

Demosthenes, born in the fourth century BCE in Athens and a contemporary of Plato, grew to be the most famous orator in classical history. When young he suffered from a speech defect, for which he was mocked by his classmates. Plutarch describes the disability as 'an inarticulate and stammering pronunciation'. It was a severe impediment. He conquered it through a drastic regimen of self-improvement. Shaving half of his scalp, he made himself look so ridiculous he could not venture out. He spent days in his room, speaking into a large mirror with pebbles in his mouth. The discipline was wholly effective in outcome. He became a speech writer, politician and leader of the democratic party in Athens.

Why, more than 2,000 years after his suicide by poison, Demosthenes should manifest himself in the Midwest to take charge of Victoria's career is not apparent, and Colonel Blood might well have resented his intrusion. The instructions he delivered were unusually specific for a spirit guide, and included an exact address: 17 Great Jones Street. Blood was not privy to his wife's visions, but he loved her more than she did him and was ready to follow where she led.

The two made a reconnaissance of the city. Finding the

rather grand house TO LET furnished, they rented it on the spot, sending word to the family to join them. The Claflins may have been indignant at losing their comfortable situation and the novelty of security, but they were used to packing, dodging their bills and moving on. Relocating in New York, they turned the mansion into the usual slum – except for the ground-floor consulting rooms. These were clean, well-furnished and calm, unpolluted by the tribe.

Here in the Big Apple, Victoria practised as a consultant, a healer who could draw on the spiritual world to provide advice. Tennie supplied the physical therapy she was so adept in. She too had benefited from Blood's tutelage along the way. She presented quick and smart, she absorbed the dress and manners of the city within days and raised her game accordingly.

Victoria, straight-backed, upheaded, serene and beautiful, had natural style. With Blood's guidance she learned fashion and politesse. Her clothes were the height of metropolitan chic. Her face was open, gaze direct. No backwoods twang remained detectable in her warm voice, no trace of Hicksville in her manner. She was immune to doubt, confidence in her spirit guide and her own destiny remained total.

Was it Demosthenes who flagged Cornelius Vanderbilt as a mark for Team Victoria to hit upon? It was not Roxanna, she couldn't read a newspaper. Not Colonel Blood, he had principles. Buck Claflin seems more likely, he possessed a criminal mind. Or Victoria herself.

'The Commodore', as he was known, was the third richest man in the US after John Rockefeller, founder of Standard Oil, and Andrew Carnegie. Born on Staten Island, at sixteen Vanderbilt borrowed $100 to buy a two-masted sailing vessel which he ran as a ferry to Manhattan. By 1840 he controlled most of the steamboat traffic on Long Island Sound and the Hudson River, and owned a fleet of ocean-going steamships. He then either constructed or took over rail lines leading from their stopping points into the heartland of America. He became a 'railroad baron' with a princely fortune to match. At the date he met the Claflin sisters in the winter of 1869–70 this amounted to more than $100 billion in today's money.

Vanderbilt's wife, by whom he had thirteen children, had died nine months before. Living at his mansion on Washington Place, looked after by servants, he spent his days playing the stock market. He owned horses, attended the races, vacationed at Saratoga Springs, played bridge with other oldsters in a regular game where they discussed their common ailments… but there was a hollowness in his life.

Victoria's approach was forthright. She and Tennie cold-called him at the Park Avenue mansion, presenting Victoria's card identifying herself as a psychic healer to the butler, who asked them to wait.

Victoria was thirty, a handsome woman in her prime wearing a skirt that revealed her well-formed calves. Tennessee twenty-two, a bright-eyed, rosy-cheeked tomboy devoid of inhibition. The butler returned to say the Commodore would receive them in the morning room.

Vanderbilt was a crafty old fox who'd amassed a fortune through ruthless opportunism; in business he was no one's fool. But failing health had rendered him susceptible. He was consulting a doctor in Staten Island, but conventional medicine had not cured his low blood pressure and circulation problems. When playing the stock market he appeared sharp as ever, but in matters of the heart old age had rendered him a sucker.

Rich old men in the last passage of their lives are not seeking simplicity when they engage in relationships with young women. They want action, scenes, drama, and the illusion they are still players. They crave control, but meet defiance. Are possessive, but jealousy only spurs blood through their shrunken veins. The price is high, for they have given the loved one a weapon that may be used capriciously to make them suffer.

Vanderbilt was lucky. He was spared the indignity suffered by most, and got prime value from the sisters in a two-for-one deal. Victoria relayed advice from her spirit guide. Not restricted just to the medical, this soon extended into what might now be termed lifestyle coaching. Very quickly Vanderbilt came to trust her. Her manner was so open, so warm, her good humour and sincerity so evident it was hard *not* to trust her. She became a confidante, privy to all aspects of his life.

Tennie too was billed as a healer, though her method was more hands-on. She took care of his circulatory problem by her signature method. Her tonic routine developed to include playful tickles, slaps and romps. After a while it became more convenient to move into the mansion to share his bed. 'Old Boy', she called him, while he named her his 'Little Sparrow'.

These dual paths of treatment worked wonders on the Commodore, they made a new man of him. The transformation was noted by all, and excited comment. A new decorum and self-conscious gentility had come to inform social life in New York and other eastern cities since the Civil War. Victorian values and conventions were imported from Europe to replace the raw brashness of early capitalism. Women played a greater role in this area, if in no other. Dignity and respectability were prized. Men might have constructed the class system, but women ruled it.

Cornelius Vanderbilt emerged no longer a recluse. A dapper oldster with a spring to his step, he re-entered the social world. Resuming his pleasure in the racetrack, he was seen at the best meetings looking ten years younger than before, always with Victoria and Tennie in attendance, dressed and hatted in the latest style. Everyone stared, though covertly, not wanting to distinguish this pair with a look. No one seemed to know who they were or how they had gained such intimacy with the Commodore. The beau monde gossiped with lively malice.

Serenely rich, Vanderbilt gave not a damn for disapprobation. He had found a new interest in life. An additional benefit the young mistress can provide is to enable her patron to re-experience his own youthful ambitions by furthering her career. One may well be sceptical of Victoria's direct line to the other world. What cannot be denied is the skill both she and Tennie possessed for promotion and salesmanship. It required only one step in the Commodore's imagination to realise they might perform wonders by deploying these skills on Wall Street, then as now the nation's financial capital.

In January 1870 the brokerage firm of Woodhull, Claflin and Company opened for business in the Hoffman House in the financial district. The *New York Times* chose to ignore the aberration, but James Gordon Bennett, editor of the *New York Herald*, seized on the news:

> The general routine of business in Wall Street was somewhat varied today by...two fashionably dressed ladies as speculators. Who they were few seemed to know. Where they obtained their knowledge of stock was a puzzling conjecture... After investing shares in

some of our principal stocks and selling others, and
announcing their intention to become regular
habitués of Wall Street, they departed, the observed
of all observers.

The following day the *Herald* ran a prominent piece on the
'she-brokers', who had dared to intrude upon the segregated
Exchange. It described their office:

> The parlour is...decorated with oil paintings and
> statuary, furnished with sofa, chairs, a piano and the
> various other articles...which go into the makeup of
> a ladies' drawing room.

A potential punter was only soothed by the tasteful gentility
of the surroundings and further reassured when his eye lit
upon a couple of conspicuous details. The wall facing the
visitor as he entered displayed only two images. One was a
portrait of Commodore Vanderbilt, his face a study in power,
wisdom and bewhiskered gravity. The other a tapestry embroi-
dered with the motto SIMPLY TO THY CROSS I CLING.
The happy twinship of God and Mammon inspired confidence.

The association of Vanderbilt's name with the firm ensured
respectful treatment in the press, nevertheless polite society
was hostile. In the States at that time prejudice against women
grew thick as a privet hedge. Their place was the hearth, the
household, and with the kids. Business, most particularly
finance, was off limits. It was unseemly that any woman
should set her dainty foot upon this hallowed soil. One
might think that to open a female brokerage house at the
core of Manhattan was an enterprise doomed to catastrophe
in the prevailing climate of the times.

Not so. That hedge of bigotry might still appear solid but

already had been breached. The first articulate assault upon male dominance had been made by Mary Wollstonecraft in *A Vindication of the Rights of Woman*, published in 1792, but not until a half-century later did women muster into a distinct body. In 1848 Lucretia Mott and Susan B. Anthony organised the first Equal Rights Convention in New York, defining the Movement's purpose: *Men and Women shall have Equal Rights Throughout the United States.*

By this point in Victoria's career the Movement's first magazine, the *Agitator*, had merged with the *Women's Journal*, whose writers included the best-educated women in the US, together with a few token males. Now, across the country discrete groups of women came together to launch the *Woman Voter* in New York, the *Western Woman Voter* in Seattle, and the *Maryland Suffrage News* in Baltimore. The gender characterised by males as 'the fair sex' succeeded in establishing a beachhead in US media.

Victoria's – or was it Vanderbilt's – decision to set up a female task force in the financial district proved astute. Male reaction the length of Wall Street confirmed it: *Sexual prurience trumps prejudice.*

Such was the level of curiosity that the Hoffman House could not contain the tide of visitors. The business relocated to 44 Broad Street, around the corner from the Exchange. Every newspaper sent a reporter to cover what the *New York Sun* titled NEW FUROR ON THE STREET.

Rival brokerage firms each despatched a scout to report on the invaders' stronghold, together with its breastwork. The sidewalk overflowed with sightseers, their offices literally besieged by 'a miscellaneous throng of 4,000'.

The steady stream of callers included Commodore Vanderbilt on an almost daily visit. This aroused some comment due to his recent marriage – with Victoria's counsel and encouragement – to Frank Crawford, a pious southern belle, from Alabama. This had not affected his relationship with Tennie, who continued her treatments, remaining close to the Old Boy's heart.

No one was more highly regarded than he for his market acuity. The sisters – seen as his protégées – found themselves running the hottest shop on the Street. A cartoon in the New York *Evening Telegraph* depicts the pair sharing the driving seat of a cart pulled by a team of bulls and bears with identifiable human faces. Victoria firmly controls the reins, Tennie the long whip with which she is lashing the leading bears, while a scatter of rival brokers lie crushed beneath the wheels.

Asked by a reporter if she was bothered by remarks made about her in society, Tennie tossed her curls to reply, 'I despise what squeaky, crying girls or powdered, counter-jumping dandies say of me.' What a world of class distinction lies in this telling phrase.

During the three years following its debut the firm made $750,000 in profit, equivalent to almost $14 million today. A whisper among the gossip circulating in the better-informed salons of fashionable Manhattan was that 'they sold more than just market shares'. It did not affect their trade; no one complained of being short-changed, of whatever nature it comprised.

Among Victoria's several gifts was a talent for using the press and – long before the invention of PR – to *work* it. The *New York Herald* had been the first to take her up and continued to follow her, as did the *Courier*, the *Telegraph*, the *Evening Post*, the *World* and the *Evening Express*. Only the *New York Times* remained too snooty to mention her. The city media had made her into a story and were committed to follow it. The next news of her was domestic. She moved herself and family from Great Jones Street to East 38th Street. The tribe by now included Buck, Roxanna, Tennessee, four sisters from failed marriages they had contracted on the road, together with their and Victoria's children, and husband Woodhull. Also domestic servants.

Larger accommodation enabled her to give houseroom to a new and influential inhabitant, who had left his wife of thirty-five years to move in with them. Stephen Pearl Andrews, a scholar and anarchist, could read thirty-two languages. He had published a textbook on Chinese and another on a method of shorthand. Still, he'd found time to devise a comprehensive system to govern the recently united States. He initiated Victoria in politics, the next step in her career.

Andrews ghosted a series of articles for the *New York Herald* under her byline. These expressed her own views, though now supported by reasoned argument and better syntax. In the role of mentor he supplanted Colonel Blood, whom she'd outgrown yet who remained resident in her house.

Andrews occupied his own room, resented fiercely by Roxanna. He became in effect director of policy, shaping Victoria's radical views into a political platform with intellectual foundations. Aged sixty-three, but looking much older, physically he was strikingly unattractive. The singularity in Victoria's relationship with him is that, among all the men with whom she had dealings – spiritual, financial or political – he was almost the only one with whom she did not have sex.

Aged thirty-two, in full bloom and possessed of her own fortune, she was now a respected figure on Wall Street. Respected also by groups of women throughout the land, to whom she was an inspiration. 'All this talk about women's rights is moonshine,' she told a reporter. 'We are doing daily more for women's rights, by being here on Wall Street, than all the speeches will do in ten years.'

She published a book, *Origins, Tendencies and Principles of Government*. Drafted by Andrews, its authorship was credited to her alone. The house on East 38th Street served as editorial office and activist HQ, while Tennie ran the brokerage business downtown. On Murray Hill, the divorced sisters turned their hand to whatever was required. Blood acted as office manager, the children could run messages and deliver mail. Only Woodhull was useless.

In 1870 Victoria brought out the first edition of her own newspaper, *Woodhull & Claflin's Weekly*, selling for five cents a copy. Its editor presented herself as 'the most prominent representative of the only unrepresented class in the Republic', and its leading voice. And a pretty damn assertive voice it was. The weekly's slick-paper pages carried articles on spiritualism, magnetic healing and exposés of banker shysters. It ran pieces arguing for easier divorce laws, birth control and self-help advice on abortion; editorials promoted political reform, short skirts, legalised prostitution and Free Love. Women loved the paper, less so men. Much less. Then, to the outrage of almost everyone, she published Marx's *Communist Manifesto*.

Victoria's life follows an exemplary dramatic arc. At this moment her career line displays a boldly rising curve. Her ascent is steady, unfaltering, but never fails to surprise. On 2 April 1870, readers of the *New York Herald Tribune* confronted her First Proclamation:

> Having the means, courage, energy and strength necessary for the race...I now announce myself candidate for the Presidency.

At a time when women did not have the vote, to announce a new political party in skirts together with her plan to lead it as First Executive provoked male fury. Though not *all* men were appalled: a few even endorsed the proposal. One such was General Benjamin Butler, representative for Massachusetts, who was particularly roused by meeting Victoria in the flesh.

Fat, pugnacious, cross-eyed, he would appear an unlikely convert to her cause, for he'd earlier demonstrated an attitude to women less than gallant. As military governor of New Orleans, he had imposed manners on the city's snooty southern belles when they'd snubbed federal soldiers. He ordered that any who did so should 'be treated as a woman of the streets plying her occupation'. Yet contained within Butler's bellicose exterior was an enlightened soul who believed in full rights for African-Americans and equal rights for all. He fixed for the House Judiciary Committee to invite

Victoria to make a petition to Congress. The hearing would take place on the morning of 11 January 1871.

The date, chosen by Victoria, was tactically astute, for that same afternoon the National Woman Suffrage Association planned to stage its third annual convention in Washington. Mightily disconcerted by the coincidence, Susan B. Anthony, Paulina Wright Davis and the formidable Isabella Hooker, leading figures in the Association, resolved to attend Victoria's hearing.

She entered wearing a plain dress, necktie and Alpine hat cocked at a jaunty angle on her auburn curls. Deliberately, slowly, she removed it to set it upon the table as the focus of all eyes. Introduced by Senator John Harris of Louisiana, she rose gracefully to begin, 'The right to vote is denied to women citizens of the United States...'

She showed not a flicker of nervousness. Her clear musical voice was informed by complete assurance. She spoke with the power of an idea whose time had come: 'The operator of the Election Laws...denying the right of citizens to vote on account of their sex is a grievance to your memorialist and to others, being women...'

She did not go on for more than twenty minutes of reasoned argument, commanding the full attention of the Committee, the press...and the leaders of the Suffrage Association. Such was the effect of her speech that those women could only – though through gritted teeth – invite her to join their movement and address its members at their convention later that day.

The same sisterhood of educated New England women had controlled the Association for years. That afternoon they were obliged to share the stage with her, facing a hall packed with females inflamed by her triumph at the Capitol. These were all for her, the star of the event. At the end they swarmed her, calling her name and reaching out to touch her.

A number of the suffragette leaders who'd sat by her on the stage felt differently. This brazen tart had *upstaged* them, stolen their cause and supporters. Victoria had hijacked the Women's Movement, and many of its blue-blooded principals were furious at the coup.

As were others throughout the land. She had usurped the Association and dared to present herself as their speaker. Social revolution, Communism, Spiritualism, Free Love... these were not *their* views. The press whipped up their righteous fury: *A background of prostitution... Two husbands living with her under the same roof...* She was vilified as 'a vain, immodest unsexed woman' and a 'brazen snaky adventuress'.

Worse lay in store for the tyro politician with her vaunting ambition. The thrust came from a skilled assailant with an informed readership. The leading columnist in the *Christian Union*, Harriet Beecher Stowe, attacked both Victoria and Tennessee. Beecher Stowe's name rated high, for twenty years earlier she'd written the most-read book in America, *Uncle Tom's Cabin*. The work occupied a position in the home and national canon second only to the Bible.

Now Harriet brought out a new comic novel, published in serial instalments in the newspaper. *My Wife and I* satirised the fads and follies of fashionable life. One of the characters was Audacia Dangereyes, a parody of the 'new woman', opinionated, attention-seeking, pretentious and promiscuous. Very many readers identified her as Victoria, and giggled. Another character mirrored her supporter and friend Elizabeth Cady Stanton, caricatured as Mrs Cerulean, a rich oversized philanthropist overflowing with imbecilic zeal for *REFORM*!

Unfortunately for its targets, *My Wife and I* was very funny; its serialisation caused the *Christian Union* to double in circulation. Victoria could deal with abuse, it bounced off her. Mockery was harder. It stung, and prompted too hasty a reaction. Andrews, General Butler and Blood all tried to dissuade her: best to ignore the satire with disdain. She would not listen to their counsel. She coveted the world's most powerful job. That compelling ambition made her deaf to reason.

She had nothing on Harriet personally, but she possessed a secret that could disgrace and ruin her esteemed brother. To reveal it in an attempt to bring him down constituted an undeserved and wholly disproportionate reprisal to the indignity she'd suffered, yet pride and fury drove her into war.

Henry Ward Beecher was the most popular and respected Christian leader in America. He had made his name crusading for the abolition of slavery. Honoured throughout the northern states, he was correspondingly hated in the South, where many had vowed to kill him. In the Civil War he'd raised money to send rifles – known as 'Beecher's bibles' – to abolitionist forces and, learning of two escaped female slaves who'd been recaptured, he raised $2,000 to purchase and free them with considerable publicity. Later, he famously auctioned another slave from his pulpit to promote his sister's book, *Uncle Tom's Cabin*.

Now fifty-nine, Beecher had been married for thirty-five years in a union later described as 'the classic marital cycle of neglect and nagging'. The couple had eight children, of whom four had died, and shared little in common except a prosperous well-staffed home, for Beecher was highly rewarded for his speaking engagements across the country. He presented as a progressive saint, preaching about discrimination and exploitation in all its forms, and his renown had made him President of the American Woman Suffrage Association, rival to the National Woman Suffrage Association, which Victoria had effectively shanghaied. He had already come out as her opponent, condemning her views on Free Love.

Now she had information that could expose him to the nation as a hypocrite and fraud. On 20 May 1871, the *New York Times* and *New York World* ran identically worded letters from her:

> Sir, Because I am a woman, and…hold opinions somewhat different from the self-elected orthodoxy which men find their profit in supporting…various editors have stigmatized me as a living example of immorality and unchastity… I know that many of my self-appointed judges and critics are deeply tainted with the vices they condemn… My judges preach against free love openly, practice it secretly… I know of one man, a public teacher of eminence, who lives in concubinage with the wife of another public teacher of almost equal eminence. All three concur in denouncing offenses against morality…

She followed up the strike. Later that same morning the letters appeared Victoria sent one of the family with a message to Theodore Tilton, editor of the *Golden Age* magazine (owned by Beecher). When he appeared at her office somewhat puzzled, she handed him the *New York Times*, asking him to read the letter aloud.

He did so, while she watched closely. 'Do you know, sir, whom I refer to?' she asked.

'How can I tell...?'

'I refer, sir, to the Reverend Henry Ward Beecher and your wife... And I read by the expression on your face that my charge is true.'

Tilton's wife Lib confessed the affair to him, as she had to Elizabeth Cady Stanton, who told Victoria. The Tiltons had been married by Beecher fifteen years before and remained practising members of his congregation. Beecher obtained Tilton his first editorial job on the *Independent*, later founding the *Golden Age* for him to edit. He was Tilton's benefactor and patron. Tilton, who concealed the resentment he felt toward Beecher at appropriating his wife's affections, nevertheless had compelling reasons not to want their *ménage à trois* to become public knowledge.

The issue was not resolved in that first meeting, but next morning Tilton called on Victoria again to beg that the affair remain secret. He implored her to consider the many victims who would be hurt by the revelation: his own and Lib's children, Beecher's wife and family, and the famous reformer's church and congregation, who venerated him for his achievements. By the time Tilton reached the end of his appeal he was in tears. Victoria consoled him.

Two days later, he called round again, meeting Andrews, Blood and the rest of the family, all busily at work on her political campaign. He visited once more, when he and Victoria went rowing together on the Harlem River to escape the frenzy of the office. Another day, they bunked off to Coney Island to picnic on the beach. He was a handsome man of thirty-five with the body of an athlete but – as Victoria pointed out – the closed mind of a conventional male, governed by prejudice and received opinion. She told him he was a tight-assed bigot.

Roughly, Victoria teased him. His marriage to Lib had

produced children but provided little physical pleasure to either of them. Had he not enjoyed his own brief affairs while away lecturing? What was sauce for the gander was sauce for the goose, no? She laughed at the perceived affront to his macho sensibility at his wife's affair. He was exhibiting 'maudlin sentiment and...*dreadful suzz*...over an event the most natural in the world, and the most intrinsically innocent... He did not *own* his wife; he was demonstrating the attitude of a slave-holder.'

Under the lash of such correction of course he fell in love. Exposure to her had the same effect as it had upon Blood: it capsized him, overturning his persona and ordered life. For the next eighteen months he served as her disciple. He attended political rallies, drafted her campaign speeches, dedicated the *Golden Age* to her cause, attacked Harriet Beecher Stowe for 'writing furiously and unwarrantably about her in the *Christian Union*'.

Tilton would script a hagiography – quoted in this book – that portrays her as Joan of Arc, *sans peur et sans reproche*. He was besotted. Much later, when hostilities with Beecher had ended by damaging everyone involved but most of all herself, Victoria explained in the *Chicago Times*, 'He was my lover for more than half a year... So enamoured and infatuated with each other were we...we were hardly out of each other's sight... He slept every night for three months in my arms.'

Throughout those months Victoria was otherwise single-minded in her campaign for the Presidency. This was run by Andrews and General Butler from the house on East 38th Street, where the whole family assisted. Nevertheless the campaign cost a deal of money, and she could no longer count on backing from Vanderbilt, whose wife had come between them. Meanwhile, the brokerage business was failing. She and Tennie were fully occupied in campaign politics, and it fell on Blood to run the office downtown but, though competent in accounts, he was no salesman and was ignorant of the financial products he was peddling. Nor was he helped by Buck Claflin, who took it upon himself to swagger down to Broad Street to offer liquor and wisdom to a diminishing trickle of clients no longer seeking to invest but anxious for their money.

Tilton's pleas to relent in the war against Beecher did not stay Victoria's hand, but expedience did. She found she needed him; as President of the American Woman Suffrage Association he was the leading spokesman for women's emancipation. The rival National Woman Suffrage Association stood at odds with it over a range of issues. Victoria aspired to effect a rapport between the two groups and merge them into a political party – which she would represent for government. She planned to propose such an alliance in a forthcoming appearance at Steinway Hall and wanted Beecher to introduce her to the audience. He had every reason to refuse, but she believed she could pressure him into acceptance. At her urging, Tilton set up an encounter with his patron, advising him to 'treat her with kindness'.

The two met in the parlour of the Tiltons' house, where she opened her arms to embrace the pastor warmly. Alone together, they enjoyed what politicians call 'a full and frank discussion', based on facts known to both that did not need to be spelt out. Commending Beecher for his stance on female rights, she reproached him for not going further in preaching what he believed – and secretly practised. Shifting uneasily in his seat, Beecher replied, 'If I were to do so, I would preach to empty seats and it would be the ruin of my church.'

He knew she was due to speak at Steinway Hall; now she told him that 'what I say or shall not say will depend largely on the result of this interview.' She wanted him on stage to endorse her – or else.

Beecher was appalled. 'He fell upon the sofa on his knees beside me and, taking my face between his hands while the tears streamed down his cheeks, he begged "Let me off! Let me off!"' He pleaded for mercy, he threatened suicide, but he 'could not, would not face it'.

She was pitiless. Calling him 'a moral coward', she told him, 'If I am compelled to go onto that platform alone, I shall begin by telling the audience why I am alone and why you are not with me.'

On the evening of 20 November Victoria, Stephen Pearl Andrews, Blood, Tennie and their sponsors stood in an ante-room to a packed Steinway Hall at 8.05p.m., still waiting for her presenter...but Beecher failed to show.

'There isn't a brave man in the circle of two cities to preside at my meeting,' she declared, and stepped toward the stage. She was angry, set to make trouble. The crowd was made up of both sexes, with many of both against her. Hecklers shouted or jeered. A voice yelled above the din, 'Are YOU a Free Lover?'

'Yes!' she called back in defiance, 'I *am* a Free Lover!'

Yells and boos greeted her declaration. Raising her voice, she continued, 'I have an inalienable constitutional and natural right to love whom I may, to love as short or long a period as I can, to change that love every day as I please! And with that right neither you nor any law can interfere.'

The meeting broke up in disorder. Next day her speech was reported in every paper. She was a headline, a scandal, a prostitute *and this hussy was a candidate for the Presidency...*?

Early in the New Year of 1872 Victoria's supporters staged a rally at the Apollo Hall in New York to announce the foundation of a new political entity, the Equal Rights Party. To organise the extravaganza required the cooperation of all the Claflin family, who went on the stump. Buck exalted in his element, dressed up as Uncle Sam with a bullhorn whipping up supporters, almost all of them women. The hall was jammed to capacity. Judge Reymart of New York presided, proposing they name themselves the Equal Rights Party. The motion was carried to applause.

Judge Carter of Ohio leaped to his feet shouting, 'I nominate Victoria C. Woodhull for President of the United States. All in favour say Aye.'

'Aye!' the crowd roared, stamping, shrieking, waving hats and scarves. Then from behind sounded a deafening blare of raucous brass. Down the aisle came a stomping band with 400 black soldiers marching six abreast. The parade was led by the irrepressible Tennie costumed in full fig as colonel, prancing at their head.

Victoria's resolve to punish Beecher remained strong. She decided to publish her denunciation in *Woodhull & Claflin's Weekly*. Andrews, Blood, even Tennie did their best to dissuade her; all were aware the move was liable to backfire upon her. She would not be moved.

The American News Company got wind of the content and refused to distribute the issue. The whole print run, four times the usual number, was instead sent in bulk to the office on Broad Street. The entire Claflin family plus volunteers combined to distribute it to news-stands throughout the city. These sold, the word spread rapidly and all copies were bought up. Prices rose from $5 to $10 to $20 a copy. The scandalous issue became, and remains, a collectors' item.

Victoria's exposé was described as a 'most abominable and unjust charge against one of the purest and best citizens of the United States', a criminal slander. The District Attorney agreed to press charges but was pre-empted by the Federal Commissioner, who despatched two armed US marshals to arrest the perpetrators.

The pair found Victoria and Tennie seated in a carriage outside their office with 500 copies of the newspaper stashed at their feet. A small crowd gathered as one of the marshals climbed up to seize the reins. The other entered the carriage to restrain the offenders, but – lacking two pairs of handcuffs – he 'politely disposed himself' across the laps of the two women to prevent them bolting from the cab…as it carried them off to prison.

On 5 November when General Ulysses S Grant was elected President of the United States, Victoria and Tennie were still locked up in Ludlow Street Jail.

The charge against them was for distributing obscene material through the US Mail – but only after six months in prison did they appear before a jury. The trial was covered by every newspaper, reiterating the shameful details in their background. The court finally accepted that the text in the *Weekly* was neither salacious nor pornographic, therefore not obscene. They were found not guilty – but it made no difference to public perception. In the media they 'had escaped only on a legal technicality'. The *New York Times* – so slow initially to take her up – now featured her on the front page: Her attack on Beecher had 'disgraced and degraded the female name'.

In the course of this three-year period, the lengthy trial, Victoria and Tennie lost everything. They were anathematised. The family was evicted from their home on East 38th Street. Roxanna and Buck found lodging with a married daughter, Canning Woodhull was now dead and Andrews back with his wife, but Victoria, her children, Tennie and Blood were homeless. They ended up penniless, squatting in the brokerage office on Broad Street, where the *Weekly* had ceased publication for lack of funds.

Victoria's fame had turned to iniquity but Beecher's bloomed wonderfully well. *Everyone* wanted to see and hear him. Demand was so great he could now charge $1,000 a lecture. The trial won him national stardom.

'There are no second acts in American lives.' In her first, Victoria climbed from the bottom of the pile to very near the top before falling into disgrace and penury. Yet she did achieve a comeback, if not in America.

Her former patron Cornelius Vanderbilt provided the key to her restoration from beyond the grave. On his death in 1877, his estate was valued at $100 million. $95 million went to his eldest son, William, $5 million to be divided between his other son and eight daughters, who all contested the will. He left Tennie an oil painting of himself, and to both sisters 'certain large sums to be used to promote spiritual healing'. Soon after the will's publication, Victoria and Tennie paid a house call on son William to inform him that certain affairs between themselves and the Commodore remained unresolved. They had filled the roles of therapist, healer, intimate and confidantes to the Old Boy and knew so many details about his life and dealings… Wisely, William paid up handsomely for their discretion, setting only one condition: that they leave the country and live abroad.

Victoria found the terms acceptable. The Claflin ensemble had played out their run in the USA and sailed for England in style, requiring six first class staterooms. The party included Ben Tucker, Victoria's nineteen-year-old 'boy lover' of the period, whom she had told soon after initiation, 'You are going to love Tennie this afternoon.' When he demurred she informed him, 'No one can love me who does not also love Tennie.' A touch too conventional for Victoria, he did not last and is of note only because he later revealed she'd conducted a sexual relationship with her nemesis Beecher during the ten months between meeting to threaten him with exposure and then doing so by publication.

At the first of these encounters Beecher had gone on his knees to beg, 'Let me off! Let me off!' His entreaties cast her in the dominant role, and throughout their subsequent trysts the power balance remained the same. It clearly worked for *him,* as she wrote later of 'the immense physical potency of Mr Beecher', but, though prurience forbids, one cannot help speculating how that dynamic expressed itself in their practices.

The Claflins resettled in London, where Victoria rented a large house and resumed lecturing. Shortly before Christmas 1877 she spoke on 'The Human Body: The Temple of God' to a full house in St James's Hall. In the audience was one John Biddulph Martin, a scholarly city banker whose hobby was coin collecting. Once again her magic worked. As he recalled, 'I was charmed with her high intellect and fascinated by her manner. I left the lecture hall that night with the determination that, if Mrs Woodhull would marry me, I would certainly make her my wife.' Tennie pre-empted her in marriage. At their London address she continued to provide full-contact spiritual healing to a number of wealthy patients, but she was aware time was not on her side and it would be wise to ensure her future. From her list of patients she selected Sir Francis Cook to share breaking news from the spirit world that he and she were linked by fate. This same ploy her sister had used on Colonel Blood saved time on unnecessary courtship and soon after, she became Lady Cook, chatelaine of a county seat and a small but exquisite castle in Portugal.

Between Tennie's marriage and Victoria's, old Buck Claflin died of a stroke and Roxanna moved in with the Cooks, where she occupied her own quarters, but Sir Francis must have loved Tennie very much to put up with the arrangement. When he expired in 1901, Tennie flung herself into activity in the woman's cause, where she had to be restrained from grabbing the lead role at their demonstrations. In the Great War she attempted to raise an army of 1,500 female soldiers and held a one-to-one with President Teddy Roosevelt at the White House to hector him prettily on the Woman's Vote. She died in 1923.

On the passing of Victoria's own husband when she was fifty-nine, she moved into his country seat in Worcestershire, inviting her daughter and son Byron to live with her. She bought one of the first open sports cars and roared through country lanes headed for London, urging her chauffeur to go faster. She briefly considered flying the Atlantic solo before dying in 1927, just as Charles Lindbergh succeeded in doing so. Set amid that news in the *New York Times*, her obituary describes her as pioneer suffragist, banker, publisher and nominee for the Presidency. The *New York Herald* honoured her as the 'American Mother of Woman's Suffrage', while another reprised the view that 'she ought to be hanged, and then have a monument erected to her memory at the foot of the gallows'.

By one single misjudgement she wrecked her career. Had she not exposed Beecher…what then? Since its foundation, the office of the First Executive has been occupied by actors, showmen, crooks, liars, megalomaniacs and reality TV stars. Despite the odds against her, it is not beyond the bounds of imagination that Victoria Woodhull might have fulfilled her destiny as President of the United States. Had she done so, America would now be another very different land.

Victoria and Tennie.

3

LIBERTY, EQUALITY
and… *WHAT?*

By 14 July 1789 the oppressive walls of the prison have
reared there for so long that many inhabiting their dank
shadow in the warren of mean houses, shops and narrow
alleys clustered around their base imagine they have stood
in place forever, a fact of life.

In Paris, affrays, looting and sporadic musket fire have continued throughout the previous night and a crowd has been gathering outside the walls of the Bastille since early this morning. At 10.30, when two delegates from the people are allowed in to negotiate surrender with the governor, a mass of them jostle their way into the external courtyard to the fort. The yard is filled by almost a thousand rowdy protesters. The price of bread and with it the level of grievance stand at an all-time high.

The throng is made up of local artisans, shopkeepers, tradesmen, army deserters, thieves, felons and shoeless youths in torn breeches. Also women armed with kitchen knives or hatchets, a pike, a few with a sword. It is a raucous disaffected rabble packed shoulder to shoulder, thigh to thigh, bodies rank with sweat in the rising heat. Their mass is swelling by the minute with the arrival of volunteers of the citizens' militia, jubilant with firearms and two cannon ransacked from the armoury at Les Invalides. The dissident horde includes more than twenty barkeepers and owners of local wine shops, doing brisk trade amid the tumult. Very many are drunk. Despite the menace, there's the feel of celebration, a riotous party slid out of control. It is a warm July morning, growing ever hotter in the blazing sun.

The Bastille is armed with fifteen eight-pounder cannon poking from the embrasures in its towers. Twelve 1½-pound guns stand on its ramparts, with an arc of fire covering the whole *quartier*. A further three eight-pounders loaded with grape-shot are lined up at the rear of the inner courtyard that contains the governor's residence, with their guns aimed at its sealed gate. The garrison inside the fortress consists of eighty-two *Invalides*, easygoing fellows in a normally undemanding job, reinforced by thirty-two Swiss soldiers and their captain. Most of these mercenaries, impressive in their showy uniforms, carry in their packs suitably tattered rags to change into if it looks expedient to alter sides, as it has of late. Neither the rabble at the gates nor the garrison within have had any sleep. The Swiss soldiery spent the night shifting 250 barrels of gunpowder – delivered the day before and stacked uncovered in the yard – into a windowless dungeon beneath the citadel, as more secure from detonation. All are exhausted.

Between the insurgents and the fortress itself stands a gate barring access to the governor's courtyard – external to the fort – then two drawbridges across a moat clotted with garbage and excrement. The stench is compounded by the reek of unwashed bodies, soiled clothes and two carts of burning horse dung. Set on fire to provide smoke cover for the besiegers, it chokes the throat and scalds the eyes. In the crush and hubbub there is hardly room to move, but the mob are shaking their crude weapons and screaming abuse at the armed soldiers on the ramparts high above them.

There is no shade in the yard. The midday sun beats down. No news comes back from the two delegates who went in to negotiate surrender a half-hour ago. Word races through the crowd that they are being held hostage. They attack the gate with axes, attempting to smash the locks. A handful of army deserters try to make a ladder up the wall by hammering their bayonets into chinks between its stones. Three youths have climbed onto the roof of a parfumier's shop abutting the compound and are edging their way across the tiles toward the roof of the gatehouse.

Then a shriek of utmost terror, so shrill it cuts through the din. For an instant the mob is struck still, then all eyes look up to the Bastille's towers, whose cannon protruding from the slits are being drawn back. *To load them*, the mob thinks. They fall upon the gate with axes and sledgehammers, hacking it down to surge into the governor's courtyard in a mass, howling and firing their muskets as they rush in…

★   ★   ★

The mob are mistaken in their assumption. In fact, the people's delegates were received courteously by the troubled job-serving governor – who would lose his head meta-phorically then physically in the next few hours. He was about to start lunch – then eaten at about 10.30 – and invited them to join him. Taken aback by the suggestion, they found themselves doing so while, in a show of calm and courtesy he surely did not feel, he explained that his sympathies were entirely on their side. He was prepared to hand over the keys of the fortress and ready to capitulate but could not do so until he'd received orders from the King – which he was expecting at any moment… Meanwhile, the pair of delegates was hastily wolfing down everything set before them, for they were starving.

The Bastille was provisioned with supplies only for two days and had no independent source of fresh water. The governor knew he could not withstand a siege.

In marked contrast to the bedlam outside the walls, discussion at his table was conciliatory and reasonable. Toward the end of the rather lengthy meal – for the Bastille was known for its kitchen – he confirmed that the garrison had no hostile intentions to the Republican crowd, and no wish to fire upon them. To demonstrate his peaceable intent, he ordered the cannon in the towers to be drawn back from their embrasures. It was this manoeuvre the besiegers had seen and misinterpreted.

As the mob surge into the inner courtyard through the broken gate the officer commanding the four cannon loaded with grape-shot yells the order, 'Fire!'

A flash and roar. Blast of shot and gun smoke. The front rank of the assailants are mown down, but impetus of mass drives the horde over the bodies of the fallen to swarm the guns and cut down their crews. First blood spatters the assailants, drenching the cobbles. Seconds later, the youths on the roof drop down to smash the door to the guardhouse in order to seize the keys to the further gate, which gives access to the fortress. Unable to find these, they use axes to smash the pulleys to the chains securing the bridge. It crashes down and the mob pours onto the span under crossfire from the towers and blasting down upon them from the parapet above.

A moat and drawbridge hold them trapped, but the range is short and a volley of musket fire shatters its pulleys. It too thuds down, killing a man standing too close and disabling another. The mob swarm across to attack the main door with axes, till its timbers split. An unstoppable mass of bodies bursts in to swamp the hall, swelling outward and upward to occupy the fortress. Accompanied by screams of vengeance, blood and shrieks of pain...then exultant yells of triumph.

The Bastille has fallen. Its prisoners are set free and its store of gunpowder will be used to fuel the revolution that eradicates the Old Regime.

The image of Liberty, born in the French revolution.

A new age has dawned.

Or had it?

There was still no bread. A succession of poor harvests had depleted the granaries, but fact held no ground in these days of rage and rumour; the shortage believed to be a tactic of the monarchists to starve the poor into submission and crush their revolt.

Young single women came together to force action. Their lowly jobs paid them barely to subsist, their future contained only servitude, destitution and continuing oppression. They had no children and nothing to lose except their lives. These women, many still in their teens, formed into same-sex gangs. They were well armed – since the sacking of the armoury at Les Invalides and fall of the Bastille, Paris was a toyshop awash with weapons. Lying in wait on one or other of the routes into the city, such a gang would hijack one of the few carts of grain still entering Paris. Then, putting their shoulders to the wagon, they forced its horses into a trot and, whooping in triumph, rushed the vehicle to the *place* in front of the Town Hall, where they threw open its contents to the cheering crowd. They took a wild joy in their actions; this was the greatest escapade any had ever known and a licence to run amuck.

A band of these young women pounded their fists on the locked doors of the Town Hall, clamouring for access. They wanted to confront the mayor face to face. Their message: he, his male councillors and men in general had no grasp of the current situation and had shown themselves unable to solve the problem. They demanded 'a role in affairs'.

Two weeks later they seized that role by force. At dawn on 5 October the inhabitants of the city centre, rich and poor, woke to the loud banging of a drum. Those of the rich still remaining in the *quartier* – for many had fled to their country estates – checked their closed shutters and their locks. For the irregulars of the female militia, so recently come into being, that insistent drumbeat was a call to arms.

The solitary drummer stood in the *place* confronting the Town Hall was a young woman, poorly dressed but sporting a tricolour cockade, symbol of the revolution. She was already surrounded by working women who had been setting up their stalls in the nearby market. An hour later the crowd of women numbered more than 2,000. Children scampered around Les Halles, blowing pipes and whistles to summon fresh recruits. Their number grew, as did their anger. They smashed the doors of the Town Hall and forced their way inside. Only night staff were there, all male. These were flung out, hooted and jeered as they scurried off, but unharmed. Women occupied the rooms, appropriating anything of use. They gathered paperwork and files to build a bonfire of the records. No men were allowed entry to the building.

The Town Hall was wrecked. The *place* outside could not contain the yelling mob, the adjacent streets thronged. What next? *The Palace of Versailles*. Site of the National Assembly and residence of the King, the destination was the ultimate bastion of authority. No one commanded this multitude, which fused together as one mind. No order was given, but the mass stirred into motion, uncoiled and began to march...

Versailles was 14 kilometres from Paris, and it was raining. The column stretched interminable; by the time it cleared the city limits it contained 6,000 women. Men who tried to join its ranks were shoved aside. Men followed after, and so did a regiment of the National Guard, commanded by General Lafayette. His troops – only recently conscripted and unreliable in their loyalty – had orders not to oppose the demonstrators but to conciliate and maintain order. An irregular cadre of drummers preceded the cavalcade, beating on instruments ransacked from Les Tuileries. They were followed by two gun carriages, hauled by relays of women. Others rode the cannons, waving swords and leafy branches. The legion that came after was variously equipped with weapons looted from the armoury, or knives and meat cleavers snatched up from their kitchens. As this army marched through the rain, they sang songs of the market, with rude ditties mocking the rich.

Dusk had fallen across the scene when the lead troops tramped up the wide avenue to the palace. From its windows the occupants looked down in horror at the mob gathering below and the endless vista of their coming, extending far as the eye could see.

The National Assembly sat in session in one wing of the building. The insurgents smashed their way in to swarm the hall and take over the meeting, shoving aside the members to make room on the benches. The president, Jean-Joseph Mounier, was removed bodily from his seat, replaced by a woman, and forced to lead a deputation to meet the King. None of the Royal Guard made a move to intervene. Had any tried they would have been butchered and trampled by the mob.

King Louis had only moments to prepare for the confrontation, which took place in the Great Hall. The most articulate among the women was chosen to voice their demands, and it is indicative of their median age that she was only seventeen, a flower-seller from the market. Like the rest, she had not eaten that day. Pushed forward to represent them in these sumptuous surroundings, she fainted at his feet.

Noblesse oblige. Louis responded with the faultless manners of his caste. Calling for smelling salts, he went on one knee to tend to her.

So volatile is the mood of a mob that in the gesture, that single image of him knelt by her was enough to disconcert and switch their emotion. It was a God-given opportunity, but the King's reaction was probably spontaneous. When he stood up, he'd gained control. He listened with courtesy to the women's demands. He agreed at once to sign the Declaration of the Rights of Man and the Citizens, which had been on his desk for weeks. He agreed to issue an order that all granaries release their reserves of grain immediately, and that stores at the palace should be sent to Paris. He agreed to move the site of the National Assembly to the city. He agreed that he, the queen and their son, the Dauphin, should vacate Versailles and return to Paris. Those currently living there and forming his court would accompany them to the capital. The whole party would be packed and ready to depart next day.

The delegation of women went back to their sisters occupying the National Assembly to report that the King had acceded to every one of their demands. The news spread to the mob outside: capitulation. They had won.

It was not enough; the drama had not been fulfilled. It required more, there had to be blood. That night rioters broke into the queen's private quarters and went in search of Marie-Antoinette, long the epitome of privilege and ostentatious wealth. Two of her bodyguards who tried to prevent them were killed and decapitated. Bearing their dripping heads on pikes, they tracked their quarry to her bedroom. She fled barefoot and in her nightdress, while they chased her, baying in pursuit, down the long corridors of the palace to the safety of the King's apartments.

As promised, next day King Louis, his queen, son and court evacuated Versailles, together with all of the National Assembly and Lafayette's troops.

With them went the mob and the royal bodyguard, disbanded overnight. Before them, two women held aloft the severed heads of their fellow soldiers killed in the affray, yet their mood was jubilant as the rest. The cavalcade, which numbered fifty or sixty thousand, was headed by the two looted cannons, now hauled by horses from the royal stables. Green foliage concealed their barrels, women rode the gun carriages waving leafy branches.

So they returned to Paris in a victorious throng. As they entered the city all within earshot gathered to watch their triumphant passage. Women wore articles of military uniform or soldiers' hats, others strode arm in arm with them. As they went past some of the women lifted their skirts and flashed their bottoms in scorn for the craven bystanders who had not been there, but shirked their part in the glorious event.

King Louis gave too little and too late. What he conceded counted not enough to save his head. It required royal blood to satisfy the voracity of the mob. On 21 January 1793 he was driven in a hackney coach to be sentenced to execution in the renamed Place de la Révolution. The casements of houses overlooking the route remained sealed on orders of the Commune, but one of the spectators at the windows of 22 rue Meslée was Mary Wollstonecraft, an English writer, who had just published her own revolutionary manifesto. In her diary she remarked on the King's dignity and composure on the way to the guillotine.

She had arrived in Paris only days before, pursued by the derision and vilification of those condemning her radical manifesto, *A Vindication of the Rights of Woman*. As they would her move to France in support of the revolution. Aged thirty-three, Mary had been member of a group of people in London known as 'Johnson's circle', who gathered regularly around the dinner table of her publisher, Joseph Johnson. Occasionally women would be invited to join them, but Mary made the only regular female guest. Others included mathematician John Bonnycastle, the doctor George Fordyce, artist Henry Fuseli, and the visionary William Blake – then at the start of his career – who illustrated one of Mary's early books. What bonded those dining at Johnson's convivial and well-supplied table was not only their literary and philosophic interests but the radical political views they shared. Which here they could discuss openly, as they could not elsewhere in England at that point due to censorship and repression of free speech.

Mary dedicated *Vindication* to the French statesman, Talleyrand. Bitterly so – his views on women, in the new constitution, had incited her to write the book. An ambitious club-foot cleric in his fifties, his concerns lay in this world rather than the next, and he'd maintained a series of mistresses throughout his ascent to bishop. At the start of the revolution he resigned from the Church to take up the post of administrator of Paris and its surrounding *département*.

Women fighting shoulder to shoulder with men had *made* the revolution, but in the republic that followed it was men who set the rules. The demand had been clear: Liberty, Equality, the right to resist Oppression…but it took only two years for the men – they were all men – who composed the constitution to delete the last phrase, substituting the word *Brotherhood*. For the army of women who marched on Versailles to confront the King, brotherhood was not the goal they sought.

The Bastille had fallen, but less tangible walls remained afterward, segregating half the citizens of France. High among women's demands featured the right to an education. In the new constitution Talleyrand promised representative government and equality for all. But on the subject of education he dictated:

> Let us bring up women, not to aspire to advantages
> which the Constitution denies them, but to appreciate

those which it guarantees them... Men are destined
to live on the stage of the world. A public education
suits them: it early places before their eyes all the
scenes of life... The paternal home is better for the
education of women; they have less need to learn...
than accustom themselves to a calm and secluded
life.

Women have less need to learn...reading these patronising words
provoked Mary's fury. Snatching up her pen, she wrote to
refute their bigotry and sexual bias. 'I here throw down my
gauntlet...'

She argues that reason – the capability to think rationally
– is the prime essential for a woman. Only by means of
reason can she achieve independence, rather than remain the
casual pastime of men – a 'toy' or 'spaniel', as she puts it.
Or else become an 'object', a possession of her husband.
Women's perceived inferiority to men was false, based on
conditioning and culture. Women who develop the ability
to think clearly and to *reason* become independent individuals, equal in every way to men. They evolve into 'rational
creatures and free citizens'.

She proposed that children attend school at the age of
five, and their education remain free until nine. Classes should
be mixed-sex and courses the same for both. Girls and boys
should be brought up in a similar manner and governed by
identical standards. She called on men to consider her
proposals:

> I appeal to their understanding...I entreat them to
> assist to emancipate their companion, to make her a
> helpmeet for them! Would men but generously snap
> our chains, and be content with rational fellowship

instead of slavish obedience, they would find us more observant daughters, more affectionate sisters, more faithful wives, more reasonable mothers – in a word, better citizens.

Mary's proposals appear so rational and self-evident it is hard to comprehend how they inflamed such execration as they did. She was dubbed 'an impious Amazon of revolutionary France', and mocked as a 'hyena in petticoats'. She became a legend of impurity, a woman deserving no less than damnation.

She was born in London in 1759, the second child of an uneducated Irish mother, Elizabeth, whom she described later as 'vague and weak'. Her father Edward was a silk weaver, who inherited a substantial legacy from his own father, consisting of three blocks of flats near Spitalfields market. At the date Edward came into their possession these were rented out profitably to some thirty tenants. The bequest had been divided three ways; the property and income shared between the deceased's daughter (Mary's aunt), his son (her father Edward), and a grandson (her elder brother). But Edward had control of the boy's funds until he reached twenty-one. A responsibility he would abuse, misapplying the money to his own schemes.

Edward showed himself a drinker, unstable in his moods. Discontented with the humble trade of weaver, 'he had ideas above his station' – in the term of the day – and nurtured the concept of becoming a 'gentleman'. Borrowing against his share of the property he'd inherited, he rented a farm in Barking, a rural village near London. He had no training in land management, agriculture or business, and the farm failed. Restless and irresponsible by nature, he moved on, leasing another farm in the north of England. This was no more successful than the first and he relocated again (leaving unpaid debts) in a series of such moves, each far distant from the last so he could reinvent himself in respectability with no backstory.

In the course of these peregrinations he incontinently sired six children on his wretched wife. He proved an abusive husband, an increasingly impoverished and embittered drunkard with a chip on his shoulder and a violent temper. Mary's first biographer, William Godwin (whom she would marry when she was thirty-eight in the same year as she died) records:

> Mary would often throw herself between the despot and his victim, with the purpose to receive upon her own person the blows that might be directed against her mother. She has even laid whole nights upon the landing-place near their chamber-door, when, mistakenly, or with reason, she apprehended that her father might break out into paroxysms of violence.

Mary too was beaten, and more often than her siblings. She received no affection from either parent and was particularly susceptible to her father's cruelty. A craving for the love and approval he withheld would scar every future relationship with men she contracted.

It took several years for Edward Wollstonecraft to whittle away his fortune to the family's destitution. Despite his failures and their successive moves, Mary attended school in each resettlement. And somehow she prospered in her education. She had inexorable will, focus, courage and endurance – all nurtured by adversity. On return from class, she was allowed no time for prep but set to work in the house. Her additional reading – she was an avid reader – she pursued in bed by candlelight into the early hours of the morning.

The same relentless domestic regimen accompanied every new habitation. Her unhappiness was compounded by the responsibility she felt to protect her two younger sisters, who continued to burden and sponge off her for years. She gives an indication of life at home in a later letter to a friend, Jane Arden:

> It is almost needless to tell you that my father's violent temper and extravagant turn of mind, was the principal cause of my unhappiness and that of the rest of the family. The good folks of Beverley…were very ready to find out their Neighbours' faults, and to animadvert on them; many people did not scruple to prognosticate the ruin of the whole family, and the way he went on, justified them for so doing.

When Mary turned seventeen, she made an attempt to leave home on the suggestion of a job as 'companion' and carer to an older woman. The role was one of the few paid occupations open to her or to any other woman at the period. However, her mother's 'intreaties and tears' blackmailed her to turn down the offer and remain with the wretched family. Not for a further two years did she make her escape, becoming just such a companion to a Mrs Dawson, in the fashionable resort of Bath.

This prided itself as an elegant town where the best people came to 'take the waters' – which were held to be therapeutic – to maintain or restore their health. In season, the aristocracy and the new-rich aspirants to that class flocked to the town for the society it provided even more than for the waters, which they both drank and bathed in. For Mary, a country girl raised on a farm, the fine buildings and hyperactive social scene made for a bewildering experience.

Mrs Dawson, a demanding and difficult widow, had gone through a number of companions before Mary's appointment to the post. Her employer showed hard to please. She lived at the hub of the place, 'whether in or out of Season…the very magnet of Bath, and if there is any company or movement in the city, Milsom Street is the pulse of it.'

Mary, the future writer, was in an ideal vantage spot from which to spectate the fashionable show. She was allowed a presence at Mrs Dawson's frequent 'At Homes' and could listen in to the lively conversations – though not encouraged to contribute to them herself. She conceived a loathing for every aspect of the modish scene. Particularly for the chattering wives who made up at least half the company. She found them idle, frivolous, barely educated and contemptible in their dependency upon their rich husbands. These women did not even fulfil their function as mothers, but consigned their children to a nursemaid and servants to look after.

Mary detested the subservient nature of her job. To Jane Arden she wrote, 'I hinted to you in my last that I had not been very happy – indeed, I have been far otherwise. Pain and disappointment have constantly attended me since I left Beverley…'

Another letter to her sister Eliza flags the uneasy relationship she enjoyed with both siblings, as it does estrangement from her parents:

> I this morning received your letter…as I found by
> it you still remember me; but I must say, I should
> like to be remembered in a kinder manner. There is
> an air of irony through your whole epistle which

hurts me exceedingly... As to Everina's illness my Father only mentioned it in a careless manner and I did not imagine it had been so bad...

The happiness of my family is nearer my heart than you imagine – perhaps too near for my own health or peace. For my anxiety preys on me, and is of no use to you. You don't say a word of my mother. I take it for granted she is well – tho' of late she has not even desired to be remembered to me...

Mary remained in Bath working for Mrs Dawson for only two years, before being obliged to return home to help nurse her mother, who had fallen sick of 'a dropsy attended by many other disagreeable complaints'. On her death in 1782, Mary quit the parental home for the last time, going to live with her friend Fanny Blood and her parents in Walham Green on the outskirts of London.

The Bloods were even poorer than the Wollstonecrafts, but in Fanny she had someone with whom she could discuss her thoughts. The two conceived the notion of starting a school, which would also provide a living for Mary's sisters, who remained miserable under their father's rule.

Mary and Fanny had been doing needlework from sunup to sundown to survive. They were unable to work into the evening, as they could not afford the cost of oil for lamplight. They had no money at all, and funding for the school was provided by a loan from a Mrs Burgh, mother of two of its pupils. Opening the establishment first in Walham Green, they soon transferred it to a rented house in Newington, the district where Mrs Burgh lived herself. Eliza and Everina moved into the house, helping to manage the school though not teaching; this was done by both Mary and Fanny.

Mrs Burgh, a kindly and openhearted woman, was the

widow of an intellectual who had authored a bulky work, *Political Disquisitions*. Through her, Mary met a group of people whose minds and interests closely matched her own. Among them, Joseph Johnson, who would publish her first book. For the first time in her life she found herself in congenial company and engaged in a job worthy of her: teaching, which she enjoyed.

Then came a major setback. Fanny left the school, ran off to get married and move to Lisbon with her husband, who was in the wine trade. Mary felt desolated by what she saw as her best friend's defection from both responsibility and the possessive love she bore for her. When Fanny died in childbirth less than a year later, the loss crushed her. In a letter to Fanny's brother George, she wrote:

> I have lost all relish for life and my almost broken heart is only cheered by the prospect of death. I may be years a-dying tho', and so I ought to be patient.

Two weeks later she added:

> My spirits are fled and I am incapable of joy…we have so many tattling females – I have no creature to be unreserved to. Eliza and Everina are so different that I would as soon fly as open my heart to them… I am resigned to my fate, but 'tis that gloomy kind of resignation that is akin to despair. My heart – my affection cannot fix here and without someone to love this world is a desert to me…

Funded by another loan from Mrs Burgh, Mary had sailed for Lisbon on learning of Fanny's ill health, but reached the city only on the day after her death. On getting back to England six weeks later, she found the school in disarray. The mother of three boarders there had fallen out with Eliza and Everina – who had been teaching during Mary's absence – and removed the children without settling their fees. Other pupils had also been withdrawn, and rent was owing on the house. Mary was further troubled by her debts to Mrs Burgh, which she now could see no way of repaying. Fanny's brother George, who had taken a job in Ireland, suggested she come stay with him, but conscience made her turn down the offer:

> I am indeed very much distressed at present, and my future prospects are still more gloomy – yet nothing should induce me to fly from England. My creditors have a right to do what they please with me, should I not be able to satisfy their demands... I cannot even guess what the girls will do. My brother, I am sure, will not receive them, and they are not calculated to struggle with the world – Eliza, in particular, is very helpless. Their situation has made me very uneasy...

Moving back into the Blood family house in Walham Green, where she scraped a bare living from needlework, Mary wrote a short book, *Thoughts on the Education of Daughters*. Very different in content to other works on the subject – which concerned advice on manners and the social graces that would enable the young to land a husband – Mary's guide insists on the importance of the intellect. 'I wish them to be taught to *think*... Above all, teach them to combine their ideas. It is of more use than can be conceived.'

Mary's experience of teaching children was limited to the three years of the school's existence; the book derived from

private reading combined with her own radical ideas on the
subject – which were startlingly progressive for the period.
'Whenever a child asks a question, it should always have a
reasonable answer given to it.'

   She wrote well and she wrote fast; at the age of twenty-
seven she had found her métier. On finishing the work she
gave it to Joseph Johnson to read. He agreed at once to
publish it, paying ten guineas for the rights, a generous
advance for a writer's first work, which enabled her to
discharge most of her debts. However, it left her with no
cash remaining and, unwilling to impose further on the
Bloods, she took up the offer of a post as governess to the
children of Lord and Lady Kingsborough in Ireland. Her
salary was to be £40 a year; accommodation and meals
would cost her nothing. According to William Godwin, she
resolved to remain in the job only for a short time:

> Independence was the object after which she thirsted,
> and she was fixed to try whether it might not be
> found in literary occupation. She was desirous
> however first to accumulate a small sum of money,
> which should enable her to consider at leisure the
> different literary engagements that might offer...

A job with the Kingsboroughs would underwrite her future
career. Nevertheless, it meant a return to the same subservi-
ence she had known as a 'companion'. Mrs Burgh loaned her
cash to cover the journey to Ireland, and she arrived at the
splendid country house in its 1,300-acre estate 'with the same
kind of feeling as I should have if I was going to the Bastille'.

★   ★   ★

Viscount Kingsborough, a second son, had become rich not through inheritance but by marriage to an immensely wealthy heiress. Mary was, as ever, unlucky in her employer's character, finding her to be a bossy, overbearing woman with a vile temper, and an imperious snob. 'A clever woman...but not of the order of being that I could love... With his Lordship I have had little conversation.'

Their four children, three girls and a younger brother, struck her as 'unformed', wild and hostile, but within a few months they had come to love her – and she them. She taught them according to the principles outlined in her book. The effect upon them in result was satisfying, though every other aspect of her life dismayed her.

Lady Kingsborough was determinedly social; her 'At Homes' followed frequent. The house was filled with guests, children and dogs – upon which she lavished greater affection than on her offspring. Mary was obliged to attend the many parties, but found the company despicable.

> Confined to the society of a set of silly females, I have no social converse, and their boisterous spirits and unmeaning laughter exhausts me, not forgetting hourly domestic bickering. The topics of matrimony and dress take their turn... Lady K's passion for animals fills up the hours which are not spent in dressing... Life has lost its relish, all my faculties languish...

She mixed and talked with the guests at the many parties, though not on the same footing. William Godwin recalls

> the ludicrous distress of a woman of quality, whose name I have forgotten, that, in a large company, singled out Mary, and entered into a long conversation with

her. After the conversation was over, she enquired whom she had been talking with, and found, to her utter mortification and dismay, that it was Miss King's governess.

Yet, despite its humiliations, life at the Kingsboroughs provided opportunity. At night, with the children in bed, Mary had time to herself and, with it, lamplight. She used both well in writing another book, *Mary: a Fiction*. In a year she had completed the work, bar revision. At that time she was about to accompany the family and children on a European tour, which would offer an experience of travel in a wider world. But, at the last moment, Lady Kingsborough cancelled the trip.

Disappointed, Mary resigned her post. Packing her few clothes and fewer possessions into a suitcase along with the handwritten draft of her novel, she set off for London. There, she gave the manuscript to Joseph Johnson. On reading it he agreed to publish, going on to suggest she stay in his house by St Paul's Cathedral while establishing herself as a professional writer.

Writing and publishing in the late eighteenth century were no more reliable or profitable occupations than they are today, yet Johnson made a success in his trade. Now fifty, he had begun as a printer, then opened a bookshop in the City. As a publisher he earned sufficient to live in some comfort, and to entertain. He had a love for his work and an eye for talent. His interest in Mary was entirely benevolent, he believed in her talent and wanted her to succeed. She was more than fortunate to find him.

She stayed at Johnson's until he found her nearby lodgings

of her own. As a means of earning money, he suggested translation. Many books published in England at that time were by continental authors. Mary could speak French, though not well; so, alone in her room, she studied to perfect herself in the language with customary diligence. Her first commissions for translation came from Johnson, but she soon acquired others.

In 1788 her publisher started a magazine, the *Analytical Review*, which expressed the liberal thinking of his circle, and carried reviews of European books. Mary wrote these while working on her second title, for children, *Original Stories from Real Life*, illustrated by William Blake.

Blake engraved a number of Johnson's publications, and formed part of the circle meeting regularly at his house, where Mary first encountered him. She too was now a respected member of the group, which included the Swiss-born painter Henry Fuseli, who dined there frequently, dominating the table with his sparkling conversation and often cruel wit.

Fuseli, then about fifty, had recently married, and stood poised on the brink of fame as an artist. A worldly, well-travelled man with a quick mind but explosive temper, he enjoyed the reputation of a ladies' man, despite standing only five feet two inches tall.

As Godwin explains,

> Mary…had hitherto never been acquainted…with an eminent painter. The being thus introduced…was a high gratification to her… She visited him; her visits were returned. Notwithstanding the inequality of their years, Mary was not of a temper to live upon terms of so much intimacy with a man of merit and genius, without loving him… What she experienced in this respect, was no doubt heightened, by the state

of celibacy and restraint in which she had hitherto
lived... She conceived a personal and ardent affection
for him. Mr. Fuseli was a married man, and his wife
the acquaintance of Mary...

Mary's unwise passion effected a remarkable change in her appearance. Till now, she'd held contempt for fashion, devoting
no care to her looks. She wore thick worsted stockings, sturdy
shoes, and the same drab black dress and a beaver hat, with her
hair hanging lank about her shoulders. Now she smartened
up, remarkably.

The portrait of her by John Opie, where her auburn hair is
powdered in the style of the day, was painted around this time.
   Fuseli, who despite marriage continued to have sex with
other women, started a casual affair with Mary...only to

discover with dismay that she was a virgin and, further, that she had fallen deeply and possessively in love with him. Her first experience of sex unhinged her judgement. One day she called on Sonia Fuseli to propose that she should move into their marital home to live with them, as she could not exist 'without the satisfaction of seeing him and conversing with him daily'. Sonia, married to him less than a year, threw her out. Fuseli was livid afterwards, refusing to see her despite her entreaties. His biographer John Knowles – who describes Mary as 'plain' – says she complained that Fuseli neglected her and carried her letters unopened in his pocket for days. Desperately needy, to Fuseli she represented an importunate pest. It made for a disastrous pattern of relationship, which, despite her high intelligence, she was doomed to reprise.

Lightning struck, the revolution broke out in France. Talleyrand's constitution for the new republic so incensed Mary she broke free from depression to write her most famous book, *A Vindication of the Rights of Woman.*

The revolution triggered considerable alarm in the British government and the country's landed class. Among Johnson's circle it was reason for celebration. The infant Liberty had clawed her bloody passage into the world. Prudently, they did not broadcast their reaction but kept it to his dinner table, where exhilaration ruled – a mood Mary shared. 'The French revolution, while it gave a fundamental shock to the human intellect through every region of the globe, did not fail to produce a conspicuous effect in the progress of Mary's reflections. The prejudices of her early years suffered a vehement concussion. Her respect for establishments was undermined.'

Mary wrote in a state of hot indignation, finishing her

book in six weeks. Johnson published it in January 1792. Soon after, a translation came on sale in France, where it spoke to those literate, mostly upper-class women who had supported the revolution from the start. Mary's demands echoed resonant to them. In England, reception proved hostile. The book was condemned as a seditious rant, particularly by those who refused to read it. Its author was vilified, denounced as an 'unsexed' woman, a traitor to her gender; she suffered from the attacks upon her. Frustrated and tormented by her unsatisfactory relationship with Fuseli, she determined to cut herself free from him and turn her back on her detractors. She moved to live in Paris, where she was already famous and could count on good reception in the most tumultuous, exhilarating capital in Europe.

She lodged at 22 rue Meslée in the heart of the city, but when in February France declared war on England she transferred to Neuilly, a suburb where she felt more secure.

Nevertheless, she walked into town almost every day – on one occasion through a crowded square, whose cobbles were freshly splashed with blood from an execution. In contrast to the glee of the rest, she showed visible distress at the sight. Someone advised her to conceal her feelings for her own safety.

She wanted to report on what was happening in the city during that seminal period of reinvention. She had many invitations, indeed was a sought-after guest, a famous writer. Her book had caused a stir, and many wanted to meet her. To one who had smarted so often in the condescension paid to a governess, the attention she received must have been gratifying.

She met many new people. Among them, Captain Gilbert

Imlay, who had fought in the American War of Independence. He had largely invented his past but was now in the timber business, shipping wood forested in Scandinavia to France through the port of Le Havre. On first meeting him in April, she disliked him. By June she was sharing his apartment, and registered at the American Embassy as Mrs Imlay. By August she carried his child.

Aged about forty, he was handsome, dressed well, could converse with intelligence and wit; he was an accomplished liar. He had read a number of books and published two of his own, which failed to sell. He'd known a lot of women in his past, grew bored quickly, was moody, short-tempered and on occasion violent − exactly the sort of older man Mary had been conditioned since infancy to fall for.

In September, three months after they had rented a small Paris apartment together, Imlay announced that he must go to Le Havre on business. He stayed away for several months, while she wrote to him almost every day. 'I have not caught much rest since we parted. You have…twisted yourself more artfully round my heart than I supposed possible.' Three weeks later, 'though I cannot say I was sorry, childishly so, for your going, when I knew that you were to stay such a short time…I could not sleep.' And again, 'You tell me your exertions are necessary! I am weary of them!… There is nothing picturesque about your present pursuits…' And again, 'I can…find food for love in the same object much longer than you can…I think there is sometimes a shorter cut to yours…'

She continued to write though she knew her letters irritated him, she begged him to 'cherish me with that dignified tenderness which I have only found in you, and your own dear girl will try to keep under [control] a quickness of feeling that has sometimes given you pain.'

Six months pregnant, Mary went to join him in Le Havre, where their daughter Fanny was born in May. The following September, Imlay decided to expand his business and run it from London. Mary and the baby returned to Paris. By now the revolution had turned on its own leaders and segued into the Terror. No one felt safe. All lived in fear of the bangs on the door at 4a.m., of arbitrary arrest, prison, torture, worse. It was no place for an illegal alien. At Imlay's suggestion she moved to London, where she arrived to find he 'had already formed another connection...with a young actress'.

Mary was suicidal, but Imlay persuaded her he needed her. Not at his side, but he required someone reliable to go to Scandinavia as his agent to obtain new contracts. It was an obvious stratagem to get her out of the way yet, taking the baby and a maid, she went. And she showed diligence in the mission he set her. She visited Sweden, Norway, Denmark and Germany; in each she effected a meeting, negotiated and agreed the deal. She used the experience to put together an epistolary book on her travels. This does not contain her anguished, largely one-way correspondence with the father of her child – published only after her death as *Letters to Imlay* – which is all too revealing of the desperate insecurity that twinned her formidable intellect and capability.

She was away for three months, returning to London in September. Rather than welcome her and Fanny home, Imlay placed them in lodgings. From his cook she learned the true situation: he had set up his mistress in an apartment nearby. She called on the address, finding them together. Her control snapped and she assaulted the pair in an ugly scuffle that culminated in her storming out of the house distraught. She hurried to Battersea with the intention of drowning herself but, finding it too public, hired a boat and rowed to Putney. There, she ran to the deserted centre of the bridge and flung herself into the Thames.

Mary's unconscious body was recovered by a waterman, who brought it to shore where she was revived. Imlay sent a doctor, fixing for her and Fanny to stay in the care of friends, where he did not visit her. Providing no support, soon after he moved back to Paris with his mistress. Mary fell into despair but Joseph Johnson came to her rescue by providing editing work and commissions for the *Analytical Review*. She had moved into lodgings of her own with Fanny, now almost two. Her publishing advance for a new novel went to repay debts; she was short on money and lonesome. Many of her friends, while admiring her work, had come to find her intensity and dominance of every conversation exhausting. Looking for companionship, she renewed an acquaintance-ship with William Godwin whom she'd met years before at Johnson's house, when she initially disliked him, and he her.

Godwin was forty. Ordained to the Church in youth, he had renounced God to become a radical philosopher and writer; many labelled him an anarchist. He had written a book, *Enquiry Concerning Political Justice*, which narrowly escaped prosecution, though he achieved this by collaborating on Tom Paine's much more famous work, *Rights of Man* – burned by the public hangman. Godwin was courageous, but egotistical, humourless and something of a prig. He possessed a cold nature together with a hot temper. He and Mary were temperamentally unsuited, though intellectually had much in common. The two of them came, each in their fashion, to love one another. But they deliberately did not make the mistake of living together: '...we were both of us of the opinion that it was possible for two persons to be too uniformly in each other's society.'

The arrangement suited them. Mary worked in her own quarters through the day while the maid looked after Fanny. She saw her daughter at a set time, when they played or she talked and told stories to the little girl. Come evening, she changed and walked the short distance to Godwin's house to share supper with him. At table they talked – and Mary was unstoppable once she got going. They argued fiercely, though Godwin never turned abusive as had her previous lovers. In this last chapter of her life she found a man worthy of her, who cared for and loved her. Moreover, showed himself proud of her. Her raging insecurity, never fully assuaged, quieted to a sort of peace.

Mary enjoins women 'to calmly let passion subside into friendship', but clearly the couple stayed sexually active for she fell pregnant...and married him. In secret, for both publicly had denounced the institution as 'bondage'. Now they ate their words in privacy. The marriage persisted only for a tragically short time as she contracted blood poisoning while giving birth to a daughter – also named Mary. She died eleven days later on 10 September 1797, aged thirty-eight.

She had raised such odium in the course of her career that her writing did not remain in print. Godwin's biography only confirmed the prejudice its readers held against her. Ignored then forgotten, her legacy lay buried. Yet she had written a seminal work, arguably the most influential book in women's history. *A Vindication* represents the first declaration of female independence, based upon reason rather than emotion. Exposing the hypocrisy and double standards separating the sexes, it forms the manifesto for what, decades later, would name itself the Women's Movement. The book was not reprinted until the middle of the nineteenth century, when it inspired the suffragist Lucretia Mott, together with Elizabeth Cady Stanton (the supporter and ally of Victoria Woodhull) to organise the first Women's Rights Convention in 1848, which declared: 'We hold these truths to be self-evident, that all men and women are created equal.'

In the first chapter of *Vindication* Mary argues that natural rights are given by God; to deny them to half the population is a sin. Yet God's message reached women only through the mouths of men, who had adapted its text to their own agenda, and only a male could be ordained a Christian minister with authority to preach His word. Thus far in history, God himself remained exclusively men's prerogative...

4

HOLY-ROLLING IN
CARMEL LOVE NEST

Welcome to Ingersoll – dullest town in North America. Perhaps it is an excessive boast; there are thousands of towns and self-styled cities spread across the continent's rural hinterland that are just as dull – Ingersoll, Ontario is only one of them. It's the week before Christmas 1907 and Aimee, a moody red-haired teenager in a homespun dress reaching to her ankles, comes slouching down Main Street wearing farm boots. Nothing's happening as always, and sure she's bored. The town's so small she knows everyone in it, but this is seven in the evening and most folks are back home and already had supper.

The only people around are on their way to the Pentecostal meeting – as herself. Apart from Main Street the settlement contains a scatter of dirt roads, a church, general store, barber's shop and men-only saloons. A small town surrounded by farmland, the place offers no culture, no entertainment, only seasonal diversions, and a single newspaper for the region. The spectacular success of Pentecostalism at the start of the twentieth century can be largely attributed to the stupefying dullness of rural life in North America.

The ecstatic faith, which told of end times and miracles, swept up from the southern states to horrify and destabilise established churches in its path, wherein boredom ruled. The movement snatched quiet orderly converts from their flock to get them throwing trances, stomping and yelling *Hallelujah!* in the aisles.

In the drabness of domestic life, land labour, and tedium, Pentecostal meetings offered an electrifying emotional release. They rated good as a raree-show, delivering all the drama and craziness a farmer and his family could hope to experience in a lifetime of early nights. Better than a circus, for the audience participated in the performance. The show, which followed no set pattern, could be counted on to deliver wonders: healing, prophecy, speaking in tongues, catatonic trance, spontaneous mass dancing, occasionally a miracle.

As Aimee saunters down Main Street in bad temper toward the mission hall and her first Pentecostal meeting, people headed for the same destination grow more numerous. Others, including her parents who have driven into town in the pony cart, will be there already. Only their insistence has got her here tonight. Her father, a farmer, is a practising Methodist, her mother in the Salvation Army – and Aimee is a dutiful though simmering daughter. She's had it with religion. Since infancy she's listened to the tale of how God created the world in seven days, and Adam and Eve and the serpent and all that bilge…and wasn't sold. Soon after starting school, where she showed herself preternaturally bright, she read Charles Darwin's *On the Origin of Species* and learned the creation myth was a load of bunk. She's a sceptic, a smart-ass teenager who questions everything and is hard to handle. Not unruly but, so far as the very limited bounds of Ingersoll permit, rebellious. She smokes cigarettes and drinks Coca-Cola (which still contains cocaine and delivers an authentic buzz). She attends barn dances, flashes a shapely calf and gets off on the effect she has on older boys. She is exceptionally pretty with animated face, bee-stung lips and a mouth made for kissing. At school theatricals – limited to end of term and Christmas – she loves nothing more than to dress up in costume, invariably to play the lead. She can sing, dance, tell stories, crack jokes and make 'em laugh. She's a born performer, her ambition to be an actress.

Her parents stand waiting outside the mission and in they go together. The plank-walled hall is full, but neighbours shift to make space, and they pack in on one of the benches at the back. The mood rides high, expectant; people gossip together in anticipation. Tonight the meeting is to be led by an itinerant visiting minister, Robert Semple, who has a reputation for great works. That common thrill is not shared by Aimee, whose limbs droop in apathy as she slouches on the hard bench, languid, sulky and already bored to death.

Robert Semple, an Irish immigrant, had heard the call while working as a sales clerk at Marshall Field's department store in Chicago. Impulsively, he threw up his job and enrolled in a seminary run by Charles Parham, a founder of the Pentecostal Movement.

Parham, another ambitious club-foot cleric with a taste for authority, had quit the Methodist church to establish his own more rousing form of religion in a derelict neo-Gothic building known as Stone's Folly, in Topeka, Kansas. Although the place was in ruinous condition and by any standard uninhabitable, it functioned as a theological college where he taught some thirty student evangelists the charismatic practices just described.

Semple showed instinctive flair for the theatrics required to lead a revival meeting. He could project a charismatic presence, which he learned to harness and perfect from Parham, his drama coach. He possessed a good voice with nothing preachy about its soft Irish brogue. He had a gift for rousing his hearers to an ecstatic state and inciting them to 'demonstrate the spirit' and testify spontaneously, seemingly inspired by its power. After graduating from Stone's Folly, Parham despatched him to a mission in Toronto, where he gained a reputation as a thrilling and effective preacher.

When he came to speak at Ingersoll as a visiting minister shortly before this Christmas, he was in his mid-twenties. Tall, slim and handsome, with a lock of long dark hair falling across his noble brow, his face in photographs bears a striking resemblance to a thinner, finer and altogether more wholesome young Oscar Wilde.

The mission hall on Thames Street was packed full. Many there were already ardent converts, others drawn by curiosity and the promise of marvels. The meeting opened and passed to Semple, who started to speak... Aimee wrote afterwards, 'I had never heard such a sermon. Using his bible as a sword, he cleft the whole world in two... Why it just looked as though somebody had told him I was there, so vividly did he picture my own life. His words rained down upon me and every one of them hurt...I could not tell where I was hurt the most.'

And then Semple's face began to glow with light. His voice changed and he started to speak in another language. The words were unintelligible, 'but they seemed to pierce like an arrow through my heart'.

From the moment I heard that young man speak with tongues to this day I have never doubted for the shadow of a second that there was a God, and

that he had shown me my true condition as a poor,
lost, miserable, Hell-deserving sinner. My very soul
had been stripped before God – there was a God,
and I was not ready to meet him.

Aimee had fallen in love with God, and/or Robert Semple.

Aimee and Semple were married six months later at the
family farmhouse Kosy Kot (so named by her formidable
mother, Minnie). The service was conducted by Colonel
John D. Sharpe of the Salvation Army (in which Minnie
held the rank of sergeant-major). The bride wore a white
silk gown trimmed with lace. It was a sunny day and the
happy couple stood in the shade beneath the spreading
boughs of a cedar tree, surrounded by a crowd of fifty guests
togged up in their Sunday go-to-meeting best.

The newly-weds had no money. They rented rooms in
nearby Stratford, where Semple worked at a boiler factory
in a grimy job, then preached in mission halls at night. Aimee
attended every meeting, her fervour matching his own. God,
by means of Semple, had granted her a revelation as powerful
in effect as that experienced by the apostle Paul on the road
to Damascus. The couple's divinely appointed task was to
spread the Word, reveal signs and wonders, and gather converts
into the fold.

Eighteen months after the Semples' marriage, Charles Parham
– who remained Robert's mentor and spiritual director –
instructed him to go to China, to reinforce an emergent
mission in Hong Kong. It is not for a soldier of Christ to
query his orders. The Semple couple packed their few clothes

and sailed for Liverpool. Aimee, who was pregnant, passed most of the crossing in their cabin, seasick.

From Liverpool they took a train to London, where Parham had secured them an invitation to stay at the plush town house of a millionaire convert to the Pentecostal church, Cecil Polhill. They were met at King's Cross station by a car and chauffeur, and conveyed to his residence, where their host welcomed them warmly into his well-staffed household. For five days, until their ship sailed for the Far East, the pair enjoyed a belated honeymoon in a luxury neither had encountered before, but which Aimee found she rather enjoyed.

Polhill, an older single man of bewildering sophistication, showed himself attentive to Aimee, rather disturbingly so. He made it clear he considered her physically attractive, but also spiritually gifted. His wealth had already enabled him to promote and stage galas exhibiting speaking in tongues and healing, along with other demonstrations of the faith. One such was already set up in the Albert Hall, coinciding with the last day of the Semples' stay. He asked Aimee to stand in as one of the speakers to 'deliver the message' to its audience.

Polhill sprang the suggestion on her only on the morning of the event. Her husband had already gone out to receive a briefing on China at a mission in east London. She had only that afternoon to prepare but, before her conversion and marriage to Semple, she had set her heart on becoming an actress. As she saw it, the role proposed to her represented a casting offer from God.

By 4p.m. that day, when she and Polhill were driven to the Albert Hall, Semple still had not got back. Two hours later Aimee, who had no idea of the scale of the event, found herself on stage confronting an enormous hall rising tier upon tier toward its domed roof, and an audience of some 7,000 people.

The Royal Albert Hall.

If she had made notes, their headings were forgotten in the shock of facing that sea of faces before her. Her part-prepared text left her mind. She began to speak spontaneously. It was not in a foreign language, but her and her hearers' own tongue: articulate English with an American accent, delivered by a speaking voice that reached every section of the hall.

Spontaneous utterance is not a recent phenomenon. It

has biblical precedent. Acts II describes how, on the day of Pentecost following Christ's death, he appeared to the eleven apostles gathered in an upper room in Jerusalem, which then was filled with a 'rushing mighty wind'. They were all 'filled with the Holy Ghost and began to speak as the Spirit gave them utterance'. The *authority* for an individual to do so is provided by St Paul: 'Now there are diversities of gifts, but the same Spirit...to one may be given the word of wisdom, to another knowledge ... healing ... miracles ... prophecy... divers kinds of tongues... But all these worketh the same Spirit, dividing to every person severally as He will.'

Aimee's speech excited enthusiastic *Hallelujahs!* and applause. She showed herself to be an exhilarating preacher, gifted with presence and charisma. Whether her performance came from above or resulted from quick-witted improvisation and ability to command the stage, it was a triumph.

Fortunately, Robert Semple had reached the Albert Hall in time to witness her success. It was the first and last time he would ever listen to his wife speak in public – which that night she discovered to be her vocation.

In her memoir, *In the Service of the King*, Aimee described her marriage to Semple as 'Joy. Blissful happiness. Wonderful, sustaining love.' Even with her recently found faith, these were not enough to sustain her in Hong Kong. At the Pentecostal mission they joined a task force consisting of two male missionaries and a woman, Phoebe Holmes, recently arrived from Chicago. Phoebe and the Semples shared the rental of a cheap flat next door to a Hindu temple in a street leading to a cemetery.

The location did not provide tranquillity or peace of mind.

From the temple came a continuous din of chanting and drums. In the crowded street the air was foul, thick with a miasma of cooking smells, charcoal fumes and the reek of excrement. Their flat had no proper bathroom, no WC but a latrine in the yard, no air conditioning or refrigeration. Its primitive kitchen was infested by flies, every sort of crawling insect and the occasional snake.

Aimee was nineteen and seven months pregnant. The heat was overwhelming. Semple was out all day protected by a cork sun helmet and green-lined parasol, preaching to unresponsive natives with the aid of an interpreter. Phoebe Holmes was working at the mission. Aimee had no one to talk to, and only a few basic phrases in Chinese. Ingersoll, where she'd spent her entire life before marriage, did not offer much but it did provide human company and a breeze fresh from the prairie. In Hong Kong the contrast to home could not have been more extreme. As she wrote in the story of her life, 'Certainly the powers of hell seemed to hover over that heathen land whose flaming sky burned like the lid of a burnished copper cauldron.'

In her later career as charismatic preacher, Aimee's power lay in her ability to excite a crowd to a high state of emotion, when her hearers lost their identity in mass reaction. She could evoke hysteria in others, for it derived from her own. One morning, alone in the house as usual, she caught the most delicious smell of cooking. Going to the window, she looked for its source. In the courtyard of the Hindu temple a body was burning on a fire of blazing charcoal doused with kerosene. Instantly the scene called up her primal religious image: the flames of hell awaiting her, a sinner. And then, while she watched paralysed by horror, the legs of the burning figure jerked and he sat up, apparently still alive.

Aimee's control snapped. She started to shake. Semple on

his return found her in convulsions. 'Don't touch me,' she hissed at him. 'Don't touch me or I'll scream.'

He tried to calm her, explaining that the burning figure was already dead, that heat causes the sinews to contract in spasm. He moved to soothe her, but

> His sympathetic caress touched the match to the pent-up powder keg of my emotions, and immediately I was in the grasp of violent hysterics. It seemed as I listened to the high-pitched wails and wild laughter that come from my heart that the screams came from another person entirely.

Aimee was falling apart and headed for a nervous breakdown. One of her daily tasks lay in shopping for food in the local market, where the jostle of the raucous crowd, the smell and continuous body contact provided an assault upon the senses. She chose fruit and vegetables for the home while an interpreter bargained for the produce, which grew in fields fertilised by human excrement. But hygiene, along with mental illness, was poorly understood at that time. She washed and boiled everything, but that was not enough. Soon, all three occupants of the flat fell sick and developed dysentery. Then both Aimee and Semple came down with malaria. A doctor was called out and ordered them to hospital. The patients were laid in hammocks slung on poles, then carried up the steep streets by coolies through the colonial area and further up the mountain to Matilda Hospital and separated in different isolation wards. On their second wedding anniversary they were allowed only to exchange written notes. Semple's fever did not abate, and five days later he died. Aimee had $60 in the world; the sum proved enough to pay for his coffin and burial costs in the Happy Valley cemetery. She remained in hospital, too ill to attend the ceremony.

On 17 September, exactly one month after her husband's death, she gave birth to a 4½-pound daughter, Roberta. Passage money was sent by Aimee's mother, Minnie, in two instalments and, six weeks later, she and the baby sailed for San Francisco aboard the *Empress of China*. 'It seemed to me…my heart was left in China with Robert and that my arms would be empty forever. But I looked down… my arms were not empty. Hugging Roberta close, I sprinkled her dear face with hungry kisses; how precious she was.'

Aimee fell into deep depression, bereft by Semple's death. Although she later would have husbands and lovers, never again would she feel so whole and complete as she'd been with him. Now the future stretched unknown and she was without resources. Despite her grief, were she single and without responsibilities, her fundamental *joie de vivre* and positivity might have come to save her. *But with a six-week-old infant…?*

She inhabited an anxious desolate state but one Sunday roused herself to entertain her fellow passengers by playing the piano and singing hymns. She did so only at the urging of the purser, who knew her story, but once on stage her zest for performance kicked in. She found her voice and sang with emotion that reached into her hearers' hearts. From then on, for the rest of the voyage, she and Roberta were the darlings of the ship. Everyone befriended her, brought her treats, toys and clothes for the baby.

★   ★   ★

When the *Empress* docked in San Francisco, the Purser handed her an envelope of money, a collection taken on board. It contained $67, sufficient to pay her rail fare across the country to New York, where Minnie now served as an officer at the Salvation Army headquarters in the city. Moving into her mother's small apartment with the baby, Aimee was issued with a uniform and put to work serving food at a midtown rescue mission for the homeless. This was well before any benefit for the unfortunate in the US and the customers included many starving.

On Sundays, she and Minnie attended service at the army barracks. The rest of her days she cooked, washed diapers, and looked after Roberta. She remained ardent in her faith, but yearned for some more significant role in life than mother and waitress. 'It seemed an impossible situation; so disheartening; such devastating loneliness. Possibly, had my heart been happy, I could have surmounted my difficulties. But...everywhere, the world was one big ache for Robert... Loneliness. Oh, the poignant, terrifying grip of it; and Roberta's dire need for a home and better care that I could give her without one...'

It was at this time that I married again... That is all she says of the event in her autobiography, going on to add: 'I took up my household duties with the understanding that I should go back to the Lord's work if ever the call came.' She doesn't even give her husband a name.

He was Harold McPherson, cashier in a fashionable restaurant, on the make and ambitious to improve his status. Very soon Aimee was again pregnant. She gave birth to a son, Rolph. For the next two years she did duty as a wife and mother. She'd married out of desperation and loneliness; following Rolph's birth she sank into an enduring depression, trapped without money in a domesticity she abhorred. She could not settle, could not rest. Housework bored her, baby care and routine lay at odds with her nature. She felt a compelling urge to *do* something and kept hearing the voice of God telling her, 'Go preach.'

> Then came sickness. Inside of one year I underwent two serious operations [hysterectomy and appendectomy]. It seemed there was not a sound part left in my body. For a year I grew weaker and weaker. At times it seemed I would lose my reason. The hand of God was heavy upon me, and His voice rang continually in my ears, 'Now go and preach the Word'... At last, when taken off the operating table more dead than alive, I answered the call and said 'Yes Lord, I'll go'. From that moment I began to improve...

Soon after leaving hospital, one evening while McPherson was at work, she packed a suitcase, called a taxi and quit home, taking her two infants to return to her parents' farm at Ingersoll. From there she cabled her husband: *I have tried to walk your way and have failed. Won't you come now and walk my way?* He replied with a letter demanding she return at once to 'Wash the dishes, take care of the house and act like other women.'

Aimee experienced a wave of relief and lightness of spirit after walking out on him. She missed nothing from her marriage, nor did she ask for child support. Then and for the rest of her career, she stayed confident that God would provide whatever necessary. She was in that respect entirely carefree and reckless of the future.

She accompanied her mother Minnie to a tented revivalist jamboree in Kitchener, Ontario, where 'the old-time power rested on me... Before I knew it I was on my back in the straw, under the power.' With Minnie's encouragement she spoke next day – and the day after to double the crowd. She proved a natural at the game.

She was invited to preach at Mount Forest, a small farming town. The mission hall was tiny and attended by only a handful on the first evening, as it was the following night. 'Where are the rest of the congregation?' she asked.

She learned this *was* the congregation. She enquired how long the mission had been in operation and was informed for more than one year. Promptly, she picked up a chair, announcing she was off to raise a crowd. Her hostess declined to accompany her, so she set off into town alone, carrying the chair. In Main Street she set it down outside the Town Hall and climbed onto it, as upon a rostrum.

'When in doubt, pray, was my first thought.' Lifting her face to heaven, she raised her arms, closed her eyes and began to pray in silence. She continued, and the sound of passing feet altered in pace or ceased as pedestrians paused to stare. She sensed a gathering crowd and heard its voices speculating on the sight of this rapt figure with arms lifted to the sky. She kept still, eyes closed, kept praying. The crowd grew, the buzz of curiosity rose. At last someone poked her with a finger. She opened her eyes to see she was surrounded by some fifty people.

Jumping down from the chair, she picked it up and shouted, 'Quick! Come with me!' Pushing her way through the crowd, she set off at a run down the street, carrying the chair. Led by the kids, the throng chased her. They followed her through the open door into the mission hall. 'Shut the door,' she ordered the usher. 'Don't let anyone out till I'm through.'

She said 'From that day on I've always preached to crowds.'

In 1915 Aimee bought a car, a 1912 Packard convertible that could carry eight passengers (three of them uncomfortably on dickie seats) plus the driver. Along one side was lettered WHERE WILL YOU SPEND ETERNITY? Along the other JESUS IS COMING SOON – GET READY. It was known as the Gospel Car.

She found a second-hand tent 30 by 60 feet in size, but in poor condition. With help from her mission group it was patched up then bagged. Loading its bundles into the Packard together with her children, Roberta (five) and Rolph (two), she took off into middle America to preach the Word.

She went where the spirit moved her, parking in the main street of towns she passed through. Standing on the back seat of the car, she preached through a megaphone. She stopped for two or three days in towns where she knew there were several churches or a small mission at which she could find volunteers to help erect the tent and provide support. On occasion she encountered reluctance, their ministers could display envy, rivalry, even hostility.

'A woman preacher was a novelty,' she said. 'At the time women were well in the background. Orthodox ministers… disapproved of a woman minister. Especially this was true when my meetings departed from the funereal, sepulchral ritual of appointed Sundays.'

Depart they did, but her audiences loved them. She delivered first-class entertainment that literally took people out of themselves. They provided welcome emotional relief from the placid tedium forming the default setting of small-town America.

The cost of the Packard had come from collections, and collections funded her travels, but it was a hand-to-mouth existence. She never took enough to cover more than a couple of days ahead. Yet her mission touched a nerve in her audiences. They gave not just cash but blankets, clothes for the children, a roast turkey, a ham, a can of gasoline. Aimee was a pioneer – a national brand Americans respond to – but also a resexed version of the medieval travelling friar, here with wheels. Once they heard her speak, no one could doubt the sincerity of her calling.

For three years Aimee criss-crossed the US in a succession of lengthy tours with herself at the wheel. Between these, she returned to Ingersoll to print new pamphlets for distribution, have the car overhauled, the tent repaired or replaced – then load up with supplies, promotional material, spare cans of gas, and resume the trail. On some tours her children accompanied her, during others they remained on the farm. When with their grandparents at Ingersoll, they attended school. With Aimee on the road they enjoyed the gypsy life as a thrilling vacation. They loved their mother and never doubted their security. As grown-ups, both Roberta and Rolph recalled the period as a wonderful adventure. It is worth noting that, despite their erratic education, both prospered happily as adults.

News of the healings at Aimee's meetings spread. Her arrival in any town guaranteed a crowd. This included people on crutches or in wheelchairs, bolder members of local churches, curiosity seekers and a rabble of kids, hecklers, drunks, nutters and pickpockets. Over the smaller meetings she could keep a degree of control, with a crowd above a thousand the meeting developed its own dynamic, resulting in chaos. Time and again she notes, 'The Spirit took control in such a way that preaching was impossible.'

On one occasion she was arrested for causing a riot. A couple of hours later she appeared in court before the magistrate, together with local mission supporter Sister Sharpe, to provide cause for disturbing the peace by 'praising Jesus in a loud voice'.

'Oh what glory filled my soul when I took that paper from the police constable for the sake of Jesus. The Lord was good to me; I danced around the constable in the Spirit.' This caused Sister Sharpe to join her and dance around the bewildered constable as well. The two left court free of charges and equipped with a licence to preach in public. Sister Sharpe wrote later, 'I hitherto had possessed a man-fearing spirit, but I praise the Lord for sending Sister McPherson into my life… she taught me how to praise the Lord and get out of bondage to Man.'

Not all saw Aimee as a preacher and healer with a direct line to God. A number of WASP citizens of the eastern seaboard (mostly male) considered her a dangerous woman. Many ministers of the Protestant church viewed her as Satan in a plain white dress, devilishly gifted with a most beguiling tongue. The dean of the Denver Bible Institute said, 'I am compelled to give it as my calm, unbiased judgement that… there has not been a more dangerous religious teacher in the United States for the last 200 years.' His opinion: that her words 'must come from the Devil'.

Aimee's tented Pentecostal rallies now drew several thousand people, two-thirds of them women. She could reliably work them into a shared frenzy marked by histrionic displays of irrational behaviour. Her critics accused Aimee of hypnotism. A mob is not moved by reason, only by emotion. Which, in the case of these rallies, they came pre-prepared for, because they knew the preacher could deliver. It could be said they craved the release of letting go. But how was that effect achieved?

The historian Matthew Sutton compares Aimee's technique to the methods laid down by the legendary advertising guru Bruce Barton in 1925: 'start with an attention-grabbing opening, or a joke. Get the reader [listener or viewer] on your side. Be sincere. Use plain language. Provide a clear, simple message. Use repetition, repetition, repetition.' These basic rules have underpinned every successful ad campaign since. But in Aimee's case — and notable others — the formula does not fully explain the ecstatic mass response and take-up on the offer.

The orator/dictator/prophet requires a further gift which, though tangible, cannot be defined in words. It can only be *felt*, because you are there. It is personality at max wattage, the blaze of tangible charisma. Historically, possessors of this gift include Martin Luther King and Billy Graham, but also a stable of notorious dictators familiar to all. Instructions on how to utilise and employ it were first set out by Adolf Hitler in *Mein Kampf*, the basic guide to group-mind control and political advertising to this day, whose evidential truths were last proven by President Trump in 2016.

There was another strand to Aimee's mesmerising allure. In the summer of 1918 she did a tour of Florida, Miami and

Key West, where her mixed black and white congregations briefly integrated for the duration of the services. These included music (piano, guitar and drums) which got the crowd dancing in the spirit to ragtime.

Her next performance was at a mass rally in Philadelphia, numbering several thousand. An enormous marquee had been put up, supported by field kitchens, canteens and dormitory tents. City water had been piped in to the giant site. It was billed as a nationwide event; families had driven from all over to attend, bringing provisions for several days. The first of these had gone badly, for the rally was disrupted by a gang of local Catholic youths with whistles, who jeered, catcalled, drowned out the speakers and jostled the audience.

Day two, when Aimee was due to speak, soon developed into a similar climate of intimidation and hostility. To calm the scene, the preacher called for prayer. The crowd dutifully sank to its knees on the grass, but the hoods strutted among them, mocking and abusing the postulants in an attempt to provoke a reaction. The mood was tense, and a brawl about to erupt, when...

> Aimee had moved to a space at the far end of the rostrum. Damp with sweat, her white dress clung to her. Her wide eyes, flashing, sought out the centre of concentric spheres. Raising one arm high, she touched the axis of the innermost sphere, lowered her eyelids, and spun gracefully beneath the pointing hand. All eyes immediately fixed on her. With both hands above her head, palms facing the crowd...her body began rhythmically to sway...shoulders counter to hips. Somewhere there was music, a slow pronounced drumming...Aimee danced, her eyes half-closed.

She danced for a long time until the beat she was hearing became audible to the several thousand people under the tent. They fell into a physical rhythm, snapping their fingers, swaying from side to side. Without missing a beat Aimee moved to the piano. With both hands she came down hard on a dissonant chord. It was sure and defiant. She hit another chord, and another, maintaining the beat, nodding in syncopation to the rhythm... E-flat blues progression and diminished chords, brought from the Deep South. The hoodlums meanwhile had gone beyond hostility to fascination...caught up in the music, they started to move and clap on the down-beat. She began to sing an improvised song in perfect rhythm... Now she had them in the palm of her hand...

The drama is described by a witness cited by Daniel Mark Epstein in his study *Sister Aimee*, but many reporters covering her meetings remarked on her body, abundant auburn tresses and huge doe-eyes expressive of a melting softness. All made a point of her sex appeal.

'Miraculous' healings formed the most controversial aspect to Aimee's meetings. Crucially, these did not take place until near the end of her performance when the audience was most emotionally receptive. The *Mercury Herald* reports on a revivalist rally at San Jose where the 'front row beside the altar resembles a great convalescing ward. In wheelchairs, on stretchers and crutches, others hobbling and almost unable to walk, they rise to their feet at every prayer.'

Louise Weick of the *San Francisco Chronicle* covered the

same meeting, which she compares to a country fair. A sceptic by nature and profession, she watched as hundreds were carried, wheeled, or limped their way to Aimee at the altar.

> What followed…will probably sound like the veriest hocus–pocus to many. But nevertheless it did happen. It happened not in the misty, nebulous long ago, to white-robed men and women we cannot quite visualise as ever having had reality, but to children and men and women who had street addresses and telephone numbers, who came in automobiles and not on camel-back, as it was said they did long ago. The blind saw again; the deaf heard. Cripples left their crutches and hung them on the rafter.

These widely reported 'miracles' irritated the Protestant establishment to exasperation. There had been a time and place for miracles, but that barbaric nonsense did *not* convey the image the modern Church wished to project to post-Great War America.

One year after the San Jose rally, Pastor Towner of the First Baptist Church conducted a survey of 2,500 individuals who had attended in the hope of being healed. Six percent confirmed that they had been instantly cured; eighty-five percent said they had experienced a marked improvement in their condition and continued to grow better; less than one percent that they'd benefited neither physically, emotionally, nor spiritually. Not surprisingly, Aimee's reported success rate piqued medical curiosity. The American Medical Association investigated a wide sample of those cured. Though its report does not ascribe percentages, its findings appear to endorse Towner's. For some the cure had not lasted, but the majority reported an immediate significant change, and that they continued to grow better. The AMA report, published in 1921, concluded that Aimee's healing was 'genuine, beneficial and wonderful'.

Toward the end of Aimee's prolonged odyssey through the US, her husband Harold McPherson filed for divorce. Citing desertion, he claimed that, prior to abandoning him, she had treated him with extreme cruelty, had frequently beaten him up and that she and Minnie had each on separate occasions vowed to kill him.

Throughout the last year, Minnie had accompanied her daughter in the Gospel Car. She had taken over her management, a very necessary role for her meetings now attracted 15,000 to 20,000 people and required venues that had to be booked well ahead and promoted fully. Minnie was more than capable in this work; long service as a sergeant-major for the Salvation Army had taught her how to boss people around very effectively.

At the end of that year on the road they fetched up in Los Angeles, where Aimee decided to build a permanent home for them and her two children. The plot was donated by its owner, and money for construction subscribed piecemeal by her congregation. One of its members pledged the cost of the kitchen, another the living room. A plasterer, a carpenter, a roofer offered their services for free.

Next, Aimee determined to build her own mega church in LA. She bought a tract of land by Echo Park and raised $5,000 to begin work. The money was sunk into constructing a huge hole for the foundations. The contractors took on the project on her blithe assurance that God would provide further funds as required. Which indeed He or her congregations did, as costs mounted over four years to a quarter million dollars. The building grew into a vast structure capped by an immense dome 125 feet high, coated with powdered abalone shells that glistened, scintillating in the sunlight. The auditorium beneath was painted sky blue with fleecy clouds. It held 5,300 people. Angelus Temple was dedicated on 1 January 1923 and soon filled three times a day, seven days a week.

Aimee's spiritual abode lay fixed in the 'city which is above', but in settling in Los Angeles at the start of the 1920s she sure came into her worldly home. No place was more fitting and the timing of her move faultlessly opportune.

Only sixty years earlier LA had been an accumulation of adobe buildings on dirt streets surrounded by orange groves, vineyards, farms and lumber mills run by Yankee immigrants, many thrown up here in the wake of the gold rush. Its lawless manners characteristic of what a local doctor described as a 'cow town where gambling, drinking and whoring are the only occupations'.

Then, at the start to the twentieth century the recently invented movie business located here, swiftly to develop into the fifth largest industry in the US. At the same time the Chamber of Commerce set out to rebrand the rudimentary city to attract both retirees and entrepreneurs. Incessant boosting hyped the concept nationwide: this was the ultimate destination to thrive and prosper – or die in the sunshine. By the time Aimee moved here, the population had grown to 650,000 and was swelling as fast as her congregation.

Meanwhile, something unprecedented had happened in America – nothing less than the dawn of the modern world. This was the start to the era and ethos we inhabit today. It was mechanisation and the production line that made it possible, technology that powered what followed. Clothes, goods, appliances, *things* became cheap and available to all. Products and services of unimaginable luxury transformed into affordable must-haves. In 1913 the Ford factory had taken fourteen hours to assemble a car; by 1925 it was turning one out every ten seconds. In 1910 an auto cost $950, in 1925 $290.

The Great War in Europe involving two million US servicemen was over. America wanted no more to do with pesky foreigners and their problems. God's own country rejoiced in isolationism. A warm tide of prosperity swelled across the land, carrying many with it to southern California where the Sears Roebuck catalogue gained a place in the home beside the Bible. The Twenties were an affluent untroubled decade where little existed to distract Americans from the swell of modernity as it engulfed them in affluence.

In 1923 wireless and commercial radio signalled the appearance of mass media, followed by the gramophone with its silver soundhead undulating across a thick wax record. Dozens of new tabloid newspapers catered to a whole new readership. Hearst's and Scripps Howard agencies controlled syndication to 230 daily papers with a combined circulation of thirteen million readers. A rush of novelty swept away the torpor of the everyday, replacing it with a torrent of images and information: best-sellers, record charts, competitions and prizes. By mid-decade one in three owned a radio and three out of four went to the movies at least once a week.

This was the golden age of American advertising. Ad revenues went from $682 million in 1914 to $3 billion in 1929. The recent invention of plate glass created a new activity: window-shopping. The instalment plan encouraged people to buy on credit with money they were sure of tomorrow. As Woolcott Gibbs put it in the *New Yorker*, launched that same decade, 'Advertising was the new giant loudspeaker of

American free enterprise, the full-throated blaring horn telling millions what to eat, what to drink, what to wear.'

'America told the world what was fashionable and what was fun', says Scott Fitzgerald. 'The country was going on the greatest, gaudiest spending spree in history...the whole golden boom was in the air.'

Anyone could become an American by choice. He could not only make a life, he could make himself over, and California was the place to be reborn. New buildings of glass and steel went up to transform the skyscape, but what defined the rebranded Los Angeles was the automobile. Motor cars united a sprawl of expanding suburbs around no distinct centre to create *the* prototypal city – which was not habitable without a car. Limos, roadsters, touring cars, sedans formed a kaleidoscope of colour, chrome, plate glass, hoardings, electric signs, sunshine and clear blue air scented by the whiff of gasoline that was LA.

The mood went upbeat to the sound of ragtime. Store windows sold clothes and new devices, but also lifestyles. Girls in light dresses and young men in straw hats crowded the drugstores' soda fountains. Movies, mags and tabloids provided models for a new personal identity. Men sported wristwatches and fountain pens, both sexes flashed cigarette cases and lighters. Everyone smoked.

Media images showed a new way of being a woman. She had her hair bobbed, then shingled in 1924 (effected at home by combing it with tongs heated on a spirit flame). She wore her eyebrows plucked to a line and Cupid's-bow pouted lips. Skirts grew shorter year on year. Young women declared themselves a different race, quite unlike their parents. Hedonistic and reckless, these so-called 'flappers' thumbed their noses at propriety. A flapper claimed the right to wise-crack with a man with her foot on the same brass rail, to drink, smoke, say 'Fuck' and quit pretending her desires, appetites and satisfactions differed in any way from his own. The Dutch cap had come available in the last year of the war; it was reported in 1925 that one out of three unmarried women carried one in her handbag.

Flapper fashion in Twenties America.

'I was never exactly a flapper,' Aimee told a journalist, who noted that she looked 'wistful' while recalling her own brief bad-girl adolescence, mild as it had been with the strictly limited opportunities her hometown had offered.

In her signature outfit of flat shoes, white dress and blue military cape – the look of a frontline nurse adopted by all the women at the Temple – she preached against the flapper and her wanton ways. She preached against drink, cigarettes, gambling, dancing in couples and Sunday entertainment, but she never spoke of hell. The message she retailed was joyful: the freedom, grace and wholeness possessing the individual who embraces Christ.

Hollywood was inventing the future just down the road, and she co-opted all its tricks to get her text across. Her illustrated sermons involved music, sets and costumed cast. The scene for one was a boxing ring with seconds, umpire and clanging bell to call the rounds. In shorts, ankle boots and six-ounce gloves, she sparred with Kid Satan to a final knockout. A summons for speeding – she was always speeding – prompted her to dress up as a cop and roar up the ramp onto stage on a motorbike with howling siren, skid to a halt and signal STOP…to the worldly life of sin.

Aimee staged elaborate operas at the Temple, some with a cast of hundreds. Construction crews and scene painters built the sets, and film technicians lit these sacred dramas. Her audiences were almost entirely low-class, but included school-girl Marilyn Monroe, Des Moines broadcaster Ronald Reagan and tyro politician Richard Nixon, who was baptised a Christian at the Temple. Also Charlie Chaplin, who later told her, 'Half your success is due to your magnetic appeal, half due to the props and lights... Like it or not, you are an actress.'

She'd already launched a magazine, the *Bridal Call*, which along with its religious content carried articles on women's suffrage and equal opportunity. Its editions and phonograph records of her sermons were distributed to Pentecostal communities around the world. She had an acute instinct for her times and instantly spotted the potential in commercial radio; the medium could have been designed for her. She knew nothing about the business – and still less did Minnie – but she did her research. She was looking not for an employee but a partner, someone who shared her vision.

Kenneth Ormiston did not, in that he was not religious. In other respects he was well qualified for the role. In his early thirties, he worked as director and news editor of KHJ, the radio station owned by the *Los Angeles Times*. His job paid well, but the station was subject to the paper's editorial and financial control; he had little autonomy. The opportunity to open an independent channel with a celebrity – an established brand – was irresistible. She had a listener base already; the scheme looked a sure-fire thing.

Aimee would not have poached Ormiston from the *Los Angeles Times* unless she'd sensed a kindred spirit. He shared her belief in the new medium and its vast unrealised power. She wanted not to dabble in the business but to start big, and ample funds lay in the Temple treasury to do so. They worked well together, they sparked each other off, jointly engaged in entirely new territory. There were no precedents, no rules to guide, no frontiers to restrict them. They were mutually absorbed in what they were doing, and to be absorbed is to be happy. For a man and woman to share such exhilaration inevitably creates a bond…

Station KFSG came on air in February 1924. Its state-of-the-art premises had been constructed within the Temple and equipped with services more usual for a movie studio. In addition to the technical staff, it employed an experienced publicity director and used a dozen freelance press agents. The new station transmitted from twin 250-foot towers flanking the Temple's shimmering dome, and its range covered California, Hawaii, the western states and Canada.

The Temple's media centre stayed open all hours, serving fresh coffee and bagels. West Coast editors loved Aimee, the

East's less, but she provided a dependable source of copy
with her series of new enterprises. One was the newly built
four-storey Life Bible College, where young women were
coached in how to dramatise and sell the Word. Another,
her refuge for homeless young women fled to LA to hide
their shame of pregnancy, many of whom she took in to
share her own and children's home at a high cost to personal
privacy.

Aimee had a demanding public life. Her energy was
boundless but the schedule exhausting. Officers of the Temple
noticed her loss of weight and short attention span. They
suggested delicately that she had earned a vacation. Rather
to their surprise, she accepted with alacrity. On
12 January 1926, she and Roberta set off on a three-month
holiday. They visited Paris, the Riviera, the Holy Land, Venice,
Rome, and on the way home London, where the *Literary
Observer* noted her slimmer modish figure and lustrous
chestnut hair arranged in a 'coiffure that might have been
done in Bond Street, pale yellow silk jumper, black silk gown,
short skirt, and flesh-coloured silk stockings'. Also her
perfume, Quelque Fleurs, by Houbigant of Paris, a chic and
costly fragrance of the day.

During Aimee's vacation, Minnie received a visit from Ruth,
Kenneth Ormiston's wife. Her husband had stopped working
for KFSG several months earlier and she had reported him
missing to the police ten days after Aimee's departure on
vacation. Suspecting him to be with her in Europe, Ruth
informed Minnie she intended to sue for divorce, naming
Aimee as co-respondent. Discussion between the two women
was unsatisfactory, resulting in a second meeting where

certain financial arrangements were agreed, for Ruth dropped
the threat of a messy divorce and soon after emigrated to
Australia to live with her parents.

On Aimee's and Roberta's return to Los Angeles, she was
greeted at the railroad station by the mayor, members of the
Chamber of Commerce and an ecstatic crowd of 1,200
devotees. Temple novices in regulation white showered her
with rose petals as a brass band blared her welcome. Media
flagged her 'the One Who Paved Women's Way into the
Pulpit'. The mass of fans escorted her in an impromptu
parade across town to Angelus Temple. Her considerable
luggage and numerous suitcases followed, receiving the odd
comment but explained as props and wardrobe for her illustrated sermons.

Aimee relapsed into the full glare of public life. Abroad,
she had tasted the covert joys of anonymity and love's
embraces. Now she was obliged to step back into her fame
and expected role. There seemed no way to escape the
bright-lit cage of celebrity become-a-prison.

Three weeks later, Aimee drove with her secretary Emma
Schaffer to Venice Beach for a swim. This or riding formed
her usual exercise; she was good at both. After changing into
voluminous black bathing suits in the Ocean View Hotel,
they erected a canopy on the sand and sat in its shade.
Schaffer, a non-swimmer, read a book, while Aimee took a
dip in the ocean then returned to work on her notes for a
sermon she was due to deliver that evening.

After a while, she went for another swim. Minutes later
Schaffer glanced up to see her in the water beyond the pier,

swimming strongly. At 3.30 she looked again but could not distinguish Aimee's head among the waves. She walked up the beach, unable to spot her, then went to the hotel. Aimee's car still stood where they had parked it, and no one had seen her. The manager alerted the coastguard station then called Minnie to break the news: Aimee was missing.

The conclusion was unavoidable. It was Minnie who took the service at Angelus Temple that night and preached the brief sermon, in which to everyone's consternation she announced, 'Sister is with Jesus.'

Lifeguards and coastguard launches searched the Pacific edge for five miles north and south of Venice. Hearst's *Examiner* headlined the news, while the *Los Angeles Times* chartered a plane with a photographer and a parachutist prepared to jump for Aimee's body. Fishing craft dragged the shallows. A hastily assembled flotilla of glass-bottomed pleasure boats scanned the sea floor, each crowded with passengers at $10 a head. Venice Beach drew pilgrims as to a shrine. The entire congregation of the Temple and its several branch churches gathered by the shore in a crowd of 10,000. They lit candles and bonfires, played music, sang hymns, prayed, wept and hugged each other indiscriminately. They remained in place on a vigil that would continue for thirty-two days.

Sightings of Aimee occurred all across America, with sixteen reported in one day alone. They continued so numerous the coroner refused to issue a death certificate. Radio and every newspaper carried a daily update, though there was nothing but rumour to report. Even the *New York Times*, which chose to ignore miracles, stuntmen and Hollywood celebs, followed the story on its front page, running more than one hundred pieces on Aimee in that year.

The Balkan émigré journalist Louis Adamic floated the idea that her disappearance was a publicity stunt. 'She and the Lord can "handle" the press to perfection', he wrote in *The Truth about Aimee Semple McPherson*. 'Not a single publication dares to say an unfavorable word about this astounding spiller of bunk and baiter of boobery.' Then she was reported to have been kidnapped. A ransom note reached District Attorney Asa Keyes demanding $25,000 to release her. Minnie received another from a gang signing themselves 'The Avengers', upping the ransom to $500,000. She disregarded both, advertising a reward of $25,000 for her daughter's return, dead or alive.

Aimee's memorial service drew 8,000 people to fill the Temple, plus an estimated 14,000 who listened to the ceremony on loudspeakers in Echo Park. The service continued for all of twelve hours and the collection brought in $30,000.

In the half-light before dawn three days later, a dusty figure stumbled out of the desert at Agua Prieta, Mexico, to bang upon the door of an isolated farmhouse, then collapse. The peasant and his wife covered her with a blanket, loaded her into their donkey cart and drove across the border to the hospital at Douglas, California.

Within a couple of hours the *Examiner*, the *Record* and the *LA Times* each had a plane winging to Douglas to snatch the first pix. Next day, Minnie and the two children pitched up, accompanied by the Deputy District Attorney and a senior detective in the LAPD. Plus, in the course of that day, several hundred hacks, photographers and newsreel crews. Western Union assigned eight extra operators to twenty-four-hour duty and the press, who had taken over every habitable shelter in town, competed to spend

$5,000 on a total of fifty-five hours of telephone calls in two days.

The train carrying Aimee and her family back to LA was preceded by a pilot engine and force of armed guards to protect her safety. Also, as many of the press corps as could cram on board. As it drew into Los Angeles, an airplane flew low over the scene, scattering a ton of rose petals. The mayor, the entire Fire Department, a brass band and 50,000 people joyously welcomed her return in a blizzard of virgin white.

The *Record*'s airplane had come down with a broken radio, but the news wired by the *Examiner*'s and *LA Times*' reporters on reaching Douglas was that Aimee was suffering from dehydration, blistered feet, rope bruises on wrists and ankles, a cigar burn to the back of one hand and 'marks of torture on her body'. As she told it, she'd been approached on Venice Beach by a couple imploring her to pray over their dying baby, tricked into a car and chloroformed. On coming round, she'd found herself held in a shack in the desert while her captors attempted to extort a ransom from Angelus Temple. While her abductors were briefly absent, she severed her bonds on a jagged tin, escaped through a window and walked through the desert all night to the first settlement she came to.

She was questioned by District Attorney Keyes. A grand jury convened but adjourned after only one week, stating that there was insufficient evidence to proceed against her kidnappers, as the shack where she'd been held could not be located. Fourteen of the seventeen jurors disbelieved Aimee's account of her ordeal. On 3 August Aimee and Minnie were subpoenaed, along with Ormiston and five witnesses who alleged they had seen Aimee and him together in Carmel, on the Monterey peninsula, where he had rented a holiday cottage under an assumed name.

Ormiston admitted to the rental but claimed he was there with another woman.

At this point in the trial, Aimee had a choice. She could plead the Fifth Amendment and decline to testify. Both Minnie and her attorney begged her not to repeat her kidnapping story under oath. However, she chose to reject their advice and take the stand.

Why she should decide on this disastrous course is hard to comprehend. By now the supportive tone she was used to in the media had begun to shift and snide articles about her started to appear. She was overwrought and in an unstable state of mind; maybe she saw these as betrayal by a press she had always treated as a confidante and ally. To her, the witness box was another pulpit, and by this stage her confidence in her own charisma and power of rhetoric was total.

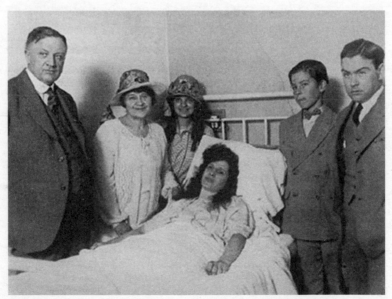

Aimee recuperates in hospital following her 'kidnapping' in 1926. Roberta and Rolph stand closest to their mother.

In presenting his evidence, Keyes exhibited a grocery list found in the Carmel cottage, allegedly in Aimee's handwriting. He had five witnesses who said they'd seen her there with Ormiston. He recalled Lorraine Wiseman, a witness from the previous hearing, where she'd claimed it was she and her sister who had shared 'the love nest' with him. Since then, she'd come to his office to retract her testimony and swear an affidavit against Minnie saying she had bribed her to lie in an attempt to exonerate Aimee. On 16 September Keyes issued warrants to arrest Aimee, Minnie and Wiseman.

The case came up for trial ten days later. Bleachers had been erected in Division Two of the LA Superior Court, but they proved inadequate to accommodate all the crowd, who slept out to catch a glimpse of the principals in the drama. Scalpers sold seats at $25 apiece. It proved impossible to maintain decorum and little attempt was made to do so; this was Hollywood and a scandalfest fit for the big screen.

The day before the trial, the *Record*, the most intelligent and restrained of West Coast newspapers, published an editorial warning that the proceedings threatened 'to split the country wide open in religious warfare'. It noted that both Keyes and his assisting attorney were Catholic, but the divide was not just sectarian. The Church Federation of Los Angeles, comprising some 250 Protestant churches, labelled Aimee 'neither honest nor genuine', describing her 'hypnotic power almost unbelievable... Her strange power was very closely related to her sex appeal.' In a rare show of ecumenical unity, Presbyterian, Methodist, Baptist and Catholic churches agreed, condemning the 'McPherson movement as disastrous' for the city of Los Angeles. It was a view the Chamber of Commerce had come to share. They had been among her most ardent boosters, the Angelus Temple had resulted in redevelopment of the whole area of Echo Park. Now the mayor and city dignitaries were mocked for their role in promoting this farce. Previously an asset, Aimee became a liability to be disowned.

The trial continued for six weeks, each day marked by a front-page update. Proceedings were not confined to the courtroom but continued over the airwaves as Aimee used KSFG to publicise her version of the 'crucifixion' she was undergoing. In response, Keyes gave interviews on rival channels substantiating his case. Aimee continued to preach on the subject, attracting the curious to swell the congregation gathered to hear her sermons over loudspeakers in Echo Park. A further crowd of prurient pilgrims was drawn to Carmel, where the owner of the 'love nest' conducted tours at $5 a head for 75,000 people, who were invited to decide whether 'the dents in the mattress fit Aimee's caboose'.

Aimee and her mother in court in Los Angeles, 1926.

The historian Carey McWilliams says in *Southern California* that, 'Sister's trial was really a lynching bee', and in *New Republic* reporter Morrow Mayo writes that the powerful forces against her colluded in 'an under-cover attempt to suppress her – and later an open civic crusade to punish her – for making a monkey out of Southern California'.

On 3 November the judge announced that there was sufficient evidence for a jury trial. Aimee and Minnie were charged with criminal conspiracy to obstruct justice and suborning perjury. All fear of libel was effectively removed, and the public invited to speculate on the $75,000 of Temple funds Aimee allegedly spent on fancy lingerie she wore beneath her nurse's uniform.

Louis Adamic had tried to expose her for two years, while grousing that she 'had the newspapers gagged'. Now he could freely vent his accumulated bile. In *The Truth about Aimee Semple McPherson* he described her congregation as 'drudges of the farms and small-town homes, victims of cruel circumstances, victims of life, slaves of their biological deficiencies. They are diseased, neurotic, unattractive, sexually and intellectually starved, warped and repressed, most of them now no longer capable of either sexual or intellectual enjoyment.'

In court Aimee had no choice but to sit silent as a parade of maids, bellhops and house detectives testified to have seen her with Ormiston in a suite at the Ambassador Hotel. There were eighty-eight witnesses. The prosecutor called her a fake, a hypocrite, a liar. Headlines labelled her a tart, a home-wrecker, a Jezebel, but it was left to the *San Diego Herald* to discharge the final shot.

> The failure, or innate inability of some women to keep their legs crossed has been the cause of more

wars, murders and crime than all other reasons in
the catalogue. This failure of women, most of whom
have been redheaded, has caused the downfall of
civilisation…

The paper names Aimee 'the most chuckle-headed liar' of
the lot, who rejoices in 'her publicity, the cash and notoriety…in the boudoir of the Lesbian Venus…where red-haired
women most assuredly do not keep their legs crossed'. It
climaxes by naming her 'the vilest female ever…the most
horrible creature, the most unnatural woman and the unlove-
liest object that man has ever fondled'.

Abuse heaped upon her. Aimee was insulted, vilified,
ridiculed, defamed. It takes a trouper not to flinch under
such personal abuse, but trouper she was. Chaplin had not
called her an actress for no reason. In court she did not wear
a nurse's uniform but the latest fashion, latest shoes and
modish hat, and she *always* knew how to handle the press
face to face in her own sassy style.

Wearing a cloche hat and short skirt, perched on the edge
of a desk with one leg swinging, surrounded by reporters
questioning whether she'd *really* been kidnapped, she bats
her baby blues as she drawls from the side of her mouth:
'That's my story boys, and I'm sticking to it.' An editor on
Outlook magazine noted, 'Not for a moment does she drop
the reins.' Ever a pro, she knew the show must go on but
confessed that

> there were nights and nights when my couch was a
> rack of anguish. As long as I was able to bear the
> physical inactivity I would lie still…wide, sleepless
> eyes staring up into the blackness of night…then I
> would get up and walk the long upstairs corridor,

up and down, to and fro in ceaseless pacing, hands
pressed first over my eyes, then over my mouth to
keep back the little cries and moans I feared would
awaken the household.

The LA Chamber of Commerce, the Protestant Church and
the Babbits of Middle America combined to crucify Aimee
even before her trial had ended. And – if the word 'crucify'
can be used to denote public exposure, ridicule and mortification – then they succeeded in the deed.

However, not *all* media combined to hammer in the nails.
The East Coast intellectual press, which had held aloof from
covering the ballyhoo, found it irresistible to mock the
Babbitry and boobery, boosterism and hype that had given
birth to such a circus. H.L. Mencken, writing in the *New
Yorker*, praised Aimee's courage and intelligence. From the
start of the proceedings he'd predicted that ultimately she
would win 'because she has the radio'. He identified the
vital resource that made it possible: she owned her own
media channel. In the whirlwind of controversy, in her own
voice, in her own inimitable delivery, *she could tell it how it
was*, in her own version of the truth.

Mencken, a sardonic critic of the foibles of American culture,
was an unexpected convert to her cause. But the trial resulted
in a whole new breed of supporters who sprang to her defence.
Sadie Mossler, writing for the *Record*, observed that criminal
trials normally draw an equal number of male and female
spectators. For this, the audience was 99 per cent women. She
speculated, 'What would be the vote of a jury composed solely
of women if they had to decide Aimee Semple McPherson's
fate?' During the lunch recess, she asked around, discovering
that 'the answer, invariably in favour of McPherson, came
from young, attractive women, while those opposing her are

not so attractive and generally past middle age'. She went on
to describe these new supporters as 'manifestly happy...well
and modishly dressed, with a laughing, dancing light in their
eyes'. While Alma Whitaker of the *Los Angeles Times* noticed
in the press seats 'a marked accession of newspaper girls...
young, stylish, flapperish'. Almost all of them wore their hair
cut short in a bob like Aimee's, and most were chewing gum.

Aimee, who had restyled herself fashionwise for her court
performance, abruptly found herself in an unanticipated role.
Viewed through the lens of mass perception, her image had
altered. In a significant shift of angle, she was recognised as a
bold exemplar of the New Woman. Hers was a success story
of a female who had won over fearsome odds to command a
designer pulpit in a profession monopolised by the male establishment. What's more, *she'd rattled their cage.* She was a hero.
    'Maybe she did have a love affair,' one young woman told

Mossler. 'I had a lot of them before I was married. A woman's human. So is Mrs McPherson.' This was the voice of Aimee's new fan base. She already had a loyal congregation at the Temple – whose characteristics were cruelly described a couple of pages ago – but these were another species entirely. They followed her to the Temple to take part, but the two groups were so dissimilar they achieved a unity only in segregation. Except for their adulation of her, they had nothing in common.

The trial was ended not by the judge but William Randolph Hearst. The fabulist media baron – 'You furnish the pictures and I will furnish the war' – who lived in his own designer castle, San Simeon, had long admired Aimee, not for any religious reason but due to her showmanship and ability to command the front page. Now he instructed the editor of the *Examiner* – one of his many titles – to offer Wiseman $5,000 for her story. On appearing at the paper's office to spill the beans, she was arrested by police waiting in the next room. The following morning the *Examiner* led with the news that District Attorney Keyes had dropped the prosecution against Aimee and her mother.

Keyes read the headline with some surprise; he'd done no such thing. But he learned his chief witness had changed her story once again. She'd perjured herself under oath and the prosecution had no case. He did as the *Examiner* already had announced and dismissed all criminal charges against Aimee and Minnie.

She emerged from the fray triumphant, her congregation vastly enlarged by a generation of new female fans across the country. Before the scandal she'd been a figure associated with religion. In the course of the trial's coast-to-coast publicity, she transcended that role in the popular imagination to become a star. Two movie studios bid to cast her as lead in a film of her ordeal.

Was the kidnapping story true? Her established congregation believed everything she said. To her new followers the answer was irrelevant – both kidnapping and Carmel love nest were equally gripping stories; none of them really cared which was true. Aimee was a ready-made icon for the New Woman. Perception is all. The medium is the message, image trumps truth. These are the lessons of mass media that hold good to this day: Fake News makes great news.

New Brand Aimee launched in New York six weeks later in a deliberately provocative venue calculated to shock.

A limo drew up outside the 300 Club on West 54th Street. From it she stepped into a light storm of flashbulbs, wearing a full-length fur coat over a beaded cocktail dress sparkling in the flare. Tex Guinan, nightclub queen and gangsters' moll, who welcomed everyone with the same line, 'Hello Sucker', instead embraced her warmly, led her to the dance floor, killed the music and invited her to speak.

She did so for less than three minutes, reminding the raffish clientele, 'there is another life…' and asking them to come and hear her speak next day at a revival meeting. She ended… and the crowd sat stunned in silence. Then, as Tex hugged her, burst into rapturous applause. She'd crashed through the barrier separating the pious from the louche and fairly drunk. She might be a holy roller but she was their sort of broad.

Aimee had regained her chutzpah and was back in the game. She lost weight, used make-up, the bobbed hair lightened in tint; columnists speculated on a facelift. Yet despite her fame and army of supporters, she had no close friend. She confesses to loneliness. She wrote a sacred opera whose lead, David Hutton, was a fat-ass baritone ten years younger than herself (thirty-eight). They worked together on the production in a relationship that palely resembled that which she'd enjoyed with Ormiston. Opportunistically he married her. For two years he exploited her to further his talent-free career, and embezzled her money until they split.

Sick of him, she did not languish. A workaholic, her energy remained boundless. In 1927 she established a medical clinic at the Angelus Temple providing free care to the impoverished and old. Soon after, she set up a commissary open 24/7, which distributed food, clothing and blankets to anyone in need. In the Great Depression following the Wall Street crash of '29, it did more to help the destitute than any federal or state agency. It was estimated that the programme fed 1.5 million people, who would otherwise have starved.

During these years of blithe philanthropy Aimee's relationship with her mother grew strained and she hired a manager, Ralph Jordan – who had worked for Hearst – to run the

Temple's affairs. Further disputes concerned the accounts
Minnie had managed, and she was forced to resign. A photo
appeared in the papers of Minnie with a black eye. Another
facelift – or had Aimee socked her?

Her bond with her daughter also frayed. Roberta and her
husband moved out of the family house on poor terms with
her. It was only surprising they'd stayed long as they had;
the place served as a troublesome shelter for battered women.
Under Jordan's management the Temple sank into debt in
a period of worldwide economic stagnation, as did most
businesses. The relationship between Aimee, Roberta, Minnie,
Jordan and the now-adversarial church board degenerated
into a welter of successive law suits. At one moment Aimee
was involved in no fewer than forty-five ongoing legal actions.

When the US entered the Second World War in 1941,
she stepped up to the plate as a patriot. She had the pacifist
clause in the Temple's constitution amended. She saw this as
a conflict between good and evil, and Uncle Sam was twin
with good. She hosted war-bond drives, selling more than
any other star on the circuit. Her Temple clinic extracted
2,800 pints of blood from her congregation's veins for the
Red Cross. She persuaded President Roosevelt to announce
a national Day of Prayer for the Republic. For Aimee, this
was always God's own country.

Aimee's sex life remains the subject of prurient speculation.
Following Ormiston there were rumours of many love affairs,
but she had only brief and intermittent opportunity to enjoy
them. Of two that are documented, one was with Charlie
Chaplin. In 1931 Aimee was with Roberta on a round-the-
world trip when, in Marseilles, she learned the Little Tramp
was staying at the Hotel Noailles while between wives (Lita

Grey and Paulette Goddard), so she knocked on the door of his suite – to his dismay. He knew who she was – everyone knew who she was – and, though an atheist, had visited the LA Temple to study her performance. Chaplin was in private an unkind and deeply unlovable man, yet for a week the two shared a bed and a curious affinity. As he noted, they were engaged in the same craft.

The comedian Milton Berle records another two-afternoon interlude in his autobiography. His description of their second encounter indicates the difficulty Aimee had fitting any personal downtime into her remorseless work schedule: 'This time, she just had the chauffeur to bring me straight to the apartment. We didn't even bother with lunch. When I was dressing to leave, she stuck out her hand. "Good luck with your show, Milton." What the hell, I couldn't resist it, "Good luck with yours, Aimee." I never saw or heard from her again but whenever I hear "Yes Sir, That's My Baby", I remember her.'

Following the collapse of her marriage to the ridiculous
Hutton, Aimee fell into a clinical depression that shadowed
the rest of her life. In the space of a few days she plunged
into a near-catatonic state interspersed by such anxiety she
could not function. She withdrew to a clinic where she lay
behind drawn blinds, unable to sleep, read, write or think
clearly. Emerging from these troughs of despair she would go
off alone to Europe or the East, where she could escape for
a while from a public who had surrounded her since youth.
Rebuilding her confidence in the shade of anonymity with
a new wardrobe, she could enjoy a drink, maybe two. She
was not on show. If chance showed up on an adjacent barstool
for a brief intoxicating while, she could step out of the closet
to enjoy the spontaneous sexuality she rarely found an opportunity to express. If her lovers knew who she was they did
not tell. Perhaps due to some now-obsolete reaction, *respect*?

Aimee leading a fourteen-hour service at the Temple,
18 June 1942.

Aged fifty-four, Aimee died in Oakland, after preaching at a revival. Her son Rolph found her next morning in her hotel room with a half-empty bottle of sleeping pills by the bed. She had always found it hard to sleep and managed only by increasing her use of barbiturates, prescribed and not so. The counterpole to her certainty and manic energy was insomnia, haunted by restless dread. Of what? One may wonder. She could not abide dirt, grime or anything soiled. She had the habit – at times compulsively – of washing her hands as if they held a stain she could not remove.

Her congregation grieved, desolated by her death. And so too did countless other women who esteemed her as a role model. Forty-five thousand mourners filed past her bier at the Temple funeral. Today her church commands a worldwide membership of some eight million followers. Others may rate her as a charlatan but to them she remains a saint. The two roles are not necessarily exclusive – possibly she was both.

5

'SOCIETY SHAKEN BY TERRIBLE SCANDAL'

Saints are rare, which is probably just as well. Despite Aimee's – and the impious Victoria Woodhull's – charisma, both must have been a nightmare to deal with when their blood was running. Without the very human flaws in their natures, surely they would have come over as insufferable prigs. Unrelieved sanctity is intensely irritating to others, and undoubtedly contributed to so many being martyred.

Edwina Mountbatten was regarded by many as a secular saint for the last twenty years of her life. Prior to that, the direct opposite: a flagrant worldly sinner. A thrill-seeking nymphomaniac, privileged and rich, she answered to no one – not even the King, her godfather. Notoriously, she cuckolded her husband Lord Mountbatten, last Viceroy of India, in a scandal so ludicrously shaming to all involved it caricatured him as a figure of ridicule for the rest of his career.

While as for her...

The event is billed as the Wedding of the Year. As the bride and groom stand at the altar of St Margaret's, Westminster, in the summer of 1922, they are seen by many as the flawless couple from a fairy tale: young, beautiful, titled and rich.

He is Lieutenant Lord Dickie Mountbatten, and best man his cousin, the Prince of Wales. The two are in full dress naval uniform with swords. The bride, Edwina Ashley, attended by seven bridesmaids, is twenty and well known to the public as deb of her year and the wealthiest heiress in England.

It is a clouded day, drizzling rain, but Parliament Square and Victoria Street are packed with people here since dawn. Most are women and many have camped out all night. They are equipped with folding stools, baskets of provisions, periscopes, umbrellas, paper flags, and their mood of celebration is undimmed by British weather.

The newly-weds exit the church arm in arm beneath an arch of swords held aloft by Dickie's fellow officers – a number of whom harbour a keen desire to plunge one into his gorgeously costumed body and with good reason. They climb into a Rolls-Royce Silver Ghost, Edwina's wedding present to her husband. The giant driverless car is towed away by a team of naval ratings, grunting and straining at the rope for the newsreel cameras. Someone has attached an old shoe to the back.

The crowd outside Edwina's mansion in Park Lane has grown so dense the butler had to call the police. A way is cleared through the exuberant mob for the arrival of 800 guests. The grand staircase has been transformed into a grove of orange trees in glowing fruit. The whole interior of the house is banked with thousands of blue delphiniums. The cake is so enormous it takes four sailors to hoist it onto the table. Tier upon tier of icing sugar are surmounted by a sparkling crown. Dickie hands Edwina his sword. As she cuts the first slice the room bursts into applause.

★   ★   ★

In marrying Dickie, Edwina acquired a status that was semi-
royal. Three generations of dedicated social climbing had
gone into the ascent. Her grandfather, Ernest Cassel, stepped
ashore at Dover in 1869 aged seventeen with one suitcase,
a violin and his wits, to seek his fortune. He prospered to
become reputedly the richest man in England and banker
to King Edward VII. The monarch was Edwina's godfather.
When she learned to speak she called him 'Kingy'.

Cassel came of a long line of Jewish moneylenders and
bankers in Cologne. Money he knew, though he had little
in his pocket. Without difficulty he got a job with the
financial house of Bischoffsheim and Goldschmidt in the
City. They sent him on turn-it-around assignments to Europe
and South America as a troubleshooter. Money is its own
country. It transcends frontiers to form its own discrete state.
Cassel already had links with key players on the continent;
now in London he was assiduously social. He met with
prejudice in his upward progress. The Jew, and especially the
Jewish banker, was a figure of caricature to some, though
not all. Cassel entertained, and he did so lavishly. Food and
wine were the best, like attracts like and the best people
pitched up at his trough.

At the age of twenty-six, Cassel married. His bride,
Annette, was Scottish Catholic. He formally embraced her
religion, taking British nationality. A daughter, Maud, was
born, then Annette developed TB. She died when Maud was
only two.

The child grew up with everything that could be desired,
except a mother; Cassel was devoted to her. He'd by now
acquired a country estate near Newmarket and started to
breed racehorses. Very swiftly that investment in bloodstock
paid off and he became pals with the Prince of Wales, the
future Edward VII. The two took to each other as to a

reflection in a mirror. They were uncannily alike to look at, short wide men bulked into the same shape, with identical beards and moustaches. Both spoke in the same German accent. The two shared a taste for racing, shooting and food, though Cassel was not drawn to women like the louche and lickerish Prince. His Highness developed an admiration for his friend's flair with money. Debarred from speculating with his own fortune, he asked Cassel to manage it for him.

To consolidate his new position in society Cassel acquired Brook House in Park Lane. The mansion's interior was grand, but not grand enough for its new owner. Its makeover took three years. He imported 80 tons of marble from the Italian quarry Michelangelo had used four centuries earlier. Even the six kitchens were walled in white marble. Marble was everywhere.

This was the palace of cold luxury that Edwina would inherit on Cassel's death, when she was just twenty. Human touches were absent. Brook House made not a home to live in but a venue to entertain in the grand style. In 1899 Cassel was given a knighthood and appointed to the Privy Council. The Jewish adolescent who'd walked ashore at Dover with a second-hand fiddle had finally arrived. To integrate fully with the top rank in his chosen country required only one further step – to marry his daughter into the English aris-tocracy.

Maud came out aged nineteen programmed to obey his will; she aspired to no less a match herself. And Wilfred Ashley appeared to fill the part. He was dim-witted, weak-willed and unrich, but he had prospects. He stood to inherit his father's estate and Broadlands, one of the most desirable country houses in England.

These two very different houses – indeed homes – together with Cassel's fortune comprised the heritage that Edwina

Ashley was born into in 1901. The Prince of Wales, her grandfather's closest friend, was now King. He attended Edwina's christening as her godfather, presenting her with a silver mug. She had come into the world already in possession of its matching silver spoon.

At the start of the twentieth century, parenting was not a hands-on activity among those who could afford to pay others to do the job. To banish your offspring to be brought up by a nanny, nursemaids and a governess was standard practice. Edwina was shifted between Cassel's sister's house near Bournemouth; to her cousins the Shaftesburys; to Classiebawn Castle in Ireland, home to her Pakenham cousins; to Broadlands, and a house in Stanmore that Cassel had bought for Maud.

These serial homes all were large, comfortable if unheated residences, though her quarters were a bedroom on the top floor − sometimes in the attic − and a nursery, where the only other child occasionally present was her cousin Marjorie. Her regimen was strict. She did not eat with the adults but alone or with Marjorie in the nursery, where she ate voraciously. Not until teatime was she brought downstairs to be formally presented to guests staying at the house. These included Winston Churchill, Herbert Asquith, Lloyd George, press barons and industrial tycoons. Solemnly she shook hands, meeting their eye and replying in a clear voice to what they said. Never was she shy.

Her father had become a Conservative MP. Shooting, fishing and the House took up his time. Edwina saw him rarely. Maud led a hectic social life in London; Edwina kissed her dutifully on the cheek but was not embraced. Hugs were not the done thing. Aside from teatime, it was believed

children should be neither seen nor heard. Wilfred Ashley
– 'a very pompous, rum fellow,' according to an acquaintance
– wanted a male heir. When Maud was delivered of another
daughter, Maria, he was displeased. But Edwina adopted her
sister in their shared peripatetic life, taking care of her with
the same affection as she devoted to her pets.

When she was eight, Grandfather Cassel took her with
him in his private railway carriage to join his friend the
King and Mrs Keppel in Biarritz. The monarch was not well.
Back in England three weeks later he was dying from bron-
chitis and sent for Cassel. 'I am very seedy,' he told him. 'But
I want to see you.' Cassel brought with him a package
containing £10,000 in cash. The packet remained unopened,
for the King died that same night.

Cassel withdrew from society in grief. He'd lost his friend,
his patron, his most prestigious client. A year later his daughter
Maud died from TB, caught from her mother. Edwina and
Maria were not taken to her funeral. She wrote a bleak letter
to her father, 'I am so very sorry darling mama left us all so
suddenly and for ever. I wanted to kiss her only once and
now I didn't.'

Edwina was thirteen when her father remarried. Molly
Forbes-Sempill had just divorced. She was a hard-faced
woman with a sniffy expression, loud, pretentious, pushy and
unkind – particularly to her new stepdaughters. That Wilfred
should choose for a wife a woman loathed by everyone is
inexplicable, except that he liked to be pushed around. She
moved into Broadlands and set to redecorating the place to
her own all-too-certain taste. Edwina and Maria lodged on
the top floor, supervised by a governess and female tutor.
Both of them became fluent in French and German, but

other subjects barely figured. The children were permitted down for tea but sent to bed at 6.30. 'To be out of the way,' Edwina heard her stepmother explain to a guest.

The sisters suffered greater adversity soon after. Cassel knew that war was pending. Winston Churchill had sent him to Berlin to discuss the Kaiser's expansion to his fleet, a blatant challenge to British naval supremacy. He had already subscribed heavily to the War Loan to rearm the country, now he accompanied Lord Reading – also Jewish – to America, where they obtained a half-million dollars toward the same urgent cause.

Hardly had he returned before he suffered the first attack. Cassel had made enemies in his climb to wealth and eminence, as any high achiever does who comes from such outsider beginnings. Now an MP brought a charge against him and another Jewish financier, Sir Edgar Speyer. The indictment cited the British Nationality and Aliens Act. Cassel was served with a High Court writ calling upon him 'to show why he should not be removed from the Privy Council'.

He must have seen it coming but closed his eyes to it – in the same manner as many Jews would do later in Germany – unable to believe that the civilised values of his adopted homeland could give way to xenophobia. Fanned by the press, there was a reaction against all things German. Cassel's widowed sister had already changed her name to Cassel. The First Sea Lord, Prince Louis of Battenberg, had been forced to resign due to alleged German sympathies, then chose to reinvent himself as Mountbatten. Even the royal family submitted to expedient rebranding, altering theirs from Saxe-Coburg to Windsor. Now everything German became an anathema and the public mood ugly. Dachshunds – perceived as a German breed – were kicked or stoned in the street.

Cassel was stigmatised; his friends dropped away. He became a recluse, holed up in his marble fortress in Park Lane. He could face no one except family, and the burden fell upon Edwina. Hurt and diminished, he found comfort in her nearness; she shared his mortification. Cassel and Sir Edgar Speyer were arraigned before a court of three judges, its president his friend Lord Reading. The bench found in their favour, dismissing the charges against them. Cassel received telegrams and letters of congratulation and support from his former friends, but he'd lost faith in those once-prized guests who'd flocked to guzzle his caviar and champagne. He'd been shown the nature of their loyalty. With him, Edwina gained her first experience of shame.

At Broadlands Molly found children inconvenient. Edwina (fifteen) and Maria (ten) were sent away to boarding school in Eastbourne. 'Awful time', Edwina noted. Her reputation preceded her. Others were the daughters of lesser fortunes, and resentful. She came already branded. Fellow pupils were cruel as girls of that age know how. She was rich, she was German, but a further detail reinforced their prejudice. On arriving at the school she'd been assigned a small room to share with her sister. This was unusual, for dormitories usually contained three or four girls. Very quickly Edwina was apprised why. No other girl wanted to share with her, she was a 'Yid'.

On her fifteenth birthday Edwina received a diamond and emerald pendant as a present from Cassel. She wrote him back from school, 'please take me away, dear Grandpapa, if you love me at all.'

Interceding with her parents, he helped her to leave The Links, where she'd learned nothing of academic significance, not even to enjoy reading. She moved to finishing school at Aldeburgh, where she continued to learn nothing except to run a household and plan a dinner party for twenty. Very many in England, including her father, believed a daughter's education was unnecessary, indeed contraindicated for her future married life.

When the Great War ended, Cassel determined that Edwina should visit Italy to extend her cultural horizons and circle of acquaintance. For this she must have the right wardrobe. She was told to choose whatever she wanted and have the goods sent to Brook House together with the bill. On these shopping trips in Mayfair and down Bond Street her maid accompanied her – it would not have done to go alone. She was overweight, even obese by today's standards. Her face was beefy, she had an unflattering short bob and was not allowed make-up. She was big and plain, she had no one to guide her and no interest in fashion. In many ways she was prematurely adult, but not in dress. She bought the most expensive, but she had no idea how to wear clothes and carry them off.

Cassel – who loved to organise – set up his version of the Grand Tour, deciding to come along as master of proceedings. Painting and sculpture, indeed fine art in general, did not do much for Edwina. At Brook House she'd grown up with Old Masters and statuary as part of the décor. Likewise, grand opera did not move her. In each city, staff were alerted to receive her. She was provided with an agenda, punctilio and expert guides. What the trip did not provide was excitement or adventure, and within her tightly buttoned persona Edwina had a yen for both. A pageant of experience lay just outside the bubble of decorum confining her. She was afforded no opportunity to touch, to taste what lay visible and almost within reach.

The Grand Tour rekindled Cassel's spirit and brought him back into the social world, to launch Edwina upon it. He asked her to come to live at Brook House and help his secretary organise big dinner parties in the pre-war style, and to act as hostess. The suggestion provided a ready escape from her father and stepmother and the chronic problem of 'What are we going to do about Edwina?' She went to work as his PA on an allowance of £300 a year.

Her sister once remarked that Edwina was never a child, but adult beyond her years. Responsible and well organised, she provided a human touch long absent from the marble mausoleum, taking care to win over the staff, something Cassel had never troubled to effect. She was always good with servants; it was hard to resent her. At Brook House, Cassel's secretary Miss Underhill controlled a small army of menials. There was a butler and four footmen dressed in knee breeches and livery, who wore their hair powdered during the Season; a housekeeper with five housemaids, Edwina's maid and Cassel's valet; a chef with five assistants, three chauffeurs, a house electrician and an odd-job man.

The purpose of the house was once again as a venue, a setting to host grand dinner parties. Cassel devoted days to composing the guest list, juggling their placements. On party nights Miss Underhill remained at her post until 8.30p.m., in case of any last-minute cancellation. By then Edwina had been on duty for half an hour, receiving the arrivals by Cassel's side. At 8.30 sharp she led the way in to dinner, taking her place at one end of a table set for a hundred in the double-height room hung with Old

Masters. At the other end, yards distant, Cassel presided at its head.

The guests were all middle-aged or old and successful in their various fields. Cassel was the impresario at these soirées he'd designed primarily to bring people together and initiate a relationship leading to mutual pleasure, advancement or gain. In this role he had rivals, for a new breed of political hostess had come into existence since the war. Sybil Colefax, Elsie Mendl and Emerald Cunard were trawling the same waters of royalty, politics, the arts and people of the moment to imbue their salons with the desired tone. At theirs, it embraced youth and wit. At Cassel's table youth and wit did not feature.

Edwina was twenty, uneducated except in the social arts. She knew how to look attentive, to react. She was quick, interrogative, her expression sparked with interest. She delivered a very capable performance. The oldsters seated by her were happy to find so alert a listener as they recalled their achievements, while their glass was refilled by an ever-attendant footman.

Her manners stayed faultless, though to look at she did not fit the role imposed upon her. She was not worldly but careless of her appearance. 'At the time she didn't know how to dress herself or anything of that sort,' a female guest quoted in Richard Hough's biography recalls. 'Not at all *soignée* as I clearly remember. The fact that she had no mother to guide her was evident.'

Edwina came out in 1920. As one of a long line of debutantes, she was presented to the King and Queen. She embarked upon the Season from May to the end of June, attending three or more dances a week, each preceded by a dinner party.

The purpose of the Season was to function as a marriage

market. Coming from either 'County' or 'Society' families, the young women on display were all the same age. None had gone to university. Their destiny was to be the wife of someone rich, preferably titled and heir to a stately home and land. That topped the prize list, but rivalry was fierce. The Great War had killed three-quarters of a million men, almost wiping out the public school officer class. There was an acute shortage of males. The fracturing of social structure by the war had opened the lists to arrivistes grown rich during the conflict – most of them regarded with horror by the establishment but nevertheless possessed of advantage in what was a buyers' market.

Not so much a market as a contest. These girls were unemployable, lacking training or any useful skills. Many could not even cook. Marriage represented the only conceivable future. Their parents were desperate for them to succeed; no ignominy was more shameful than an ageing and unmarried daughter still living at home. These young women all aped the same look and manner. They had bobbed or shingled hair, pouting scarlet lips. Except when governed by the fashionable necessity to look bored, they acted roguish in their arch femininity. They were not friendly, but antagonistic to others. Rudeness was a deliberate habit of both sexes. One was rude to acquaintances, strangers, shop assistants, waiters. The put-down rated high, cruel wit was expression of the utmost sophistication.

It was impossible for a young woman to be friends with another at this time. Not one could be trusted. A woman might be an acquaintance, an ally, but she was *always* a rival. Within the ballrooms of Mayfair and Belgravia, polite society had reverted to the primal. Another woman was an enemy to be destroyed.

★   ★   ★

The press labelled Edwina the richest heiress in Britain. Her coming-out ball took place early in the Season at Brook House, where Cassel ensured it outdid all others after in its extravagance. A dance orchestra played in the ballroom and an African-American jazz band in the drawing room. On arrival the guests were shown into the lofty hall, whose white marble walls were wholly clad in red carnations. Edwina stood positioned at the foot of the grand staircase to receive them centre stage, clothed in a full-length sheath of shining gold.

All eyes fixed upon her. The herd of breeding stock in ball gowns composing her peer group examined her head to toe. Her jewels, the dazzle of that long gold sheath...yes, but as that critical group gaze scrutinised and dissected her it noted that her shoulders bulged from the drapery, that her upper arms were meaty and strong, that her hips strained against the rich material. These details were observed with intense satisfaction, for at this moment the lean, breastless, waistless, hipless look was vital. Edwina's strapping physique was discussed with breathless glee.

Yet she reigned as queen of this night. Very many men were keen to dance with her, she was the prime beast garlanded with the most rosettes. At her ball Edwina's dance card was full. She found the attention gratifying, it authenticated her. At debs' balls that followed upon hers, her card was always full. Human nature being what it is, it was not long before she was undeceived.

The dance took place at a town house in Belgrave Square, now an embassy. The band had broken and Edwina was standing sipping a lemonade when a girl by her remarked, 'You get a lot of dances, don't you?'

Edwina peered at her. A fellow deb she vaguely recognised but couldn't remember the name.

'It's only because you're rich,' the girl informed her. 'No one would ask you if you weren't. You're fat.'

The blow disabled her, she lost her voice. Like a sleepwalker she found her way out to where her car and chauffeur waited. Back at Brook House she viewed herself naked in the full-length mirror. She had no confidante, no mother, no adult mentor except old Cassel, who doted on her but whose criteria were of the Edwardian era when fullness and strong features were considered desirable. There was nowhere to go for either comfort or advice.

What Edwina did have was formidable strength of will. Her resolve was immediate. For the first, though not the only time in her career, she set out to remake herself. She purged and mortified the flesh. Many did, so urgent was the requirement to conform to fashion. At dinner parties she ate nothing, shuffling the food around her plate with a fork. She bandaged her breasts in an elastic brassiere and, however late to bed, rose early to ride in Hyde Park. Meanwhile, she put herself through a crash course in fashion with *Vogue* for a primer and focused her sharp unschooled intelligence upon self-improvement. Already she possessed quickness and wit, now she applied herself to learn the lesson that it is not *what* but *how* that matters most.

As her features fined down, she rediscovered her cheekbones. The face was still mannish with firm jaw and proud straight nose, but these distinct features visible from the gods caused Edwina to be relabelled by the tabloids as a 'beauty'. Also, 'fast'.

The men at the Season's parties were all on the 'list' in a scale of eligibility well understood by debs and their parents. By the third week Edwina had come across most of them.

The majority were in their early twenties, an older section had either survived or avoided the war. All conformed to a type. Their hair was cut short, slick with Brilliantine and combed flat. All wore white tie and tails with wide 'Oxford bags'. They spoke in affected jackass voices, their conversation essentially trivial and mundane. After the Great War to talk of anything serious was taboo. Their manner was bantering, mocking, facetious. Anything they didn't understand – such as modern art – they ridiculed.

These men constituted the pool of potential husbands for the debs, who otherwise knew no one outside their own class and race. But as hostess at Cassel's dinner parties Edwina had encountered a wider if older circle: the international rich. Among them were the Cornelius Vanderbilts, whose fortune derived from the Commodore, patron to Victoria Woodhull. They had taken a house at Cowes for the regatta, and owned their own enormous yacht – a staple collectible for the very rich, then as now. In June the Vanderbilts hosted a grand ball at Claridge's. The guests included a young man Edwina had already heard about: Dickie Mountbatten, an officer in the Royal Navy, the son of Prince Louis Battenberg and cousin to the Prince of Wales.

Naval uniform befits a man, particularly if he is tall and lean. In the ballroom of the grandest hotel in London he stood erect, unlike many there who adopted the languid droop now the fashion. There was a stiffness in his bearing, a hint of the Teutonic. It indicated a consciousness of self; he was vain about his appearance. But what Edwina saw singled him out from others at the ball. He was of a different cut.

Vanderbilt introduced him and he asked her to dance. He was not adept, but she adapted. Months later they would practise alone to a gramophone till she taught him to lead.

Four inches taller than she, he was fine-featured with strong straight nose, dark hair cut short – movie star looks. He was twenty-one, she nineteen. Physical attraction formed an immediate connection, but the two shared a deeper bond, though it is unlikely they ever discussed this. Both were *outsiders*, German and in her case Jewish, who had been dealt a very high position in British society. They held court cards, but the two were parvenus, jumped up out of nowhere.

Dickie's grandfather was the Grand Duke of Hesse, ruler of a pocket state with a token population of smocked peasants and a picturesque castle not *quite* on the Rhine. His son Prince Louis while very young determined to become a sailor, an unusual profession in a landlocked country nowhere near the sea. He relocated to London the same year as Edwina's grandfather Cassel and at the same age. Both came to advance their careers. In Louis' case, through calculated dynastic marriage to a qualifying wife. Rulers of the tiny comic opera states that made up Germany and Austria at this time were in urgent survival mode to secure their future before obsolescence. The instinct to perpetuate royally lay strong in Louis and passed on to his son Dickie, who always knew which direction was up.

The principality of Hesse subsisted penuriously unrich and in England Prince Louis found himself woefully pushed for cash, with little above his service pay. But the family future depended upon him, and he came up trumps, bagging Queen Victoria's granddaughter for the job. Humourless and Hunnish, Prince Louis did not make a popular figure among home-grown officers in the British Navy. But he was pals with the portly Prince of Wales, soon to become Edward VII. The two shared the same Teutonic accent as well as the bed of the same mistress, the famous actress Lillie Langtry. The relationship kept the two men close. Royally favoured as he was, promotion came swift to Prince Louis. Though senior officers fumed at his advancement to First Sea Lord, they kept their jaws clamped shut.

Prince Dickie of Battenberg was born in 1899, Louis and Victoria's fourth child. He grew up attended by indulgent nursemaids who feared to deny him anything. He could be one sulky little prince if thwarted. An early problem showed up in his balance. Much later, in the Second World War the ships he captained tended to capsize. King George VI groaned when he heard he had been given command of a refitted aircraft carrier. 'Well, that's the end of the *Illustrious*', he observed glumly.

Throughout infancy and childhood Dickie's home life was passed at the impoverished Hessian court and the overwhelmingly ostentatious Romanov court at St Petersburg, where his aunt presided as tsarina, attended by her rank-smelling lover Rasputin. The sumptuous setting, gorgeous costumes, grandeur and display worked a powerful effect upon an impressionable lad. He never outgrew his delight in dressing up.

This tendency to show off caused Dickie much suffering when he went to Osborne Naval College at the age of thirteen. Worse, he was German at a time when all things German were anathema. He was ostracised, taunted, bullied and accorded the same treatment as Edwina at The Links. As conflict grew inevitable, public hostility turned upon his father as First Sea Lord. In a war against Germany, how could the British Navy be commanded by an admiral who was German?

Prince Louis was forced to resign and change his name. Dickie experienced a shame whose memory would never leave him, 'It was the worst body-blow I ever suffered in my life.' He was seen standing at attention on the parade ground by the flagpole with the tears pouring down his face. The display of weakness gained him no sympathy. The 'Little Hun' was a pretty boy who from the start was subject to sexual abuse. This was standard at Osborne, part of the naval tradition described by Churchill as 'rum, sodomy and the lash'. It was thought to be character-forming and the making of a man. Very often it was, establishing his tastes for life.

Having first met at the Vanderbilt ball, Edwina and Dickie next encountered each other at Cowes, a premier event of the Season, where she was a guest of the Barings, owners of *Sylvie*, one of the huge racing yachts competing in the regatta. Edwina proved much in demand. She was a catch and drew many suitors, young and not so young, all richer than Dickie. Their attentiveness was not due only to her wealth. A rigid dieting regime had thinned her to much nearer the androgynous ideal of the day. She never seemed quite relaxed, always restless and keen to *do* something. Adding to her allure came the reputation she was fast – game for petting, maybe more.

The regatta days were passed on the lawn of Cowes Castle, watching the races while drinking lemonade or champagne. The weather continued sunny and warm. The Barings' house had a pool and tennis court. Edwina and Dickie partnered in mixed doubles. She never engaged in anything she was not already good at, but Dickie's balance was a handicap. Nor was he skilled in courtship. Nubile women were an unknown species, though he'd dated a couple of girls and been engaged to one, Audrey James, who jilted him while he was abroad on the Royal Tour, to marry the older, vastly rich Major Dudley Coats.

In the early Twenties, young women smoked, swore, flirted and petted, but few put out. The shame of pregnancy loomed as a spectre at their dalliance. Dickie Mountbatten was probably a virgin, as most men of his class and age. In regard to women, that is. He had experience of older cadets at Osborne, who hit upon the new intake when they arrived aged thirteen, to be cast in the female role. The youths who used them did not consider themselves gay; they did not fellate their juniors, instead were served by them. Yet most had come to the practice as juniors themselves in the submissive role. This could make for some confusion in future married life.

Later that summer Edwina joined the Duke and Duchess of Sutherland at their shooting party in Scotland, where Dickie was also invited. Dunrobin Castle, dating from the thirteenth century, was uninhabitable except in high summer, but formidably imposing. It even boasted its own railway station to receive guests arriving on the overnight sleeper from King's Cross; on this occasion an oddly composed bunch of aristos and establishment, including the Prince of Wales, his stammering brother Bertie (who would become George VI) and the Archbishop of Canterbury.

Dickie was a poor shot but it would have been bad form not to join the men (plus some women) in the butts, where coveys of game were driven toward them by a line of beaters. Afterwards, the company posed with their guns for a group photograph behind a mountain of bloodied flesh and feathers.

Edwina did not attend these killing fests. Not only did she love all animals, she found this male blood-bonding repellent. She leaned toward left-wing republican views, though she knew well not to express them in these surroundings. During that weekend Dickie continued his wooing; he had made up his mind to propose. The house party stood grouped in the drawing room before dinner when a flunkey appeared with a telegram for him. Opening it, he read DEEPLY REGRET PAPA DIED AT 1.20AM. He burst into tears. Other guests were thrown by his public display of grief, it showed frightfully bad form. No one knew quite what to do until the archbishop suggested they say a prayer together. Rather embarrassed, they gathered cushions, set them on the Aubusson carpet and kneeled awkwardly to do so. Hardly had the primate begun to lead them in prayer than the door was flung open and the butler and two footmen entered in procession bearing enormous silver trays of cocktails.

Dickie caught the morning train to London, Edwina remained with the house party, the next day to receive a call from Miss Underhill. Her grandfather was sick and wanted urgently to see her. She took the next train south. Miss Underhill was waiting to meet her at King's Cross. Cassel had died of a heart attack during the night.

When Dickie appeared later that day at Brook House to commiserate, all the blinds were drawn. Edwina met him in the hall and they fell into each other's arms, both of them in tears.

Genuinely bereft — for Cassel had been her sponsor and protector since infancy — Edwina inherited his country seat Moulton Paddocks and Branksome Dene, the house he'd bought for his sister. The Newmarket estate and stud went to Maria, but the villa in Switzerland and Brook House were Edwina's, plus shares and investments that would be worth almost £240 million today. She could access none of it. Not until she reached her twenty-eighth birthday would she have control of her fortune — unless she married.

Dickie was committed to accompanying the Prince of
Wales on his Indian tour, sailing on the battleship *Repulse*
on 26 October. He couldn't *not* go, it was a great honour.
Yet his absence on the last Royal Tour had cost him his
previous fiancée, and Edwina was a more valuable trophy
than Audrey Jones had ever been. He suggested she find an
excuse to visit India and join them, though 'I never thought
she'd pull it off.' For a woman who was not yet twenty-one
to travel halfway across the world unchaperoned was unthinkable. It took Edwina guile and a loan to arrange, but she set
to work to do so.

The Royal Tour had been conceived by the mandarins
of the Colonial Office as a public relations exercise – though
the word 'goodwill' furnished reason for the mission.
Goodwill was not the sentiment most Indians felt toward
the motherland and its monarchy, but instead aggrieved
resentment for the lofty authority that for so long had
dominated and controlled their lives.

The royal party's arrival in Bombay provoked riots that
spread throughout the land. Mahatma Gandhi began the first
of his public fasts in protest. The Indian National Congress
boycotted the tour, urging people not to acknowledge the
visit or attend its ceremonials. Those who did were often
murdered. The new Viceroy (Cassel's old friend Rufus Isaacs)
ordered that the political ringleaders should be locked up,
including Jawaharlal Nehru (later to become Prime Minister
of the country and Edwina's lover, so devoted to her that
on her death he sent two destroyers from India to attend
her burial at sea off Portsmouth).

People remained at home. No cheering crowds lined the
Prince's route, no one at all. The normally busy streets

stretched eerily deserted. 'A spooky experience,' the Prince noted in his diary. The Viceroy's staff had laid on the most elaborate arrangements and the royal party compensated by a frantic gaiety at their polo matches, pig-sticking, tiger shoots and garden parties. Edwina had wangled an invitation to stay with the Rufus Isaacs (now Lord and Lady Reading) at the Viceregal Lodge in Delhi. It formed a setting of palatial splendour with hundreds of servants and undeviating choreographed pomp: the Raj accoutred in what was increasingly perceived as the Emperor's new clothes. A huge bungalow had been built for the Prince and his staff, with its own private garden. He gave Dickie a key to his section of the house, where the couple could be alone.

In these optimal circumstances, on Valentine's Day Dickie asked Edwina to marry him.

On the royal party's return aboard the *Repulse* in June 1922 they received a triumphant welcome home.

The tour had been a disaster. Its misconceived grandeur and display of privilege had united all India in a fierce desire for independence. But the British public remained unaware of the flop. Television and radio did not exist. Newspapers were controlled by the press lords, reporting the tour as a splendid progress illustrated by photographs of its stars: the Prince, Dickie and Edwina. This was still the cave age of communication. Mass media – which would transform the world – had not yet been invented.

The month before the wedding, Edwina's time passed assembling her trousseau and getting to know the in-laws. She attended two lunches at Buckingham Palace, then a weekend at Windsor Castle. The couple made the hottest item in town and London's rival hostesses competed to throw the best party.

Throughout this social whirl Dickie remained officially a serving officer at the naval base at Portsmouth. His diary allowed him little opportunity for duty, and when he did drop in, his reception in the wardroom was frigid. He'd been favoured from the start, the chosen one for two royal tours. He was stuck-up, too good-looking, too up himself, too bloody German. His fellow officers made their hostility clear; some refused to speak to him. 'It was absolute hell,' he said later. He dealt with it by absenting himself and remaining in London.

The wedding at St Margaret's, Westminster composed a splendid affair. Every detail had been planned by Dickie and the faultless stage management captured by the newsreels and all the papers. For their honeymoon the couple drove to Paris in the Rolls, with the chauffeur, Edwina's maid and a mass of luggage packed into the back. They stayed at the Ritz for three nights, then motored to what had been Hesse. They then rushed south to call on the King and Queen of Spain (his Battenberg aunt). Dickie had spent an entire afternoon planning the route and itinerary, calculating optimum daily mileage. His infrequent visits to the Portsmouth naval base had been enlivened by trying to beat his own record: 'One hour, twenty minutes, and remember no front brakes.'

Edwina did not share his obsession with order, which excluded all spontaneity. She wanted to dawdle in picturesque medieval towns, stroll the cobbled market, lunch on the shaded terrace of an unpretentious café... They argued, Edwina quite fiercely. Dickie conceded at once, cancelling their forward hotel bookings without considering this was

the last weekend in July, when all France headed south for
le mois d'août.

Traffic was heavy and it was evening when they reached
Tours and no rooms to be had. Eventually they located an
attic in a *pension* 'with a so-called double bed', while the
chauffeur and maid lodged in a nearby house. The next night
at Bergerac proved even more trying, for their room lay
above the main drain and the hot water boiler exploded in
the bathroom. It did not make the most auspicious start to
a honeymoon and the drive itself was far from a relaxed
experience. Chauffeur and maid sat in the back but fully
shared Edwina's alarm at Dickie's overtaking. And to be
obliged to coordinate their rest stops and all scurry for the
toilettes together made for an unwanted intimacy in the
master–servant relationship.

And another difficulty lay between the couple. Since coming
out Edwina had been quite bold in her flirtations, though
probably still technically a virgin. She possessed a lively interest
in dalliance, if not wide practice in the actuality. Whereas
Dickie had considerable experience of sex from Osborne,
though of a different kind. He wanted very much to be a
father. 'One girl and one boy, wouldn't it be divine, darling?'
They would 'be practically founding the name of Mountbatten'.
But, like many of his class, intimacy embarrassed him. As they,
he disguised it in a jokey facetiousness. He named her breasts
Mutt and Jeff, his foreplay lacked finesse. One of the couple's
innumerable wedding presents was a silver mascot for the
Rolls' radiator, the figure of a naval rating leaning into the
wind, gripping a streaming flag. As the huge car thundered
south on the next stage of their honeymoon the lad's braced
haunches stayed central in its driver's view.

★　★　★

Edwina and Dickie returned from their continental honeymoon to Brook House in August, and Dickie moved his
clothes and few possessions into her marble palace.

His wife received an income of £50,000 a year. He had
no means beyond his naval pay, but he knew it was vital to
maintain his independence. 'Marriage to a very rich woman...
posed problems. I realised forcibly that the only hope of
standing on my own legs was to work. I couldn't hope to
produce the money that Edwina had. So I had to work...
like a beaver to excel.'

The period did not promise well for officers in the Royal
Navy. Of Britain's sixty battleships and battle cruisers, forty-
five were scheduled to be sold or scrapped. Half of the
officers of Dickie's rank would be laid off in the next few
months. No one stood more ripe for the cull than he. He'd
managed to irritate not just his seniors but most of his own
rank. Not unreasonably, they resented him. He had no experience of combat, spent little time at sea and had avoided
three years' duty by poncing about with the Prince of Wales.
On top of which, his splendid marriage and glamorous image
in the press was intensely galling.

At this critical moment it was provocative of Dickie
blithely to request four months' further leave so he and
Edwina could visit America. He remained curiously insensi-
tive to how much many longed to see him get his
comeuppance. Later, he brushed off any suggestion he was
lucky not to have been axed. His skills and leadership ensured
his future, he maintained. Far from the case – he was saved
only by royal intervention. 'He wouldn't starve if he were
fired from the navy,' the Prince of Wales said. 'However, being
related to my father, the Admiralty referred Dickie's case to
King George V...the King eventually agreed.'

So everything was hunky-dory then. He and Edwina

sailed for New York on the *Majestic*, where they had a sitting room, wardroom, dressing room and bathroom – all for the price of a single cabin. They represented a fancy couple and excellent publicity. Edwina felt seasick for most of the crossing and kept to their suite, but late at night he would stroll up to the bridge for what he described as 'a companionable yarn' with the officers on watch.

The newly-weds were, in his words, 'semi-royal' and perceived as such. When they docked in Manhattan journalists and news crews scrambled to interview them. Both adjusted quickly to what was expected. 'Simply ripping to be here,' Edwina was quoted. Next day they gave a press conference then went to the cinema with Douglas Fairbanks and Mary Pickford. They dined with President Harding at the White House and attended the World Series at Madison Square Garden, where they shook hands with Babe Ruth. Edwina watched the game through lorgnettes, having learned to yell 'Attaboy!' and 'Take him out!'

A private railroad car took them to Hollywood, where they'd been lent the Fairbanks' house, Pickfair. Both were passionate movie fans. Their host was the 'little man' himself, Charlie Chaplin. He made a short film for them as a wedding present, casting the couple in a hold-up minidrama. During the shoot 'Edwina made a pass at me,' Chaplin recalled.

On returning to London Dickie was assigned to the battle-ship *Revenge* in the Dardanelles, policing the Balkan states. Wives were not allowed, 'Too dangerous'. He set off by train with 220 kilos of luggage – he'd come to terms with posses-sions.

Edwina's sister Maria had completed her schooling and seized the opportunity to escape from her stepmother at Broadlands to come to live at Brook House. The fact that Edwina was now pregnant and for the moment single slowed her social life not at all. She received as many as four invi-tations every evening. Her escorts included the Prince of Wales and Prince George but also the Milford Havens, Dickie's older brother Georgie and his wife Nada.

Nada presented an archetype of the New Woman who had emerged early in the decade; with ever shorter skirt, Eton crop, brittle conversation and barbed wit. Though the couple kept two small children in the country, there was nothing domestic about their life in London, where both shared with Edwina a fashionable taste for perversity and transgression. As they, she found the Bad Set infinitely more amusing than the Good, and enjoyed the odd line of cocaine in louche company. These were the trendsetters, forever engaged in a restless search for pleasure and hectic gaiety, who would soon be known as 'the Bright Young Things', achieving immortality in the early novels of Evelyn Waugh.

Dickie was aboard the *Revenge* on his way home when he learned he'd become the father of a baby girl. The Prince of Wales agreed to be a godfather, 'so with his permission we named her Edwina…and we kept the name Victoria after my mother, who was of course named after *her* grandmother, the Queen.' In all his moves Dickie was alert to position himself at the heart of the royal family.

In the summer of 1924 Dickie left the *Revenge* to do a signals course at Portsmouth. Signals and wireless communication were clearly the key to naval tactics in the future. The course was not due to start for two months, so the Mountbattens and the Prince of Wales hit on the idea of making up a party to attend the Anglo-American polo tournament on Long Island. The three were in love with America, where the future was being invented in a new age of Fords and flappers and fun. The music they listened to on a wind-up gramophone came from the US, as did the newest dances. Additionally for the Prince was the priceless advantage that he'd be 3,000 miles from the disapproving eye of his father the King.

The trip rated as a vacation not an official visit and the friends put together an in-group to accompany them: Georgie and Nada, Fruity Metcalfe, the Prince's aide, Harold and Zia Wernher, plus half a dozen others. This was the core of what was known as 'the Prince of Wales set'. Also, travelling separately on the ship, was Diana Cooper – on her way to star in *The Miracle* on Broadway – and her husband Duff.

The arrival of the royal party in Manhattan generated huge attention in the press. Edwina wore a light silk dress stopping at the knee, Dickie a blazer and yachting cap, the

Prince a double-breasted suit with wide lapels and two-tone
co-respondent shoes. The party put up at a handful of estates
around Port Washington on Long Island, whose owners
competed to play host. Days were passed at polo games,
swimming, sailing, waterskiing, partying and dancing. Edwina
could spend three hours or more a night on the floor without
flagging. She needed constant activity to burn off her abundant physical energy.

Unfortunately Dickie wasn't feeling well. He was diag-
nosed with tonsillitis and put to bed. Edwina had no cause
to feel neglected; two immediate suitors were to hand. One
was Lytle Hull, a guest in the same house party, the other
Johnny Gaston, a young friend of the Vanderbilts. With one
or the other she went out to dinner, to parties and on to
nightclubs in Manhattan, returning at dawn. When Dickie
complained, she told him he was being boring. The *New
York Times* reported his wife enjoying a high time 'streaking
it up Long Island in one of the fastest motor boats extant.'

Although perfectly matched in many ways and 'a brilliant
couple', the Mountbattens were sexually incompatible. Janet
Morgan, the most insightful of Edwina's biographers, states
that 'their marriage was not a success. Frustrated, Edwina
criticised Dickie, knowing as unhappy people do, how to
cause maximum pain…she had discovered where he was
most vulnerable… He agreed he was a bore, a snob, too
fond of uniforms, a hopeless dancer, a fusspot and rotten
driver but it was unfortunate he admitted it, for Edwina
despised him all the more.'

Dickie's career always attracted rumours of homosexuality.
Letters from Noël Coward – 'Dear Dainty darling' – suggest
a camp intimacy fully condoned by Edwina. Yet the British
press was cautious. It was not until 1975 that a *Daily Mail*
exposé placed him at a Mess evening of high jinks in the

Household Cavalry's barracks, where he'd kneeled, a little stiffly due to age, to service a young trooper in riding boots and spurs.

While a member of the same house party on Long Island and in daily company with the Prince's set of closest friends, Dickie had to confront the fact that his wife was cheating on him nightly with two different lovers. Her unabashed exhilaration showed obvious to everyone.

To play the cuckold, a requisite role in farce, proved exquisitely painful for him. He could not be seen to lose face. He maintained a show of open cordiality with his rivals, and did his best to shape his stiff upper lip into an easy smile. But Edwina was showing her mettle, she had cut loose and gone off the rails, radiant and high on freedom. Dickie suffered, and it was about to get a whole lot worse.

The Prince of Wales grew easily bored, and the schedule of entertainment relentless. Though low in spirits, Dickie did his best to keep up. They were invited to a party in Manhattan by old friends Cornelius and Grace Vanderbilt. A night in the city would allow them to see how Diana's *Miracle* on Broadway compared with the London original, then maybe head uptown to Harlem to suss out the new black singer Grace Vanderbilt mentioned.

It was 2a.m. on a hot summer night and the steps down to the club on West 134th Street descended steep and unlit. In the basement area a grille flipped open on the metal door, a pair of eyes in a black face inspected the trio. 'Yeah?'

Dickie repeated the password they'd been given at the Vanderbilts'. The door opened and they walked into a waft of heat and smell and sound from the club beyond. While he dealt with cash at the desk – for the Prince was notoriously reluctant to put his hand in his pocket – Edwina snapped open a gold compact and added a dab of powder to the sculpted cheekbones that so many of the New York papers had remarked on.

The blare of jazz engulfed them as Dickie marshalled their group into the club proper. The band was hidden by dancing couples but the music bounced off the walls and vibrated in the floor. Edwina sensed her body respond, though it wasn't Dickie's sort of thing; she could see it in his face. But the Prince was already grinning and flicking his fingers to the beat.

The warm air steamed with cigarette and cigar smoke and the smell of booze. The humidity of the night was compounded by cheap scent and sweat and something more into an atmosphere that felt palpable. She sensed it like pungent breath on the bare skin of her neck. The place rocked, jammed with a mixed crush of mobsters, hustlers, bootleggers, figures from showbiz and Broadway here after the show – plus white society toffs like themselves, set among a flux of neighbourhood hookers and players, all of them black. Yet no friction grated in the mix. This was Prohibition and alcohol unlawful, but a taste for liquor and jazz bonded the clientele into a club. The cops were paid off, still there was an illicit tang to it, a shared defiance. The rules suspended here and all was swell. Sure there was trouble occasionally when someone threw a punch or pulled a gun, but otherwise respect obtained. Though it felt edgy, it was oddly safe here.

They got a table but it cost Dickie high – he was an embarrassing tightwad like the Prince. Did a small throb of irritation pulse within her as Edwina glanced at her husband? He was so obviously not at ease here. He had to shout to order drinks and the waiter found his English accent baffling in the racket. The dance floor was shifting. The black girls in their bright trashy dresses loved this music for its strut and raunch, it fit their moves. The scene was a blur to Edwina, who didn't like to be seen wearing glasses. Drinks appeared, banged down on the table without ceremony. She tasted hers, and the bootleg hooch scalded her throat. She didn't enjoy liquor, but a dive like this was not for milksops.

A hot lick caused her to look toward the band, six black guys she could glimpse only momentarily beyond the kicking couples on the floor. She didn't even know the steps to this dance, the Charleston hadn't reached London yet. Edwina adored to dance. Dickie wasn't up for it, but the Prince would ask her soon, she knew.

The number ended on a high note. A break while the couples went back to their tables or made for the bar. The Prince turned to her, his boyish face lit up in approval. Then an arpeggio of notes rippling up the scale, a beat, and the piano player took it solo, accompanying his own voice. A voice that would become famous, that would speak for this wayward age and catch its essence, but which at this time was still unknown beyond a handful of Harlem dives like this one, where Edwina sat enthralled at first encounter. The accent sounded not American but educated British, though glossed with a warmer tone. A very personal voice, it spoke close, teasingly intimate. If you were a woman, it spoke to you alone.

Without shifting her gaze, Edwina felt for her glasses in her clutch. The beam of the spotlight on the piano player was fuzzed with coils of drifting smoke. First to strike her was his looks, a second later his body ease. Sat tall in a

perfectly cut tuxedo, leaned back, his assurance showed unas-
sertive but visible. Presence – plus that voice. He had his
audience from the first bars, they were with him, and he
knew it. He was young, only a year older than Edwina, as
she would make it her business to discover a few days later.
His was a handsome gold-brown face with firm features,
straight nose, full mouth, an engaging very white smile. Its
lineaments hinted at intelligence and wit. And that nonchalance and *ease*...

Later, charm was what most remarked on as their first
impression. And they used the word 'mesmerising' about his
delivery and performance, both on and off stage. The audience tonight held captive to that charm. As was Edwina,

enslaved by the music, the voice, the man. All were foreign to her, dangerous and alluring. She wanted a part of it for herself.

'Hutch' Leslie Hutchinson, who was destined to become Edwina's lover, was born a year before her into notably less promising circumstances than she.

Gouyave is a small fishing town on the coast of Grenada in the Caribbean, known as the 'spice isle' and – except on Main Street, which reeks of fish – the tropic air wafts fragrant with their scent. Hutch's father George was a shopkeeper, a respected figure who played the organ in church, where attendance was compulsory. Dark-skinned, he'd married the daughter of a Scottish plantation owner, white and of a higher caste then himself.

Hutch was a pretty child with pale brown skin. Slavery had been abolished in Britain and its colonies in 1833 and the following seventy years saw free racial mixing, resulting in every variation of colour. The paler the better, the prevailing view. Hutch became acclimatised to whitey early. At eight he received piano lessons from an Anglican canon's daughter, whose friends composed the island's gentry. He was invited to their tennis parties, not to play but as a ballboy. Still, he learned the game, which would prove handy later when he reinvented himself as an English gentleman.

At the Anglican school he worked hard, winning a scholarship to the Grenada secondary school in the capital. There he practised dutifully at classical piano; he possessed real talent. He already knew his future lay in a wider world than the island could deliver. Inspiration came from his English teacher, who coached him in received pronunciation until he lost his Caribbean accent. 'You would have thought he

was a white man,' a friend recalled. At sixteen he took a job
as a government clerk at £5 per month, then a girl he knew
offered him a cheap ticket to New York – she'd fallen in
love and changed her mind about emigrating there.

George stepped up to the plate as a supportive father.
Hutch enrolled in Meharry Medical College in Nashville,
Tennessee, one of the few institutions open to black people.
His godfather, Dr Dunbar Hughes, contributed to the fees.
During his later English makeover Hutch reinvented his past,
as did others in this book. The hint at a professional background was subtle. Some received the impression he'd
practised as a lawyer before taking to music. But then, a
tooled leather case of surgical instruments in his dressing
room suggested medicine. Whichever – the allusion modu-
lated into personal myth.

In fact, Hutch studied only for nine months at college
before dropping out, when his father cancelled his allowance.
With only a few dollars in his pocket he headed for the Big
Apple, the magnet for every ambitious new arrival. New York
was not especially welcoming to immigrants at that time, if
they were black. Hotels, restaurants, park benches and drinking
fountains were denied them, they stayed confined to the most
servile jobs. In Grenada he'd been accustomed to security,
here he subsisted alone in an alien city. 'The walls, the
skyscrapers all round me scared me stiff,' he later told the
Chicago Defender. 'It was like being in a cage… I became an
elevator boy in a palatial New York hotel…then I was out of
a job again and absolutely broke. Imagine winter in New York
when you are down on your luck – the blizzards, the biting
cold…the grey damp pavements and oh! that smell of food
from restaurants…' He was hungry, cold and destitute.

★ ★ ★

It could not have felt so at that moment, but throughout his life Hutch had an uncanny ability to be in the right place at the right time. In New York, Paris, then London, in each he would be present at the first swelling of a wave. America was about to take off on what Scott Fitzgerald called 'the greatest, grandest, gaudiest spending spree in history'. A democracy of shared prosperity came to embrace the country, excluding only its farmers. The machine age was accompanied by its own aesthetic, Art Deco. Soaring towers of concrete and plate glass rose to overtop the Manhattan skyline, and the world was reinvented in the breathless now. Many viewed progress with a near-religious awe. For many, faith in the machine replaced belief in God.

Meanwhile, Hutch lived in Harlem in one or another walk-up room. He was short on comforts, short on decent food, short on sleep, but he possessed remarkable self-discipline. He practised daily on piano in bars or anyplace he could, sometimes with a plate on the piano for tips. He had a feel for this new music. Jazz, swing and blues soon became the defining sounds of the decade, which coincided with commercial radio in America, the advent of mass media. In 1923 'Kitten on the Keys' featured as the first number in pure ragtime to be broadcast. Wireless spread it around the world through the free medium of the air. That fall Hutch made his first recording: 'Original Charleston'.

He gained his initial exposure to white audiences at Barron's, on the corner of Seventh Avenue and 13th Street. He was filling in for Fats Waller, who said, 'I knew him when he didn't have a pair of pants to his ass.' In his eponymous memoir, the club's owner Bricktop describes Barron's as '*The* Harlem spot. Only light-skinned negroes could get in... Every night the limousines pulled up and rich whites got out, all dolled up in their furs and jewels. They were the Who's Who of New York's Roaring Twenties, gangsters rubbed shoulders with high society.'

One evening at the club on West 134th Street during a break Hutch is told of a table of Brits in the audience who want to meet him. On joining them for a drink he recognises who they are, their pictures have been in all the New York tabloids. He's not awed but easy in the meet. Charm gets him by, charm is what gets them all by.

Talk is of jazz and the new dances: the shimmy, the camel, the black bottom and the Charleston. It's the Prince and the woman who do the chat, her husband's a stiff. They're raving about the Charleston, they *have* to learn the moves... Here? No, not in public. Lunch, some swanky place on Long Island...they'll send a speedboat to pick him up. The white woman has this clipped way of speaking, tense manner, unyielding gaze, brilliant blue eyes. Maybe she's on something. Then beneath the table Hutch feels her stockinged foot brush his ankle...

Edwina met Hutch again two days later when their host's speedboat brought him to Long Island, where he taught her and the Prince to dance the Charleston. She did not get the opportunity to be alone with him but both were keenly aware of the attraction. When Dickie returned to England soon after, she remained in New York for a further two weeks before following him home.

'Home' now included a second residence, for the Mountbattens were leasing Ashdean, a large country house with stabling, paddock, riding school, golf course and tennis court. Its staff included nineteen servants and eight gardeners. Meanwhile, they kept Brook House as 'the biggest *pied a terre* in town'. Ashdean was only twenty miles from Portsmouth, where Dickie was doing his signals course. He roared off every morning in his Rolls, returning at six. Every weekend meant a house party with half a dozen guests. The couple were never alone together. A new arrangement – never discussed – governed their relationship.

With the encouragement of Edwina and the Prince of Wales, Hutch moved to Paris, where they fulfilled their promise to take in his act. They flew over with the Prince piloting the plane. On subsequent visits she was accompanied by Nada Milford Haven, who in Janet Morgan's words 'had a nose for peculiar nightclubs' and could sniff out the latest scene.

Hutch found himself in Paris in the golden age of US expatriation. The franc was at nineteen to the dollar and, per the young composer Virgil Thomson, 'Americans flocked to Paris to get screwed, sharpen their wits and eat like kings for nothing.' The cast included Hemingway, the Scott Fitzgeralds, the Murphys, Ford Madox Ford, Gertrude Stein and Alice B. Toklas. All centred around Shakespeare and Company, the bookshop run by Sylvia Beach. Paris at that period was a feast, the greatest place on earth to be alive.

Hutch's arrival in the city followed the appearance of the Ballets Nègres from America, with the nineteen-year-old Josephine Baker its star attraction. The show set a fashion for all things black: music, painting, sculpture, jewellery, interior design. In the hedonism, superficiality and cynicism of the Twenties, black was viewed as primitive and authentic. Also beautiful. Baker's audiences saw her jutted black ass as the savage real.

To date, Hutch had passed most of his life in trying to distance himself far as he could from the savage real, yet the warmth of his welcome into the fashionable milieu provided a most heartening surprise. He was taken up by Cole Porter and his wife Linda, who hosted a salon on rue Monsieur. She was worldly and rich, ten years older than her composer husband, 'a homosexual who had never seen the closet' in the words of lyricist Alan Lerner. Cole became Hutch's lover, tutoring him in cosmopolitan style and *modes du jour*. Hutch enjoyed affairs with many men, including Noël Coward. Bisexuality in both genders was considered the height of chic.

That cult crossed the Channel to launch in London in 1926 with C.B. Cochran's revue *Blackbirds*. Within days it was the rage. People went to it many times; the Prince of Wales saw it twenty times from a box curtained from the audience, where he danced and mimed the players' moves. It was a simple matter for Edwina to get Hutch to London. She asked him to perform at a party she threw with her friend Lady Gibbons. Hutch sang Cole Porter numbers he'd rehearsed with the master. 'I'll never forget the warm-hearted way they welcomed me to town.'

Edwina invited Cochran to the evening, where she suggested he feature Hutch in his new production at the London Pavilion, which promised fifty six-foot chorus girls in costumes designed by Coco Chanel. He had announced it as his farewell show. On the day of the premiere a queue formed at 5a.m. The revue proved a triumph. From their box Edwina and her complaisant husband showered Hutch in the orchestra pit with a sparkling rain of coloured sweeties. In New York the *Amsterdam News* reported, 'There hasn't ever been a pianist and singer who has come to London and achieved such wonderful success as Mr Hutchinson, also entertaining at least two private parties every night. It is Lord and Lady Mountbatten and the Prince of Wales, who have made it possible for him to get in with this class of people.'

By now Hutch had become solo entertainer at the Café de Paris and a must-have at the smartest parties. Barbara Cartland, who'd come out with Edwina, notes that he was 'the first nigger many of us had ever talked to'. He moved to Chez Victor, a more intimate nighterie for the in-crowd, where he gained another royal groupie, the King of Spain. Joan Vyvyan, a fan who followed Hutch everywhere, says, 'He was madly attractive and intelligent... He could inject more sex into one bar of music than most people knew in a lifetime. At Chez Victor he used to sing directly to Edwina Mountbatten, who on one occasion took off her chiffon scarf and put it around his neck and kissed him... How we envied her!'

Edwina gave him a gold cigarette case engraved to him with her love. He smoked often, and the accessory attracted notice. He showed the inscription to many – a rash if understandable misjudgement. The gift would prove a mistake.

Edwina's promiscuity was an open secret among her friends, her affairs gave rise to continuing gossip. Several have commented upon her casual approach to sex; if she found a man attractive she made the first move. She didn't give a toss for others' view on her behaviour – including her husband's.

'I was terribly upset and found it hard to believe,' Dickie later told Richard Hough. 'It was an awful shock.' He was deeply mortified. Since first moving into Brook House he'd had his own bedroom, visiting Edwina's only on invitation. Now he had it remodelled as the cabin on his last ship, *Revenge*. Walls and floor were sprayed white metallic to resemble steel plating, the windows converted into portholes containing *trompe l'oeil* views of Valletta harbour. Against them he arranged his miniature cut-outs of the Mediterranean Fleet. The flick of a switch changed the scene to moonlight. Soothed by the hum of a ship's engine from a gadget he'd devised himself, he could lie on his narrow bunk operating the fleet's Aldis lamps to flicker messages to each other in Morse. Here he could escape to an uncomplicated manly world where he was in command.

The view through the portholes became real when he was posted to Malta as the fleet's wireless officer. Edwina chose at first to remain in London, where she'd started an affair with Mike Wardell, manager of the *Evening Standard*. When she did move to Malta, it was with some style. They rented a large house with garden and three guest cottages beneath the walls of Valletta. The navy did not provide married quarters. It was served by two categories of officers, PO (pay only) or PM (private means). Only the richest PMs like Dickie could afford to bring out their wives.

The Mountbattens arrived on station 'with their own bloody great yacht' followed by his string of polo ponies. Dickie didn't trust his local stable lads to exercise them, so some of the POs were asked to. The suggestion set the tone and attitude with which the couple were regarded. Naval stations are by their nature suburban and dull, and the advent of this stylish couple gave the community something to talk about. In the recollection of one young officer: 'She was certainly the most beautiful woman on Malta. She had quite a fast reputation already…we were all looking forward to her parties.'

They were disappointed. Brother Georgie was already here (as gunnery officer) with Nada, and, though the Mountbattens kept their house supplied with imported guests, neither PMs nor POs got to be invited. And Dickie had no need to suck up to senior ranks, he had higher strings to pull.

He embarked on his naval duties with brio. Shipboard wireless was a new invention, and as result of his signals course he became an expert. He was invariably sure he knew more about any subject than anyone, and in this case he did. Wireless perfectly suited his fastidious taste for detail. He valued precision, order and control. A rigid self-imposed regimen governed his life. Each day was scheduled, with set times allocated to work, study, exercise, devising inventions, plus fixed periods for family and socialising. It drove Edwina frantic with irritation.

Malta could not hold her for long. She returned to London for sister Maria's wedding, then – though again pregnant, for Dickie wanted a son – took off with his sixty-five-year-old mother on an archaeological tour of Algeria in the Rolls with herself at the wheel. On the drive home across Spain the pains began. Checking into Barcelona's Ritz, she called King Alfonso, asking him to send a doctor. The line was poor; he understood her to be in danger. Very soon the hotel was secured by armed soldiery and the Military Governor burst into her suite with a drawn revolver. Shortly after, she gave birth to a daughter, Pamela.

Edwina did not feed the baby herself. To do so was unthinkable among her class and known to ruin the breasts. Pamela was raised in Malta by a nanny and nursemaids. Meanwhile Edwina embarked upon a period of almost continuous travel. With her friend Marjorie Brecknock she sailed for New York, then they moved on to San Simeon as guests of William Randolph Hearst, to Hollywood and to

New Orleans. She picked up two new beaux, one an actor, Larry Gray, the other, Ronald Colman. She and Marjorie continued to Mexico, Guatemala and Honduras, fired by a newly discovered interest in Mayan art. To recover from their discomforts in the jungle, they chartered a boat with crew and sailed the Caribbean. They were in no hurry, theirs was a cruise in every sense. Two suntanned ladies of leisure, sleek and fit from their travels, they trawled from island to island, sampling the adventure each provided. Her friends referred to these months as Edwina's 'Black Period'.

The Mountbattens were in Malta with the King of Spain as a house guest when the story broke in the downmarket *Sunday People* in May 1932:

> SOCIETY SHAKEN BY TERRIBLE SCANDAL
> I am asked to reveal today the sequel to a scandal which has shaken society to the very depths. It concerns one of the leading hostesses in the country – a woman highly connected and immensely rich. Her association with a coloured man became so marked that they were the talk of the West End. Then one day the couple were caught in compromising circumstances. The sequel is that the society woman has been given hints to clear out of England for a couple of years to let the affair blow over, and the hint comes from a quarter which cannot be ignored.

Few failed to identify 'the society woman' as Edwina, and it was clear the 'quarter which cannot be ignored' meant Buckingham Palace.

The Mountbattens were informed by telegraph of the story

in the first of a flurry of cables between family and lawyers over the following days. To react by issuing a statement or return to London was judged a mistake. The *People* was a rag known for scurrilous gossip, what it published could be dismissed. Nevertheless, waiting for copies to arrive in Malta three days later surely proved a strain. Edwina seldom went into Valletta and never to the base except to board their yacht. She could remain sequestered in the house with her royal guest, but Dickie had to continue with his duties at the naval station, where it must have been excruciating to meet the scarce-concealed smirk on the face of his fellow officers.

Yet the item was only a slur by an anonymous hack in a no-account tabloid. With no follow-up, it would have slid from recall. But it was brought to the attention of the King who was outraged, pronouncing it a libel on the monarchy that could not be ignored. The Mountbattens were told they must issue a writ on two counts: that Edwina was conducting an affair with 'a coloured man', and that the Palace had instructed her to live aboard.

The case, which came to trial two months later, had certain curious aspects. The court opened at the unprecedented hour of 9.30a.m. and no notice was given of the hearing. In result, the public gallery remained empty with no member of the press in attendance. Additionally, the plaintiff's counsel was allowed to put Edwina in the witness box to swear on oath that she had never ever met the 'coloured man' referred to. Later, she confided to her sister Maria she had lied in court.

The *People* issued an unqualified apology with 'genuine and profound regrets'. It published a retraction and Edwina refused damages. But the case ensured that all Britain – and beyond – heard about the scandal. Gossip divided on the identity of the black man. Some favoured the actor Paul Robeson, whom she was known to have slept with, for the two had caused a scandal in Jamaica by swimming naked together after a concert. The in-group bet on Hutch. In Malta the fleet ran a book on it.

The day following the trial, the Mountbattens were summoned to lunch at Buckingham Palace in a show of family solidarity staged for the media and populace, involving two hours of agonising embarrassment for all present. A photograph shows Edwina stepping into the car taking her to meet the in-laws. Her discomfort is visible, for by now a graphic version of the story has spread to reach the royal ear.

As retold in a breathless voice, it would appear that she and Hutch – or was it Robeson? – had reached the end of a light gourmet luncheon in Brook House and moved upstairs to the master bedroom where the two are closely engaged when a most unfortunate incident occurs – a mishap that more usually affects dogs. The anus contracts in spasm, the male penis is trapped in situ and the two are unable to disengage. Here, it presents the couple with an acute social dilemma, for to disconnect requires outside assistance. With dogs the traditional solution is to throw a bucket of cold water over the copulating duo, but the staff at Brook House when eventually summoned to the rescue see this as a poor career move. Delicate attempts to ease their difficulty prove ineffective so an ambulance is called and the still-united lovers are wrapped in a sheet and transported to hospital, where separation is effected.

How the bets were settled at the naval station in Malta is unrecorded, but when later questioned on the matter Hutch was wont to reply, 'It was the other fellow.'

★　★　★

Edwina could play a fair game at poker; no one guessed her hand from her face. She showed an impenetrable façade though she divined the gossip. Her self-control showed firm; she'd learned a seamless cool.

War with Germany broke out in September 1939. She sent her children to the States to lodge with the Vanderbilts and closed Brook House, moving into Kensington Palace, where Dickie's elderly mother occupied a 'grace and favour' apartment for free. Enlisting in the St John Ambulance Brigade, she took a crash course in first aid along with twenty-five female volunteers. She learned how to deal with the effects of blast and shrapnel, burns, smoke inhalation and shattered bone. *Tatler* ran a piece on her, prompting many readers to volunteer. On 4 September 1940 she enrolled in Westminster Hospital, close by the Houses of Parliament, as an intern on the wards.

Three days afterward in the late afternoon, 350 German warplanes – heavy bombers with fighter escort – followed the sunlit course of the Thames at an altitude of 10,000 feet to strafe London. The Luftwaffe's main target were the docks, surrounded by narrow streets and mean houses where the local population lived. The bombers droned overhead in successive waves, discharging their load of landmines, high explosive and incendiaries, meeting no opposition in the air or from the ground. Warehouses and homes blazed on both banks of the Thames, spilling smoke that choked the lungs. The Blitz had started; the bombing would continue uninterrupted for a further fifty-seven nights.

Edwina's job title read Coordinator and Commander of St John's Emergency Personnel. Its actuality consisted in inspecting every air-raid shelter in the East End, visiting eight or ten in a twelve-hour shift. Night after night she set out in her small Morris car with hooded lights and drove through blacked-out streets littered with broken glass and debris from the bombardment, the darkness thundering, sliced by searchlights.

Richard Hough records a fellow worker's account of one shelter she visited:

> We went first to a warehouse off the Commercial Road. It was still quite early in the night but every inch of space had been taken up by whole families with children... In the half light it was like something out of Dante's *Inferno* – people trying to sleep on deck chairs, on the wooden floor, on old crates, anywhere and everywhere. We were told that there were no lavatories for the ten thousand or so people and that was why the floor was already awash with urine and there were piles of excrement. Later Edwina managed to discover the lavatories – no more than buckets really – behind some sacking. Two of them! Edwina talked to some of the people as she walked about, touching some of the old people, reassuring them that things would be improved. And so they were – with incredible speed.

She got people to move ass because she could. She picked up a telephone and with one call got through to the top... to deploy her cut-glass accent and steely determination to obtain whatever needed doing. She could knife through bureaucratic red tape and prove supremely capable and effective. In the work she found a purpose for her restless energy, a cause outside of self, and in it pinned down an elusive purpose to her life.

★   ★   ★

Dickie too 'had a good war', in the phrase used for a few years afterward, quite without irony. At its start he went to sea in command of a flotilla of destroyers, never driving his own at less than full speed ahead. He fought with valour in several naval battles. His ship, HMS *Kelly*, was sunk by German dive bombers during the Battle of Crete in 1941. She went down gloriously with her remaining guns still firing, and the engagement resulted in a classic movie, *In Which We Serve*, with Noël Coward playing Dickie's heroic part in the action. He was promoted to Chief of Combined Operations that same year, and in 1943 became a full admiral and Supreme Commander of Allied Forces in East Asia.

In February 1947, Dickie was appointed last Viceroy of India with Edwina perched imperially on a matching throne beside him. His brief was to accomplish the country's transition to independence as a united entity, free from British rule. The Raj was bitterly resented by the entire population of some 400 million people made up of Hindus, Sikhs, Muslims, Buddhists, Christians, plus more than 500 individual princely states, each ruled by a maharajah. This diverse multitude spoke in twenty languages and divided into more than 300 separate castes. To integrate them represented an impossible task, which Dickie was temperamentally and intellectually unfitted to resolve.

One of the main players in the discussions was Jawaharlal Nehru, leader of the Congress Party, whom Dickie described as 'a great snob and pro-English...marvellous to look at... wonderful eyes, very tall and handsome. He and Edwina got on marvellously.' The other was the intractable Mohammed Ali Jinnah of the Muslim League. 'It was almost impossible to warm to him...my God, he was cold.' The two met as irreconcilable opponents.

'It was Jinnah and the Muslim riots and massacres that convinced me of two things,' Dickie said. 'The first was that we had to be quick to find a solution. The second, that it was more important to be quick than to have an undivided India. Government was losing control, I decided that we had to be out not in fourteen months but in five months.' Mahatma Gandhi's vision of a united India already lay in ruins. Now Dickie determined that the only answer was Partition: to divide the subcontinent into two separate countries, India and Pakistan.

A Boundary Commission hastily drew the dividing line upon the map. Partition was effected not on ethnic or political principles but purely on religious grounds. Independence was celebrated on 15 August 1947, but by then the country had already disintegrated into chaos. The transition came rushed and botched. The resident force of English police, and garrisons of British troops, who might have maintained some control, had been shipped back home in the haste for independence.

Riots of a scale and horror beyond human memory spread across the subcontinent. People who for generations had coexisted in an orderly manner, if not in amity, turned upon their neighbours in unholy violence. Between one and two million men, women and children were shot, hacked, or burned to death, or expired from famine. A further twelve million on the 'wrong' side of the line fled their homes for the dubious safety on the other. Not to be made welcome; the destitute refugee is never welcome, wherever their provenance.

Lord Mountbatten, luxuriously ensconced in the Viceroy's palace attended by 200 servants, was seen to be presiding over bloody anarchy. Newspapers and newsreels conveyed the horror of the riots to the British people: independence proved a disaster. The right-wing press, led by Beaverbrook's *Daily Express*, accused the Viceroy of 'giving away the Empire'. When the Mountbattens returned to England, Churchill pointedly refused to shake his hand.

From very early in the negotiations on Partition, Edwina engaged in a love affair with Nehru. Fully condoned by Dickie, it was the closest relationship she ever knew, enduring not just in India but for the rest of her life. When she died in 1960, Nehru's letters lay to hand by her bed. On 25 February her coffin was piped on board a naval frigate at Portsmouth. Escorted by another warship, it went to sea. The cortège was accompanied by two destroyers sent from India to attend the ceremony, one bearing Nehru's personal wreath of marigolds, which was cast onto the waves at the site of her burial.

Dickie's reputation emerged stained by the consequences of Partition; self-esteem though shielded him from awareness, and he remained blind to criticism. Nor did the debacle damage his career. He became Commander in Chief of the Mediterranean Fleet, then NATO Commander of Allied Forces Mediterranean in 1952. His final posting at the Admiralty was as First Sea Lord and Chief of the Naval Staff, the position his father had occupied forty years previously. He was murdered in 1979 while spending the summer at one of his properties, Classiebawn Castle in Ireland, with his elder daughter and her family. The IRA planted a bomb in his fishing boat, which detonated at sea, killing Mountbatten, his grandson (fourteen) and the boatboy (seventeen). On the same day, the IRA commemorated the atrocity by ambushing and killing eighteen soldiers in the Parachute Regiment. Dickie's state funeral, watched by the nation on TV, took place at Westminster Abbey attended by the Queen, Royal Family, and notables from around the world.

★   ★   ★

The Mountbattens made news on the day they married, and continued to do so throughout their careers. They were prototypes of a kind, celebrities in an era before there were 'celebs'. They played out their lives before a public audience. Perfectly cast, they enacted leading roles in a soap opera followed by millions.

Noël Coward, who hadn't seen them for years, re-encountered the couple he'd been so close to in youth at a reception soon after their India period. He was dismayed by how grand they'd grown. Both were vested with a bland aloof regality. No sign existed of the charm, spontaneity and wit that once made them such fun to hang out with. They had *become* the characters they portrayed and morphed inescapably into their public image. No trace of individual personality remained detectable.

A marble bust of Dickie Mountbatten stands on a plinth just inside the entrance to the RAC club in Pall Mall. Visitors encounter it as they mount the steps into the lobby. An old member of the club, who'd served under him in the war and had the habit of lunching at the club, followed an invariable routine on leaving the building afterward. He would pause in front of the statue, glare at it for seconds… then slap it in the face.

6

THE MESSALINA COMPLEX

Many of her peers described Edwina as a 'nymphomaniac'.
Although highly sexed women have always existed in history,
they were not characterised as a recognisable species until
the late eighteenth century by the French doctor Bienville
in his treatise *Nymphomania, or a Dissertation Concerning the
Furor Uterinus*.

Once named, nymphomania became medicalised. During
the following decades many doctors took up the study and
declared themselves specialists in the disease. A patient
referred to them was questioned closely on her symptoms
and activities then examined physically. The root of the
problem was soon identified as the clitoris. Physicians
expressed their shock at witnessing the arousal, 'loss of control'
and 'very evident delight' their patients exhibited on them
touching the area with their instrument.

Indications that a woman might take pleasure in sex –
within marriage or, worse still, outside it – perturbed the
early Victorian mind. The female role was submissive and
passive; anything else was deemed abnormal. The purpose
of sex was solely to conceive a child, other reasons deemed
aberrant. Sex should take place only between a man and
woman, and any variant on the missionary position was

labelled 'degenerate'. By the end of the nineteenth century
the medical profession had put together a wide catalogue of
unnatural perversions. Cunnilingus, fellatio, fetishism, homosexuality, lesbianism, paedophilia, masochism, sadism,
necrophilia, voyeurism, satyriasis and nymphomania. Those
who performed these acts were deviants, their character
warped. A woman did not *have* nymphomania, she *was* a
nymphomaniac, a pervert.

Then Freud cast a new light upon the subject. In the
middle of the twentieth century, when Edwina was in her
fifties, the psychiatrist Frank Caprio identified such 'excessive
heterosexuality' and promiscuity as the 'Messalina Complex'.
For two millennia Messalina has denoted the epitome of the
hypersexual female; she represents, as it were, the Platonic
Form of the currently labelled 'sex addict'.

Like Edwina, Messalina was born into wealth and connection. Much of her childhood passed at the court of the
Emperor Caligula. At fifteen or sixteen, she married his
successor, Claudius (forty-eight), described by his own mother
as 'a man whom Mother Nature had begun her work upon
but abandoned before completing'. He proved as unsatisfactory
a husband as Dickie, seemingly indifferent or complaisant
about her extramarital behaviour. As the Emperor's wife, she
came to think herself invulnerable. Her many lovers included
the best-looking members of the Praetorian Guard, and the
blood-smeared trophy gladiator-of-the-day in the Colosseum.
In the brothel, where for a while she posed as a prostitute,
she engaged in a contest with the reigning professional on
who could despatch the most men in succession, achieving a
score of twenty-five to her rival's twenty-four.

Messalina's increasingly brazen acts seemed to elicit no
reaction from Claudius; they were ignored. Perhaps his indifference provoked her final excess: to stage a lavish mock

marriage to her lover Silius, followed by a celebratory debauch. Claudius was quickly apprised of the sacrilege, which made him look a fool. His soldiers found her with her mother in the Gardens of Lucullus. Offered suicide, she botched the job and was decapitated by an officer with his sword.

Messalina achieved notoriety even before her death, but the fact that her name has remained a byword designating an 'oversexed' woman is largely due to the poet Juvenal, who provides a vivid glimpse of her in his *Sixth Satire*:

> ...hear what Claudius suffered.
> Soon as his august wife was sure that her husband
>   was sleeping,
> This imperial whore preferred, to a bed in the palace,
> Some low mattress, put on the hood she wore in the
>   night-time,
> Sneaked through the streets alone, or with only a
>   single companion,
> Hid her black hair in a blonde-coloured wig, and
>   entered a brothel.
> Reek of old sheets, still warm – her cell was reserved
>   for her, empty,
> Held in the name of Lycisca. There she took off her
>   dress,
> Showed her golden tits and private parts,
> Took the customers on, with gestures more than
>   inviting,
> Asked and received her price and had a wonderful
>   evening,
> Then, when the pimp let the girls go home, she
>   sadly departed,

Last of them all to leave, still hot, with a woman's
erection,
Tired by her men, but unsatisfied still, her cheeks all
discoloured,
Rank with the smell of the lamps, filthy, completely
disgusting,
Perfumed with the aroma of whore-house, and home,
at last, to her pillow.

Juvenal's verse of 2,000 years ago displays pretty much the
same reaction of prurient fascination, alarm, challenge, disgust
and lust most men demonstrate to her female equivalent
today.

'No one is more arrogant toward women, more aggressive
or scornful, than the man who is anxious about his virility',
states Simone de Beauvoir, adding, 'Men do not like tomboys,
nor bluestockings, nor thinking women; too much audacity,
culture, intelligence, or character frightens them.'

Emancipated highly sexed women have always been feared
by males, particularly if they possessed privilege and power.
Nymphomania remained categorised as a 'disease' through
most of the nineteenth century. Treatment included diet,
exercise and ice compresses applied to the genitals. If ineffective, a surgeon was called in to remove the patient's
clitoris, and cauterise her labia with a red hot instrument.
Early in the twentieth century, the condition was reclassified
as 'moral delinquency'. Delinquent, 'wayward' or 'sexually
psychopathic' girls were brought to court on charges of
'disorderly conduct', or institutionalised as 'incorrigible'. By
the 1920s (Edwina's youth), it was a psychosexual disorder.

You will not have failed to note that every one of these

diagnoses, categories and labels was devised by *males*. Meanwhile the equivalent condition in men continued to be admired and later rated an alpha male characteristic. High sexual energy informs many successful men's and women's lives. Now the word 'nymphomania' has fallen into disuse, as soon may 'sex addict'. The concept is held by many not to exist, being instead a lifestyle choice to live boldly in a manner only possible in the West today.

7

'I AM NEWS JUST BECAUSE IT'S ME'

Victoria…Mary…Aimee…Edwina…all found fame along with their share of infamy, but they earned that fame. They stood apart, were more than merely figures in an historical landscape. They showed high courage, they acted, they changed things, they achieved. Certainly, all were touched by the magic wand of charisma but they justified that gift in their subsequent careers.

Margaret Whigham did not, though it could be said she earned her notoriety. What she did possess was another quality entirely, and it was priceless. She was born on the Upper East Side of Manhattan, and the truth was revealed to her in infancy: she was better than anyone else. Self-belief stayed with her till the end of her life. She did not just feel entitled, she *was* entitled.

Nothing in the course of her well-insulated childhood in Manhattan shook Margaret's assurance of privilege; her parents' wealth guaranteed respect in America, along with prompt service. People perceived her as she saw herself. When she moved with her family to live in England in her early teens, those she met with did not necessarily share the same view on her position.

Class demonstrated a peculiarly British preoccupation. Its

system had remained set since the Industrial Revolution created a prosperous bourgeoisie in the Midlands and North who aspired to join the gentry, usually by marriage into its ranks. People felt a corresponding need to 'place' others they encountered in the same hierarchy of status and prestige. This swift assessment did not rely on knowledge of your wealth or lack of, but solely upon the image signalled by your appearance, dress, bearing and accent. Their interpretation would be later nuanced by ascertaining your background, education, profession and lifestyle.

Margaret made the grade on first impression, but she failed in background and status – she came from trade. Yet her imperious manner enabled her to get away with the bluff to those uninitiated in the code.

During her youth in the Twenties and through four decades afterward, entitlement *worked*. Others responded by kowtowing

to that chill face and air of commanding hauteur. It convinced not just tradesmen but most people she encountered. But it did not make her friends; very many detested her. With good reason; conscience was unknown to her and human empathy outside her emotional range. Lacking any sense of humour, she came across cold and rude.

WASP, privileged, beautiful and thin, her superiority was entirely sincere, she *expected* deference as her natural right. She got it. She and other privileged individuals, professions and institutions of the period continued to receive the same respect in Britain until a precise date. Between 1963 and 1965 deference was rudely and decisively abolished in England. Margaret was a key player in the events that brought about its destruction; she helped put paid to an entire culture.

The Polaroid photographs shown to the divorce court comprised a set of four. The first was of a naked man full frontal, displaying an impressive erection, but with his head cut off by the top edge of the picture. The next showed a naked woman crouched before him, gripping his penis in both hands while fellating him. In the third she was spread out beneath him, legs in the air, the faces of both obscured. The last shot resembled the first, but with the man's erection detumescing. The handwritten captions to each were: *Before. During. Oh!* and *Finished*.

Who was the headless man? The question dominated the front page in every newspaper through winter and into the spring of 1963. At dinner parties, in pubs, at launderettes and over the garden fence, it was the topic most hotly discussed in Britain.

The identity of the woman was more easily established by the court. The finger of one hand grasping that steady member was adorned with a ring recognised as a family heirloom given to Margaret Argyll by her husband Ian, the Duke. After first categorically denying the fact, Margaret admitted it was indeed she. The photos were of course of her husband and herself recording a special moment in their marital relationship; the occasion had slipped her mind. Her defence put Ian in an invidious position. He could prove her to be lying, but only at high cost of embarrassment to himself. He would have to display his own sadly insignificant equipment to the court and expose himself to public ridicule. It was an agonising predicament.

Margaret's father, George Whigham, was the last of ten children in a 'good' but impoverished Scottish family, who remembered until the end of his life the humiliation of being sent to school wearing his sister's cast-off boots. Money was short at home, yet all in it were raised with sound Presbyterian values and the work ethic. An upbringing that evidently took root, for five of the sons, including George, grew up to become millionaires.

When Margaret was born in 1912 her parents were living in some style in New York where her father, an engineer, was involved in building railways, the boom industry of the period in America, though he made his fortune otherwise. George, who had an eye for the main chance, happened to come across three Swiss scientist brothers who had invented a formula for viscose acetate (artificial silk) that would revolutionise the clothing business. At George's canny suggestion, they formed a company, naming their product Celanese – the first man-made fibre. In a single day, only six years later, shares in the corporation jumped from $1.05 to $30.

On Park Avenue Margaret's parents lived the life of the

fashionably rich. Their only child, she with her nanny accompanied them on holidays at Southampton on Long Island, to Virginia, Scotland and Switzerland. She passed little time in their presence. At the close of each day her mother wafted into her nursery bedroom in a haze of perfume to say goodnight on her way out for the evening. Helen, a cold elegant woman of unpredictable moods, married to an unfaithful husband, taught her daughter the importance of haute couture and emotional reticence, that feelings are not to be displayed and never discussed. Though she did not love Margaret, she resented the girl's attachment to her father.

At private school Margaret was materially indulged. At Miss Hewitt's academy in Manhattan other girls were as privileged as herself, and one of them, Barbara Hutton, would stay a friend forever. The million-dollar baby, as Cole Porter named her, stood to inherit the Woolworth fortune. She shared much in common with Margaret: 'the rich are different from other people.' At school Margaret showed no academic talent. Naturally left-handed, she was made to write with the other, which resulted in a verbal stutter that would remain with her for life, conveying (to men if not to other women) an impression of vulnerability that was wholly misleading.

By the time she was fourteen, Margaret had made the same number of Atlantic crossings, on each provided with her own stateroom. Then her father bought a country house at Ascot near London, where she lived until she 'came out' to do the London Season as a debutante. Aged seventeen, she was slim, vivacious, beautiful, with a chill sculpted face and the disdainful poise then considered the height of chic. Among the horde of timid country mice emerging from remote country estates to be cast upon the marriage market, Margaret stood out proud and notably better dressed.

To promote his daughter into society George employed a press agent, Charles Lyttle. Results showed swift: 'Miss Whigham is quite the smartest *jeune fille* London has seen for a long time.' *Bystander.* 'She has leapt into the forefront of every social event.' *Sunday Chronicle.* 'Photographs of her are well known as those of every film star.' *News Chronicle.* 'A thoroughbred in a field of hacks.' *Sunday Graphic.*

Margaret explains, 'I had a knack of projecting myself. Almost like an actress...I was so terribly international. I wore make-up, nail polish, and was extremely well dressed...*nobody* dressed like I did...I suppose it was star quality...'

For her presentation at Court she wore a dress of white tulle and a headdress of ostrich plumes. It took over an hour for her car to drive down the Mall to reach Buckingham Palace, so densely packed was the crowd of spectators. Recognising Margaret, the mass of women swarmed her car, cheering and pressing their faces to the windows to gaze at her. At the palace King George V was 'unwell' that day. Unable to abide the boredom of the event, he'd gone to play with his stamp collection in the basement. Queen Mary presided alone in the Throne Room as hundreds of debs filed by to make their curtsey before her. The vast room was a blaze of colour, filled with people in full court dress or ceremonial uniform, wearing decorations and swords. On cue, Margaret advanced across the floor toward the throne. As she did so she noticed a dark young man in an Indian tunic and white turban set with an enormous emerald, who was standing just behind the Queen. For an instant their eyes met. The following night she encountered the young Indian again at a dance for Lord and Lady Mountbatten. He was Prince Aly Khan, nineteen-year-old son, heir and god-

in-waiting to his father the Aga Khan, one of the richest
men on earth, who was annually presented by his grateful
subjects with his own considerable weight in gold. Margaret
was instantly drawn to Aly.

In the weeks that followed she attended three or four dances
each night, but afterwards would escape her chaperone to
meet him at the Café de Paris or the Embassy. They danced
to the music of Cole Porter and believed they were in love.
It fell to him to pluck her cherry; he did so with both sensibility and expertise. He'd been taught by women since puberty,
showing aptitude as a pupil. Very different to the experience
of most women, Margaret's initiation involved a master in the
art of pleasing. She achieved a thrill of excitation most of her
subsequent lovers would fail to satisfy. Aly was invited to join
the Whighams' house party for Ascot races. At the end of the
week he asked Margaret to marry him. The prince was a
spectacular catch; Margaret was thrilled. But her father vetoed
the match. Aly might be wealthy beyond dreams of avarice
but as a son-in-law he was ineligible. Alas, he was a 'wog'.

Margaret's next engagement was to Glen Kidston, millionaire
sportsman and pioneer aviator, who was about to attempt a
record-breaking solo flight to South Africa. Their romance
ended when he crashed and died on the way, to maximum
publicity. In the winter of 1932 her father and mother took
her with them on a holiday to Egypt. By that time she had
already become engaged to Max Aitken, son of Lord
Beaverbrook, proprietor of Express Newspapers. About her
departure with steamer trunks and parents on the boat train
from Victoria station, the *Daily Express* said, 'Lord Reading
was on the same train, but no one took much notice of
him; after all he is only an ex-Viceroy.'

Egypt was ruled by Britain and Cairo a desirable military posting, providing polo, racing, shooting and any number of manly opportunities. Except one: it was short on single white memsahibs. Lord Fulke Greville was a twenty-year-old subaltern in the Grenadier Guards with an imperious manner and twirled moustache, a swaggering blood in breeches and riding boots. When Margaret and her parents left Cairo on the luxuriously appointed White Train for Aswan, Fulke accompanied them on board.

Other guests at the Cataract Hotel overlooking the Aswan Dam consisted in English couples taking the cure for rheumatism. To escape them Margaret and Fulke rode camels through the desert, picnicked and sailed on the Nile in boats with slanted sails. While strolling across the Aswan Dam by moonlight on New Year's Eve, Fulke asked her to marry him.

She was troubled – though not unduly – by doubts, for she was wearing Max Aitken's engagement ring. But to become the wife of an earl was a proposal hardly to be refused. Max's garnet was replaced by Fulke's sapphire, and the young lordling accompanied the Whighams when they sailed back to England. An announcement of the engagement appeared in *The Times*, and photographers and pressmen were waiting when the liner docked in Southampton. Their reception later that week by the town of Warwick, site of Fulke's family castle, resembled a royal progress. Cheering crowds lined the route and the castle staff were drawn up curtseying or tugging forelocks before the entrance. Also there to meet if not exactly welcome them was Fulke's mother, the formidable Lady Warwick. Their encounter was bruising. Lady Warwick made it clear she did not consider Margaret a suitable wife for her son: her father was in 'trade'.

For Margaret's parents the experience of getting to know

their intended son-in-law was equally unsettling. Fulke and his fellow subalterns in the Guards believed themselves above the conventions of good manners. They were disrespectful, dominated conversation, caroused, broke wind and laughed immoderately. It was not unknown for one or other of them to relieve himself onto the glowing coals in the Adam fireplace. As for Fulke, he didn't stand up when Mrs Whigham entered the room. He got drunk, threw up on the carpet and passed out, leading Margaret's father to say: 'He's so rude *now.* What's he going to be like when you're married to him?'

The Victorians laid down the rule: marry the position not the man. It meant she would join the nobility, the cream of English landed aristocracy, but the price for such extreme mobility was high. The future as countess and chatelaine of Warwick Castle looked more gross than she had imagined, yet she would have gone through with the wedding were it not for the discovery that Fulke was in love with another woman, her friend Rose Bingham.

A paragraph in *The Times* announced:

> *The marriage arranged between the*
> *Earl of Warwick and Miss Margaret Whigham*
> *will not take place*

To languish was not Margaret's wont. Six months after breaking off her engagement to Warwick, *The Times* announced her betrothal to Charles Sweeny…and Charlie was a dish. He and his brother Bobby were champion golfers, gamblers and young men-about-town, whose father had relocated the family in London. Dad had got involved in some shady business in New York that made it expedient to get out of town.

The Sweenys were Catholic and, in order to marry Charlie, Margaret had to convert. She was only nominally Christian and apostasy meant nothing to her, but she knew how to cut a deal. 'I said, "OK, I'll become a Catholic on two conditions. I wouldn't recognise the infallibility of the Pope and I wouldn't pray to a saint…if I'm ever going to say a prayer, it's going to be to the Head Man." The Church accepted me to get the publicity. And it did get tremendous coverage…'

She was confirmed as a Catholic on the day before her marriage. Next morning people started to queue outside the Brompton Oratory before dawn; by 10.30 the crowd around the church packed solid. Inside people stood on pews and clung like monkeys to the nave's supporting columns. Traffic between Hyde Park Corner and South Kensington was gridlocked and when Margaret's limousine arrived it was mobbed by women screaming her name. The *Sunday Graphic* describes 'scores of young women who had obviously modelled their appearance on hers. They had long earrings, full, rich, cupid-bow lips, and tiny hats aslant, as "The Whigham" wears them. I watched them scan her avidly to get "confirmation," for few had actually seen her except in photographs…'

After a six-week honeymoon cruising the West Indies on a yacht, Margaret and Charlie set up home in Belgravia. Their staff consisted of a cook, a parlour maid and her childhood nanny – plus a Rolls-Royce and chauffeur provided by her father. Margaret fell pregnant, lost the child and became sick with double pneumonia. Crowds gathered outside the hospital. Newspaper placards read 'MARGARET WHIGHAM DYING'… She recovered but, as she revealed to biographer Charles Castle, 'Charlie was going out to the Embassy every night in white tie…and there I was on the critical list, my

child gone... I was given up for dead and out he went to
the Embassy... I was miserable. I was crying half the night
through.'

She and Charlie made a good-looking couple. They
matched well, though better in bed than conversation. Their
income of £2,000 a year provided a large house, staff and
every comfort, and George Whigham covered the large sums
she spent on clothes, but it was not enough to throw big
parties. Charlie worked in his father's merchant bank in the
City. His and Margaret's social life consisted in inviting or
being invited by young married couples the same age and
sort as themselves. Never did they venture outside their set.
If Margaret suggested asking a writer, artist or politician to
dinner Charlie vetoed the idea. When she attempted to
discuss what she read in the *Daily Mail* with him he remarked
that she 'was getting to be quite a little intellectual'. Charlie
was a dedicated golfer, and his job allowed him generous
opportunity to compete in tournaments and to travel but,
while he was away, he forbade her to go out alone. The ban
taught her discretion, something that had never concerned
her.

Margaret's daughter Frances was born in June 1937. She
regained her slender figure in no time and featured in the
papers wheeling a pram, the tailored image of nanny-assisted
modern motherhood. An image triumphantly confirmed the
following year when she was voted into the Ten Best-Dressed
Women in the World List. Soon after, she gifted that same
world with a second baby, a son and heir.

When the Second World War broke out the American
ambassador, Joe Kennedy, telephoned Margaret, asking her
to come see him. He warned her she must pack and sail

for the US with her two children immediately. Britain was done for; he was in a position to know that the country would be overrun by the victorious German army within weeks. Margaret was magnificent in response. Disgusted by his attitude, she threw her head back defiantly and told him he was talking rot. Britons never never would be defeated, and she had no intention of leaving. Instead, she and Charlie closed up their house and moved into the Dorchester Hotel, which was built of concrete and thought safer in bombing raids.

Plans were put in hand to evacuate children from London and other major cities to the country. Under pressure from Charlie, Margaret reluctantly agreed to take her two children together with a nanny and nursemaid to Lord and Lady Aberconway's remote country house, where they would live out the bombardment. However, the reality of England's green and pleasant land so appalled her she used her hosts' telephone to send herself a telegram saying Charlie was seriously ill, and took a train back to London after only one night beneath their roof.

Then America entered the war, and US servicemen swept into town, 'Overpaid, over-sexed and over here'. Both Margaret and Charlie rallied to the flag and did their bit. He enlisted in the Eagle Squadron of American volunteers, which formed part of Fighter Command. And Margaret joined the American Red Cross. 'We had a frightfully pretty uniform. It was Air Force Blue, with a red-lined shirt or jersey and plain white stockings.' She had hers made by Molyneux, London's leading couturier. As always, she was at the heart of the action, a well-appointed house in Mayfair, which she and the wife of Anthony Biddle, a distinguished US ambassador, ran as a Women Officers' Club.

It was a time of stringent rationing, but the two bypassed

the regulations by using their own money to buy asparagus and fresh strawberries and cream from Fortnum & Mason, and the very best available on the black market. Margaret was Entertainments Officer; she fixed for Jack Benny, Bob Hope, Bing Crosby, Sid Field and Marlene Dietrich to perform. The club, which provided luxurious premises and a rotating supply of young women, proved a conspicuous success. Not least for officers who happened to be male. Margaret was awarded the American Red Cross Theatre Ribbon for raising military morale while Britain and America stood firm against a common enemy. 'It was all tremendously gay, and great fun and very dangerous. We were on 24-hour alert all day and every day... You never knew what was going to come and hit you.' She enjoyed a lively war, running the best little house in town.

VJ Day incited a spontaneous carnival in London; crowds danced and cheered in the streets exulting in victory over Japan and the end of the Second World War. Margaret Sweeny celebrated the date by moving into a house in Belgravia her father had given her. Alone. She was fed up with Charlie's infidelities and his possessiveness — he'd caused countless jealous scenes about her job, yet he behaved carelessly as she. They were squabbling in the ashes of the sexual passion they'd once enjoyed with little to keep them together.

Margaret did not exactly live alone in the large, luxuri-ously furnished house in Upper Grosvenor Street, for she had her son and daughter with her and a full staff of servants. But she had regained her independence and with it the freedom to cultivate the sort of people *she* wished to see. She relaunched herself as a society hostess, later recalling, 'There wasn't anybody in the political, theatrical, Hollywood or social world that I either didn't know or hadn't met.' She had one of the best cooks in London and – in defiance of rationing – could afford to serve the finest food and wines available. Among those who came to her parties were Jack Whitney (who had replaced Joe Kennedy as US Ambassador), the German Ambassador, Brendan Bracken, Chips Channon, Lord Kilmuir (the Lord Chancellor), Stavros Niarchos, Douglas Fairbanks Jr, J. Paul Getty, Noël Coward and Elsa Maxwell. 'I had a really wonderful time…I had a ball…I could ask whoever I wanted. Charlie was always so orthodox and boring… Nobody had as much fun as I had… Nobody. Nobody. The house was always filled, packed with the most amusing people.'

None of Margaret's marriages were made in heaven; her next was arranged by the concierge of the Ritz. She put up at the hotel during a trip to Paris to view the couturiers' collections, buying Chanel, whose clothes suited her spare lean frame. When she came to leave, naturally it was Georges she asked to book her a seat on the *Golden Arrow* to London. A routine task for Georges, but it so happened that a little later another would-be passenger strolled into the hotel to make the same request of him. Ian Campbell was a craggy Scot with a rain-soaked Highland pedigree and haunted otherness resulting from five years in a German prison camp; he'd been released only the year before. He'd married twice and had two sons by his second wife Louise, a rich American socialite. He possessed no money of his own – something he chose not to mention to Margaret on the journey to London – though he did confide that his marriage had come near to its natural end. He also told her an odd story that, because it is attested to by others, possibly is true. Fifteen years before, he'd been dining in the Café de Paris with his first wife Janet Aitken, when he glanced up to watch a beautiful girl descending the famous curved staircase to the nightclub. A young woman of such startling grace and loveliness that in a flash of Highland second sight, accompanied by the Highlander's wholesale lack of tact, he turned to his wife to say *that* was the girl he would marry one day.

That prescient vision had been of Margaret as a deb. When the *Golden Arrow* arrived at Victoria station she invited Ian back to her house for a drink. A cousin had just died, leaving him the Dukedom of Argyll along with its ruinous castle and a half-million-pound burden in death duties and debt. He had as much need of a rich wife as Margaret's desire to acquire an ancestral title. The two were ideally matched.

Six months later a bare-legged clan piper in kilt stood playing 'The Campbells Are Coming, Wahay, Wahay' as the Duke of Argyll, dressed likewise in full tartan, carried Margaret across the mouldering threshold into Inveraray Castle…and was seen to stumble. Then the sombre walls of the fourteenth-century fortress closed around the couple as Ian unsteadily deposited his bride in the Great Hall of her marital home, the Argyll family seat.

The idea of living in a castle has appeal to many, but the reality can fail to match the dream. Ian's was particularly forbidding. Not only was it located deep in Scotland's West Highlands – an area of almost constant rainfall where the natives had been long cleansed and replaced by sheep – and haunted by a history of ancestral curses, but the last of these recurrent disasters had fallen upon the place just prior to the wedding when the heap of sodden granite mysteriously had caught fire. Much of the east wing was gutted, and the roof had gone. Extensive though the damage was, it hardly altered the look of the place. Nothing had been done to maintain the castle for generations, and the 88-room building was a crumbling ruin smelling strongly of wet rot.

At Ian's instigation Margaret invited her father up to visit. George Whigham was mighty proud of his daughter, who had adorned the pages of newspapers and glossy magazines for more than two decades. Now she had capped years of admiring publicity by a trophy marriage into the top rank. But it had cost; to settle Ian's debts, pay off the death duties and put up what was needed to restore the castle amounted to a hefty sum. Fortunately, the castle's rooms were filled with decrepit furniture and paintings; mildewed canvasses by Gainsborough and Reynolds hung on the dank walls. Whigham was a businessman and cut a deal. In return for funding, his son-in-law would sign a Deed of Gift, transferring ownership of the best of the stuff to Margaret. Ian did so gladly, omitting to mention that the castle's contents belonged to a trust he did not control. The document was worthless.

Ian had always been hard up. His father died when he was twenty-two, leaving almost nothing. Nor was he equipped to *do* anything. He had moved into Whites, his London club, at times occupied an unobtrusive desk at Conservative Central Office and searched for a rich wife – finding one in American Louise Vanneck. With her he produced an heir to the title plus another son before being taken prisoner in France at the start of the war and locked up for its duration. He'd never been very bright and possessed no inner resources. Long incarceration in prison camp affected his mind. He was not one of the daring few who retained their spirit by digging tunnels and planning escape. Like most inmates he became withdrawn and apathetic, numbed and isolated. The experience institutionalised him and when finally released he remained emotionally incarcerated and unable properly to engage with life.

Margaret sent her two children to boarding school at eight; she had never been close to them. Now she quit London whose social whirl she enjoyed so much to take up residence at Inveraray Castle, where she started to pour her father's money into the place to render it habitable. Dressed uncharacteristically in wellington boots, overalls and stout gloves, she supervised a team of estate labourers, sorting, cataloguing, rescuing or burning the accumulated detritus of centuries when nothing had been thrown away. At first Ian helped her in this Augean task, but his interest waned as he became obsessed with another enterprise. It was said that a Spanish treasure galleon lay on the bottom of Tobermory Bay. Legend had it that the vessel was the payship for the forces of the Armada, wrecked with most of that disastrous fleet on the Highlands' rocky coastline, and that the ship was carrying not only gold but the crown intended for the king-to-be of Scotland.

Combining improbability and impracticability in equal measure, it was just the sort of scheme to appeal to Ian. An instinct for doomed causes flowed genetic in his Highland blood. The precise spot in the bay where the ship – if ship there was – had foundered was unknown. Another difficulty resided in the fact that countless millennia of incessant rain had stripped the surrounding mountains of their topsoil, depositing it in Tobermory Bay as mud of incalculable depth. Within which, Ian maintained, lay an embedded treasure worth £400 million and the crown of Scotland.

He set about his quest with zeal, announcing his plan to

the press. Falling in the silly season, it had considerable appeal. Reporters and photographers headed north, and he had hastily to round up a couple of dredgers from the naval base at Rossyth to convey some semblance of activity on the loch. Many photographs appeared of Margaret (who had changed from overalls into haute couture) and the laird in their romantic tumbledown castle. But soon the press departed. Months slipped by while Ian continued in his search, but no Spanish galleon was discovered. As his hopes slowly foundered in the mud he turned to drink. He grew surly and his moods became unpredictable. Margaret was irritated to come across a brown envelope behind a cushion in the library, containing a writ from the Royal Navy for £3,000, the cost of their futile dredging. Of course it was her father who had to settle it.

A headscarf and oilskins didn't suit Margaret's style, and she was bored rigid by country life. Bored otherwise as well for Ian was a dull dog. She moved back to London. Ian came down to join her for Queen Elizabeth's coronation, which coincided with their first wedding anniversary, and provided the opportunity for her to show off a diamond tiara and ermine-trimmed robe. They had to be in their seats at Westminster Abbey soon after dawn. There, among the tight-packed peers and peeresses of the realm they endured an endless wait for the ceremony to begin, while Ian sustained himself from a hip flask. Afterwards they were invited to the French Embassy. Celebrating crowds jammed the streets, and their limousine gridlocked in St James's. Ian by now had grown fractious and out of sorts, tired by the interminable performance and close company of his effervescent wife. Fumbling open the door, he stumbled from the car and lurched into the sanctuary of Whites club, leaving Margaret to enjoy herself without him. As from now on she would.

The battlements of Inveraray Castle were wreathed in mist and the chill air once again rent by the squeal of bagpipes as the band of the Argyll and Sutherland Highlanders in their barbaric costumes played in the Great Hall, where 150 guests shivered while they sipped malt whisky to celebrate the castle's restoration.

They didn't make up a fun crowd. Those at the reception were representatives from tourist boards and travel firms, plus of course the press. This was the start to a week of Highland Games and festivities to mark the official opening of the castle to the public. Tourists would pay half a crown (12½p) to look over the building and its treasures. Basing his arithmetic on a premise as fundamentally flawed as the existence of a treasure galleon in Tobermory Bay, Ian had calculated that a crowd of 300,000 people would beat a path to his renovated front door during the first summer of operation.

Margaret had come up from London to fulfil the role of hostess but found it less than enthralling to sit in the rain watching burly bare-kneed men toss logs and round up sheep. And she was seriously displeased by the presence of two among the castle's house guests whom Ian had lacked the nerve to tell her would be there. His American ex-wife Louise and their younger son. She was here to visit their older boy, the Marquess of Lorne, at school at Glenalmond in Perthshire.

Louise appeared in full bloom, complacent, confident and loud. She was about to wed a prosperous New York banker (his second, her third). She already owned a house in Biarritz and a chateau on the Côte d'Azur and planned a future of gracious living and international travel. Her intention was to visit Scotland frequently to see her sons at school here. Meanwhile she was of course *fascinated* to look over renovated Inveraray Castle – which one day would belong to her eldest boy when he inherited the place on Ian's death.

Margaret's manner toward her remained seamlessly polite throughout. Not a tremor on that perfectly controlled lifted face betrayed the utter loathing she felt for this interloper from the past with her inconvenient progeny. Her father had spent thousands of pounds restoring this grim pile, and it was unacceptable it should pass to someone else. With a house in London, a complaisant husband and a refurbished ducal seat, she finally had her own life organised on the right lines. The current arrangements suited her, and Louise and her son must not be allowed to disturb them.

That summer Margaret's daughter Frances, son Brian (fifteen) and the Duke were invited on a freebie cruise in the Mediterranean aboard Stavros Niarchos' 6,000-ton yacht *Achilleus*. Elsa Maxwell, their hostess, had been hired by the shipping tycoon and Queen Frederica of Greece to do for the Greek islands what she had done for Venice and Monte Carlo. To put them on the map. Her PR technique was straightforward: she invited 200 guests from the international A-list for a two-week jamboree. It was the sort of family holiday Margaret could handle. At the last moment Ian announced he wasn't coming, a relief to everyone.

For those on board the luxuriously equipped vessel the Greek isles at that time represented as improbable a holiday destination as Outer Mongolia. In both the food was vile, the *aménagement* to civilised life lacking and bathrooms as they understood them non-existent. But as sea-girt venues of quaint primitivism in which to drop anchor, dress up and party, the islands could not be bettered. The menus aboard ship were first class, the wine superlative, and the guests... The guests were the best too, the bejewelled beautifully groomed women and urbane men who had made Café Society what it was. Yet it could not but be noted that some walked a little stiffly now, in others the attention wandered, some you had to shout at to be understood. The *jeunesse dorée* of before the war was visibly less *jeune*. John D. Rockefeller Jr was eighty-one, Perle Mesta nearing seventy. And Prince Aly Khan, that slim youth Margaret had spotted behind the throne when she was seventeen, had grown stout and bald and was still waiting to be a god but had lost none of his charm. It was a pleasure for both to meet again. A vacation cruise requires a shipboard romance; here was one of proven quality and without strings. They embarked on it without delay.

Margaret returned from vacation looking five years younger. Ian was at London Airport to meet her and the children on their return. News from the north was not good, he confided. The Spanish treasure galleon at the bottom of Tobermory Bay still eluded his efforts to locate it, and castle-wise his forward projection of the number of tourist visitors had not been matched by the reality. The few people who had driven for long distances on bad roads to view Inveraray Castle and its treasures had, however, included a gang of burglars, who had returned the following night to steal a truckload of them.

Collecting insurance for the robbery proved to be a problem as Ian had been negligent with payments. From the start Margaret's father had been picking up the couple's bills but she was coming near to the end of her own resources. Ian was upset by her refusal or inability to pay up. He declared that he now had no option but to close the castle, removing its roof to avoid taxes. As Margaret only recently had paid to have the roof put *on* she regarded his solution as provocative. Tiresome too his announcement that he intended to move to live in her house in Upper Grosvenor Street but intended to change its address to Argyll House as more fitting for a duke. She found all this vexing and inconvenient.

Just before Christmas she took Frances on her first visit to New York to launch her in the States. There she introduced her to the Colony, El Morocco and 21, still maintaining their positions as the in-joints. Then, sending Frances to stay with friends in Palm Beach, she took the *Queen Mary* back to England. A fellow passenger, Cecil Beaton, caught a snapshot of her at the time in his diaries.

> I'm tired of seeing Margaret about 'everywhere.' She always looks wonderful but always the same with her dark eyes and nut-brown hair, her pink and white complexion, her bandbox-fresh dresses chosen with impeccable restraint... There is a dull inevitability and monotony about her beauty... I was a bit taken back when she asked if we could eat together during the voyage. What on earth could one find to talk about all the time? I believe it was the late Lord Wimborne who said of Margaret 'She don't make many jokes, do she?'

Margaret was not close to her two children but she was assiduous in her duty when it came to finding a husband for Frances. She invited the recently divorced 39-year-old

Duke of Rutland to join Ian, Frances and herself on a tour of the Middle East in 1958. No one was surprised when Ian refused to accompany them at the last moment.

Wherever they travelled, Beirut, Israel and Jordan, the press lay in wait. Which was unsurprising, for Margaret had provided London newspapers with their itinerary. The trio were followed wherever they went. In *Forget Not* she wrote of one occasion where, in an attempt to help her 'escape the harassment', King Hussein (whom she'd known while at Sandhurst) lent them a plane to fly to Petra, where a troop of cavalry and an Arab Legion officer waited to escort them to the ruined city. While trotting through the bleached empty landscape a small Arab grasping a camera was spotted crouched behind a rock. 'Mummy look, the press!' squealed Frances. A soldier captured the man and dragged him over. Terrified, on his knees, the poor fellow confessed to being in the pay of a London tabloid. 'Shall we kill him now?' the officer asked Margaret.

The Middle East tour lasted five weeks, during which Rutland and Frances became secretly engaged. Next day the news bannered on the front page of the *Daily Mirror*. The couple were married four months later.

Margaret's children had been raised by others; she had not sought to be a hands-on mother. In so far as she had a heart it belonged to Daddy. A fond papa, he had indulged her generously but, knowing her extravagance, when he'd given her the house in Upper Grosvenor Street he'd wisely kept the lease in his own name. For the last fifteen years he'd lived with his invalid wife in the Dorchester. In 1955 she died, and less than a year later he telephoned Margaret to say that he had just remarried an attractive divorcée, Jane Brooke, thirty-five years his junior and a year younger than herself. The news was ghastly. She'd always relied on him emotionally and financially. Now there was another woman to share the old man's affection and – in the not too distant future – his fortune. Margaret was distraught. 'How can you do this to me, Daddy?' she demanded.

It was known in London that Ian Campbell preferred Inveraray to the smart life. It was also recognised that Margaret required an escort to the various functions she attended. *Cavaliere servente* or 'walkers' have a role in social ecology. But Ian was piqued by the many photographs in the papers of his wife, wooden-faced as always, but evidently having a good time in the company of a stable of mostly younger men. This public display of her lifestyle riled him and stung his pride. She was bringing discredit not only to him but upon Clan Campbell and the name Argyll. There was an ugly side to Ian, a bitter edge. Imprisonment and a loser's luck, chronic deficiency and having to request pocket money from three rich wives…it takes little insight to spot how it came about. His mood swings became more marked, a trifling event could tip him into fury. He was taking Drinamyl (purple hearts) prescribed by his doctor. He had never been quite the complaisant husband Margaret imagined him and now, strung out and drinking whisky beside a dying fire in Inveraray Castle while his wife was out doing the town, he brooded on his resentments.

The amphetamines he was taking made him hyperactive. He cooked up a new plan to make his fortune. His stunts to raise funds in the course of his rather desperate life included modelling a line of Argyle socks. His projects all had been attended by various degrees of failure and disappointment but he was always game to stagger on to the next.

Ian's new Big Idea was to market himself as clan chief to

the diaspora. The land around Inveraray had not always spread desolate as now. Once this had been the home to many families who, in the Highland Clearances of the nineteenth century, had been rounded up and transported to the antipodes where they prospered and multiplied. Campbells were numerous in Australia and New Zealand. Long removed from their rain-sodden roots, nevertheless they maintained their ethnic heritage: they liked to dress up in kilts, congregate in smoky halls and listen to bagpipes when drunk.

With no one to assist him except a girl from the village who came in to do his typing, Ian launched on his campaign. His writing paper from Smythson shone glossy, emblazoned with his Campbell crest raised in colour. The prose was rich, accompanied by photographs of the castle and himself. Of course it helped to be a duke. Rather surprisingly, the pitch worked. Somehow he contrived to be invited to visit his far-flung dominions. He was determined Margaret should not come with, but she outwitted him. Sending her extensive luggage ahead, she bought her own plane ticket to Sydney.

Ian's schemes were invariably harebrained but he had a capricious flair for promotion. In Australia he'd set up what amounted to a sort of official ducal tour. At each stopover he and Margaret were met by official dignitaries and a pipe band playing 'The Campbells Are Coming'; they stayed at Government House, attended dinners and lord mayors' receptions; he delivered speeches and appeared as guest of honour at a Highland Ball for 2,000 people.

Throughout this ceremonial progress around Australia Ian stayed off speed, drank little, was presented in his costumed role, and showed himself an accomplished public speaker. He and Margaret maintained a tacit truce…which disintegrated explosively in their Sydney hotel suite when Ian came across his wife's diary while she was in the bathroom. It was a four-year journal 1956–1959 of unusual format: each page covered what she was doing on that particular date each year. It recorded meetings with six men, some of these annotated with a coded symbol that to Ian could only mean one thing. Margaret re-entered the room while he was reading the diary and snatched it back. *How dare he!* In response he challenged her with flagrant adultery.

She didn't deny the charge. What was she expected to do? He remained stuck in his damp castle, hating parties, hating guests, hating all that was carefree and pleasurable. She loved activity, loved dancing, nightclubs, travel, people. What did he expect? She was forty-seven and in full bloom; unlike him she happened still to be alive.

It made for an ugly row and the atmosphere afterwards remained so strained that Margaret chose to return on a later plane when Ian flew back to London. A disastrous call. He took advantage of her absence to search her rooms in Upper Grosvenor Street and go through all her belongings. He found her earlier diaries and a stack of private letters. At the back of a bookcase he came upon a set of Polaroid photographs – each with a caption – of a man and woman performing sexual acts. The faces of both were invisible but Ian recognised his skinny naked wife. He also found some-thing else: a sheet of hotel notepaper onto which cut-out handwritten words had been pasted to compose a text. The handwriting and signature were those of his ex-wife Louise, and the letter a confession that her two sons were not Ian's but fathered by other men. The paste-up wasn't very well done but a photograph might pass for genuine.

Ian took everything, lodging the evidence in a safe deposit box at his bank. He packed his clothes and possessions and moved into Claridge's 200 yards away in Brook Street while working out his next move...

When Margaret arrived home she discovered her husband had made off with her personal letters, the Polaroids and her past diaries — but crucially did not realise he'd found the forged confession. Blindly she continued with her devious scheme, flying to Paris to view the spring collections as was her wont. On her return she contacted the Duke to show him copies of further letters she claimed she'd seen while in France. Supposedly written by Louise, these referred to her husband as a moron and admitted that her children were not his.

Ian's reception as clan chief had done wonders for his morale, and bucked him up no end. To ruin Margaret gave fresh purpose to his life. He made copies of these letters and listened to what she told him with well-acted concern. As soon as he was alone he telephoned Louise in the States and told her what Margaret was up to. Then he took the copies and the evidence in his safe deposit to Scotland Yard.

Unaware that her game was blown, Margaret continued with her increasingly absurd machinations. She invited her old friend Diana Napier to lunch à deux, dismissed the butler and said, 'Darling, I want you to go to Venice at my expense. I would like you to use your Polish contacts to adopt a newborn child or get a newborn child over from Poland to Venice.' It was a bizarre request and Diana wanted to know why. Margaret explained, 'I have padded my tummy with a cushion and put it about that I am pregnant. I want to fake a pregnancy and go to Venice and bring back the Polish child as the Duke's son.' Who would of course inherit the Argyll title and castle if Louise's boys proved to be bastards.

It was a fatuous plot. Diana laughed in disbelief at Margaret's madcap scheme; she refused to have any part in it.

Meanwhile, in his war room at Claridge's Ian Campbell

had assembled most of the evidence he needed to divorce his wife, but he lacked her current four-year diary, which he'd had the opportunity only to glance through in Sydney before she snatched it back. Very early one morning he let himself into her house with his latchkey and stole it from her bedside table while she was asleep.

Two days afterward Margaret received a court injunction forbidding her to enter Inveraray Castle. In response she cabled the Duke: ARRIVING CASTLE FOR LUNCH SATURDAY WITH MY FATHER STOP ANOTHER COUPLE ARRIVING FOR DINNER AND WEEKEND STOP PLEASE INFORM STAFF AND TELL MACDONALD TO MAKE SURE MY BEDROOM IS QUITE READY STOP GIVE MY FONDEST LOVE AND A BIG KISS TO COLIN STOP MARGARET.

Ian cabled in reply: I CONFIRM THAT YOU ARE FORBIDDEN TO ENTER INVERARAY CASTLE.

She stormed the gates a month later accompanied by a couple of lawyers, her maid and two trucks to carry away what belonged to her. 'It was a farcical day,' the Duke reported, 'Margaret toured the whole castle, sweeping through room after room pointing apparently at random to pieces of old furniture, Campbell family portraits, and even suits of armour, "That's mine…that's mine too," she kept saying.'

They were. These things had been given her in return for the fortune her father had spent restoring the dismal fortress. They'd been transferred to her in a Deed of Gift inscribed on vellum and tied with legal ribbon, which was worthless. Ian had cheated her of all of it; she was allowed to remove nothing.

She took the defeat with the cold hauteur she could do

so well, the disdain that told other people they were worms. She, the smart one, had been outwitted by a loser who'd conned her from the start. On the journey back to London her blood seethed. *The indignity of it, the affront!* What Ian had done to her was intolerable; she would make him suffer for it.

Exacerbated by drugs – for she too was on amphetamines – Margaret's deceit and manipulation became pathological. She was also conducting a covert campaign against her stepmother. Since the date her father married Jane Brooke she had schemed to destroy the relationship. With considerable success, for three years later George Whigham was separated from his wife and occupying the mews cottage attached to Margaret's house.

In the summer of 1959 Jane Whigham, living alone in Berkshire, became aware that she was being followed each day by two men in a car. Taking its number, she traced its ownership to a firm of private detectives. Their client turned out to be Margaret. George Whigham was now eighty and ill with cancer. Margaret prevented Jane from visiting him in the London Clinic and when he died barred her from the funeral.

Stories about Margaret did not read well. George Whigham's estate proved to be worth less than expected. His widow received only £20,000 and the marital home, Margaret got the rest. Securely tied up in trusts, the capital gave her only what she considered a pittance of £18,000 a year. She went into battle with Jane in the Nassau courts, contesting the ownership of George's house in the Bahamas.

Daddy was gone, the only man she'd trusted. Gone too was his judgement and restraining influence, the knowledge that he would bail her out of any problem. She who had never suffered from insecurity felt it now like an icy draught. Ian intended to divorce her – not at all the done thing at that time; a gentleman habitually provided evidence and let his wife divorce *him*. The code required him to spend a night somewhere like Brighton and to check into a good hotel with a prostitute, registering as Mr and Mrs. But Ian wanted not just rid of her but to hurt her. And he knew where she *could* be hurt: in her pride and self-image. Emotionally she was numb but there she was vulnerable. He wanted to expose and humiliate her before the world.

Aware that Ian was preparing to go to court, she determined to be the first to strike. And to do so in the most compromising and injurious way possible. Before he could act she filed a petition to divorce *him*. Her grounds were his adultery. As co-respondent and Ian's lover she cited her own mother-in-law, Jane Whigham. As the front pages announced next day, war had been declared.

Threatened by divorce, humiliation and what she saw as poverty, Margaret embarked on a campaign of intrigue, deception and outright perjury, which by 1963 involved eleven different legal actions. She had already paid out over £100,000 in damages plus a fortune in lawyers' fees. Louise sued for defamation and was awarded £10,000, together with an injunction that meant Margaret would go to jail if she repeated her allegations. She was also suing the Duke's daughter by his first wife for unlawful entry to her house; suing the *Daily Mail* for libel; suing for the contents of Inveraray Castle; defending a counterclaim for removing paintings and silver from Inveraray; and being sued for libel and slander by the Duke's secretary Mrs MacPherson.

These various skirmishes had been well covered by the press. They fed the running story leading up to the eagerly anticipated main event: the Argyll divorce. The couple represented something more than the glossy milieu called the Jet Set. Their dukedom carried a resonance heard so long in Britain it was assumed to be part of the natural elements like the air you breathed. The blue bloodline of the nobility carried history on its flow; it bore a tradition dependable as the monarchy itself. Along with the Queen, Parliament and Church, *it was what made Britain what it was.* And aristocracy, together with those other institutions, was attended by deference.

In Britain at that time deference was struggling to draw its last breath before expiring. The organs of subversion already had undermined respect among the intelligentsia. *Private Eye* started publishing in 1961; the satirical revue *Beyond the Fringe* opened in the West End; at the Establishment Club the manic American stand-up Lenny Bruce, flying on speed, surveyed his second-night audience in suit and tie, flower-print frocks and kitten heels, then lurched from the stage unzipping his fly: 'Tonight I'm going to do something I've never performed in public before... I'm going to piss all over you.'

Britain was poised on the edge of an era that would transform everything and result in nothing less than a new consciousness: the Swinging Sixties.

Although this was 1963 the Sixties hadn't happened yet. The traditional order was very much in place and evident in the shape of the judge, Lord Wheatley, and surrounding *mise en scène* of the Court of Session in Edinburgh when the Argylls' divorce case opened on 26 February. Public and press seats were packed, the spectacle promised a hit show from curtain up.

Ian was suing her for serial adultery with three men: Baron von Braun (West German ambassador to the UN), John Cohane (an American executive) and Peter Combe (press officer of the Savoy Hotel). Margaret had argued for three years in the Court of Appeal through to the House of Lords to have the documentary evidence Ian possessed declared inadmissible because he'd stolen it – and lost. Her personal correspondence, the letter she'd forged from Louise's cut-out words, her three diaries covering twelve years, the Polaroid photographs...all could now be exposed to the court.

Lord Wheatley was a dour elderly Scot, Catholic and a Campbell on his mother's side. He listened with set face as John Cohane's notes were read out: 'Darling Margaret, you are an incredibly exciting woman...my not having written to you does not mean that you are not inflaming my imagination. I have thought of a number of new, highly intriguing things we might do, or I might do to you.' To the judge 'the clear implication was that he had already engaged in a number of "highly intriguing things".' Margaret was not amenable to cross-examination. 'I am not accustomed to being shouted at,' she told opposing counsel, 'I am not *deaf.*'

The Polaroid photographs provided the avidly awaited climax to the trial; press and public had speculated about them for weeks. As described earlier, these comprised a set of four and Margaret was dismissive of the 'evidence'. These pictures formed part of the Duke's extensive collection of porn; he'd exposed his taste to members of Whites. The face of the naked woman in the photographs was unidentifiable; she denied categorically that it was her. Unfortunately, close examination of the background revealed the location as none other than her well-appointed bathroom in Upper Grosvenor

Street. Furthermore the woman was sporting a three-strand pearl necklace Margaret wore habitually, and one of her hands grasping the man's penis showed a ring recognisable as an Argyll heirloom given her by her husband.

Ah yes...she conceded that the woman was indeed her. How forgetful of her! The photos were of course of her husband and herself. Her defence put Ian in an agonising quandary. He knew he could nail her and prove her lying but only at dire cost to himself. So determined was he to shame her he paid the price. He subjected himself to examination by a court-appointed doctor who measured and photographed him, then certified to the court that Ian was definitely *not* the male figure in the scene, for the puny ducal apparatus resembled not at all the outstanding tackle displayed in the Polaroids.

This 'Headless Man', so explicitly revealed in all but his identify, was by now a mythic figure in the press. Who he might be was the subject of avid speculation. Some suggested the War Minister, John Profumo, others proposed Duncan Sandys, Secretary of State for the Commonwealth, though this was contested by some for he was known to have stepped on a mine during the war and, even under a powerful magnifying glass, the raised buttocks in photo three appeared in good shape. Yet others held that because the Polaroids had been taken with a delayed timer – an American device unobtainable in Britain – the cocksman was Douglas Fairbanks Jr, part of a set of aged roués including Lord Astor. One thing all were agreed on however: the Headless Man was a prominent person.

Further cracks in the establishment's façade opened up at this time, flagged by *Private Eye* as a fault line in the social fabric of the nation. At a casino operated by the Kray brothers, the MP Robert Boothby, bisexual lover of the Prime Minister's

wife, was snapped in cosy company with its criminal propri-
etors. Scurrilous rumours circulated about orgies in great
houses where guests were served drinks by a naked 'butler'
wearing a mask. This was alleged to be a government minister,
but were the Man in the Mask and the Headless Man the
same? The fog of secrecy and discretion that so long had
veiled the doings of the elite in Britain was starting to shred.
In counter image to the staid gravity of the Edinburgh Court
of Session where the divorce case continued, tales appeared
of a club of special needs in Notting Hill where authority
kneeled bare-bottomed to be disciplined for the price of a
pound a stroke. A whiff of transgressive perversity was leaking
from the corridors of power that indicated something good
and rotten at the heart of the establishment.

A gleeful public awaited the next development, for the
divorce had segued into another case sharing members of
the same distinguished cast: the Profumo–Stephen Ward–
Christine Keeler scandal. Involving sex, espionage, eminent
figures, a two-way mirror and black drug dealers shooting
at each other in W1, the scenario had unusual piquancy.
The disclosures spilling from both courts appeared to under-
mine government, security of the realm and the entire ethic
of public life. The eminent High Court Judge and Master
of the Rolls, Lord Denning, was appointed by Parliament
to conduct an enquiry into the whole messy business.

His first action was to send to Edinburgh for the transcript
of the Argylls' divorce case. Very soon after he invited Margaret
to an interview. The examination took place on her own
turf, in her drawing room in Upper Grosvenor Street. Sadly
there exists no verbatim record of how it played and the
imagination falters reconstructing a dialogue in which the
West Country burr of the ever-courteous out-of-his-depth
old judge contended with the cut-glass accents of the brittle,

damaged once-a-duchess in a surreal discussion of naked butlers, headless lovers and comparative penis size.

Margaret as ever remained composed, but she was a wreck. Her divorce had ended disastrously. She'd been found guilty of adultery with all three men named in the Duke's petition. The judge concluded that 'she was a completely promiscuous woman whose sexual appetite could only be satisfied by a number of men.' He himself called it 'disgusting'. She was labelled a nymphomaniac; her daughter banned her from the house and from seeing her grandchildren. She stood publicly disgraced. The farce had stripped her of all dignity, shown her true nature to the world: manipulative, vindictive, spiteful, wholly unprincipled and a liar. A well-dressed wicked witch.

The Duke lost out too. His image as kilted treasure-hunter in a storm-tossed sea had morphed into that of a cuckold and weakling, an unscrupulous sponger with a very small cock. A duke he might be, but not a gentleman. He was blackballed by fellow members at Whites and expelled from his club. Even after the battle in the courts ended, the couple continued their war in the press. He sold his story to the *People,* she to the *Sunday Mirror.* Exhausted by the combat, each somehow found the strength to toss a last splash of petrol onto the flames merrily consuming them before the gaze of the world.

The following year the Conservative government was thrown out in a General Election. But by then Britain already had become a different country. For decades it had connoted a land of proscription and austerity regulated by rationing and the virtue of going without. Now suddenly London had split wide open and everything had changed:

sexual conduct, attitude to authority and to class, the way people dressed. A dull black and white world had switched into full colour. Not the recent scandals alone had caused it; other seminal events played their part in the transformation: the trial for obscenity of *Lady Chatterley's Lover*, the Beatles, rock festivals and drugs, the Wolfenden Report on homosexuality – above all the Pill. All combined to effect the tectonic shift in values, attitude and behaviour that went to make the Sixties' revolution.

Margaret's long-running performance in the public eye lasted more than thirty years, and she found the show's ending cruel: 'What I went through with Ian publicly was ghastly. Ghastly, ghastly, ghastly. Nothing on earth could have been more dreadful to live through. But it wasn't only because he was a duke and I was a duchess, because I had been this great star...until I married him. All of a sudden I fell from the greatest heights down to the ground with a crash. That is what made it so interesting from the public point of view. I have been in the news for a long time...wherever I go all over the world there are articles about me...I am news just because it's *me*... Nobody had ever *heard* of Ian Argyll before...*I* put him on the map.'

It was not easy to find the rent of £400 a week for the two-bedroomed suite. Yet she still dressed up to attend book launches, gallery exhibitions, first nights and promotional parties. Invitations of a sort still came in the mail. 'She was on every public relations company's list', Charles Castle wrote in *The Duchess Who Dared*, 'She would go to the opening of an envelope.'

Her clothes no longer looked in fashion, but they were classic. She held herself haughtily erect. She had her thinning hair dyed black, set in the same style as always in the mask that formed her face, the lips painted in the same carmine bow as

1930. She looked scary, a ghost from the past, and strangers trying to hold a conversation with her – people she met mostly all were strangers now – found that their party chat at times faltered into silence as they became aware with creeping horror that behind the garish mask there was…nothing. She stared back at them confused and lost, not knowing where she was.

During the night of 26 July 1993 she stumbled while getting out of bed and fell, breaking her neck. A Catholic priest administered the last rites at 1.20a.m.

So this is Margaret's life. It can be read as a parable, and its moral is biblical: *Pride goeth before destruction, and a haughty spirit before a fall.* Rate her as you will. One may loathe her or regard her with appalled awe, but she personified a watershed moment in English social history. Our betters were shown to be no better than ourselves, but with enviably greater opportunity for sin. In her fall from grace she dragged after her a whole class and culture of respect into mothballed desuetude.

8

THE BRAND BECOMES HER

Character is destiny, says Novalis. And adversity is to be welcomed for it provides the seed bed for the will. Coco Chanel was familiar with adversity; she started life in the poorhouse, though *when* is uncertain. Was it 1883, or 1893 as she maintained? She was a ready fabulist: 'My life didn't please me, so I invented my life.' Its span is riddled with alternative facts. She posed a mystery long before she became a myth.

Her unmarried mother – nineteen and already with a year-old daughter – gave birth to the baby in a charity hospital run by nuns in Saumur, a small town in rural France When the underweight infant was baptised soon after, her mother lay too ill to attend. Her father, an itinerant pedlar who spawned six children, was absent with his horse and cart. By mistake the baby's surname was misspelt as Chasnel in the church register. The error was unimportant, both parents were illiterate and of no significance. It went uncorrected until altered to Chanel five years later. By that time the slight dark-haired girl was known to everyone as Coco.

When she was twelve, her mother died of tuberculosis and malnutrition. She and her two sisters were unloaded at the door of the convent at Aubazine, in *France profonde*, before her father took off on the road with his cart. The twelfth-century abbey of Saint-Étienne harboured an orphanage run by sisters of the Sacred Heart of Mary. Existence for the abandoned siblings in the convent's stone-flagged rooms was basic and austere. The dormitories were unheated, the food meagre. Two sorts of orphans boarded there: those with relatives who paid the fees and came to visit, and the charity wards who did not – whose clothes were patched and shoes down at heel. Very early Coco learned of the divide separating the haves from the have-nots and the indignities that diminish the nots.

All the girls had to attend Matins at 6a.m. After making their beds and housework, breakfast was bread and a glass of milk. The morning consisted of schoolwork, interrupted by a short service at eight and Mass at twelve. After a frugal meal they were taken for a strenuous walk in the wooded hills surrounding the town, when conversation was permitted. On return, Vespers at 4.15. More lessons, then Compline at 6.15. Afterwards, supper, reading, or talk until lights-out. Discipline was harsh, 'I remember that they used to take my knickers down to spank me. First there was the humiliation. Then it was very unpleasant, your bottom was red as blood.'

Coco stayed at Aubazine until she was sixteen, unhappy and lonely. 'Every child has a special place, where he or she likes to hide, play and dream,' she told biographer Paul Morand. 'Mine was an Auvergne cemetery. I knew no-one there, not even the dead.'

Many girls in the orphanage would remain to become nuns, but not Coco, who lost her faith soon after her First Communion: 'The Catholic religion crumbled for me,' she confided to her friend, the psychoanalyst Claude Delay. She left to board with an aunt; there were many for her father had nineteen siblings. She shared an attic bedroom with another aunt, Adrienne, only a year older than herself. The two attended the same Catholic school in Moulins, where they learned the practical skills of sewing, embroidery and needlework; the basics required to scrape a living.

Moulins was a garrison town, populated by soldiers. The place had a number of bars, and a small leafy park contained a pavilion with dance floor and band. It also provided entertainment: magicians, jugglers, stand-up comedians and singers. Many of the acts were amateur, but prices cheap. It was a popular spot for troops to spend their pay.

Coco and Adrienne auditioned as a singing duo and were taken on as a side act – not for pay, but reliant upon tips and coins tossed onto the stage. Their performance lacked finesse, but they were teenage girls in a town where men outnumbered young women 20:1. Of course they were popular. After a number of appearances the two agreed that Coco should go on stage alone. She had a nothing voice, she couldn't carry a tune, but what she did have was brio – a vivacity and spirit that proved infectious. She was not beautiful but cute, a tomboy with thick black eyebrows and wide mouth. She was petite, scrawny, animated, with a gift for expression ranging from comic to pathos. The soldiery loved her.

Adrienne, the better-looking of the pair, showed no jealousy of her success. The two were close. In the evening they worked in their attic, altering clothes for clients or embellishing hats with ribbon and artificial flowers. Adrienne shared with Coco the second-hand books (romantic fiction, melodrama and the macabre) she had accumulated during adolescence; also magazines she'd saved and sewed together into volumes of illustrated pages, revealing to Coco a wider, more glamorous world existing outside the confines of her lot.

Her aunt and landlady Louise had succeeded in rising from her own lowly childhood among a score of ragged siblings. She'd improved her status by marrying a stationmaster on the Moulins–Paris line. Also started her own business. In a field on the outskirts of town, she managed a stable where she raised horses to sell to the army. Coco helped to look after and exercise them in the wooded country surrounding Moulins: 'I mounted our horses bareback (at sixteen, I'd never seen a saddle). I caught hold of our best animals…by their manes or tails.'

Aunt Louise's business brought to the stables cavalry officers, who came to choose a mount for themselves. These were young, well-dressed and well-heeled, for most had a family income to supplement their pay. Among them, Étienne Balsan. He was no longer a serving officer in a smart regiment, but independently wealthy. Still in his twenties, he had resigned his commission to devote himself to a bachelor's pleasures: racing, polo, hunting, food, drink and the company of women. Willingly, Coco was seduced.

Balsan owned the Chateau de Royallieu with its estate racecourse, near Compiègne in a particularly beautiful area of France. He loved to entertain and did so in carefree fashion, throwing frequent parties where his guests usually misbehaved in manly fashion. He invited Coco to move in and help train his racehorses.

Her position in the well-appointed and well-staffed household was nuanced by the fact that his established *maîtresse-en-titre*, Émilienne d'Alençon, was resident in the chateau. A big blonde with voluptuous figure in the then-fashionable mould, her teenage career had begun in a circus with a speciality act involving trained rabbits, but she caught the eye of several men, and soon her superb body and particular talents gained her fame in the métier. Now thirty-three, she'd progressed to become a *grande horizontale,* a top-rated courtesan, with her own horse-drawn carriage, coach driver and footman in designer livery. Curiously, no rivalry came between her and Coco – so very different in physical type – and the two quickly became close friends. The French are ultra-civilised in such matters and the arrangement worked smoothly – but Coco, unlike Émilienne, was deemed *pas-sortable,* and when Balsan entertained the grander and more respectable of his friends she was relegated to eat with the staff in the kitchen.

Balsan's set was made up of men the same age or younger than himself, most of them cavalry officers, and their *maîtresses-du-jour.* At Royallieu during the morning the men rode and women played cards or took the air, tripping in pairs down the garden paths in tiny steps, hobbled by their tight dresses. In summer they carried parasols to protect them from the sun. Then there was lunch. Afterwards, sport for the men, croquet, cards, tea and gossip for the women. But, happily, evenings broke the boredom of this routine. At dinner men sported dress uniform or white tie and tails. The women remained tight-laced in their corsets but not behaviour. Balsan had a fine cellar and everyone drank champagne. Drugs were to hand and used by many, including Coco.

At the start of the twentieth century morphine formed the essential ingredient in dozens of patent medicines, which could be bought without prescription. Cocaine was available over the counter. The drug was welcomed as a treatment for asthma, alcoholism, the common cold, whooping cough, dysentery, haemorrhoids, neuralgia, seasickness, sore nipples, vaginismus, syphilis, as well as a cure for morphine and opium addiction. It was further used to discourage female masturbation, since it numbed the clitoris. The habit was viewed as pernicious by the medical profession.

Coke was taken up more usually by women than men. At that period, stately dinner parties consisted of twenty or more guests of both sexes. There were many courses, a succession of wines. It was customary for men to drink copiously as they talked, and talked, and talked and women listened. Except for a smart witticism to set the table laughing, women were expected to stay silent and attentive. The heavy meal could extend for hours; it is hardly surprising a lady needed a little something to enliven the unendurable boredom. For women, cocaine was the staple perk-me-up of the Belle Époque.

At Royallieu, nightly revels were as dressy as formal dinners, but notably more dissolute and lively. Coco, who passed much of her day at the stables or exercising Balsan's horses, wore jodhpurs and a boy's shirt, in the evening a simple tunic she had made herself, with white shirt, collar and tie. The contrast between the way she dressed and the elaborate costumes of the other women, whose whalebone corsets cinched their figures into billowing caricatures of femininity, could not have shown more stark. Alone in the seraglio at the chateau, she could move freely.

Cocaine sharpened her spontaneity and wit in these surroundings, but rich food and wine had no appeal, nor did idle luxury suit her. To occupy her time she began designing hats for Émilienne. These looked very different from the cumbersome confections women wore at the time. She bought straw boaters from a department store to trim with one silk flower or a single ostrich plume. Coco Chanel was first to introduce to women's fashion qualities not seen before: simplicity, clean lines and strength.

Émilienne, who accompanied Balsan to elegant race-courses, was seen about in smart society. Her hats were noted by other women, who enquired where they might obtain them. For Coco, this made the start of her career.

Coco remained at Royallieu for six years, occupying the same between-stairs position in the household. Despite its occasional humiliation, she shared with Balsan a relationship rare between men and women: friendship, quite unrelated to sex. She was the best of company, uncontrived, independent-minded, perceptive and unabashed. She was quick; she could shaft with her wit and silence the table. And there was another element he admired in her, a dynamic he lacked himself: ambition.

Coco could be relied upon never to act tiresome and never to bore. Balsan took her with him on a trip to Pau, the best fox hunting to be found in France. The house party included Boy Capel (twenty-eight), an English businessman, whose work did not keep him from a gentleman's pursuits. Both men and women rode to hounds with the women perched side-saddle in their long skirts. Coco conformed to the convention, with her hair gathered under a bowler hat. She could ride expertly on any saddle and describes the correct posture to ride astride. A woman must imagine she possesses a pair of balls: 'Under no circumstances can you put an ounce of weight upon them.'

Coco was instantly struck by Boy, and during the week-long house party observed him closely. The French attitude to the Englishman – then and perhaps still – consisted of a rather unwilling admiration of certain characteristics: his self-possession and *phlegm anglais*. This esteem extended to his clothes, which, in those rich enough to travel abroad, were usually made in good-quality tweed. When Coco began to design couture, it was this material and masculine cut she adapted for women, in contrast to Edwardian fullness and frippery, the long dresses and hobble skirts of the era.

But it was not just Boy's clothes that held Coco's attention. 'In Pau I met an Englishman,' she explained.

> We made each other's acquaintance when we were out horse-trekking one day; we all lived on horseback... The young man was handsome, very tanned and attractive. More than handsome, he was magnificent. I

admired his nonchalance, and his green eyes. He rode
bold and very powerful horses. I fell in love with him.
I had never loved Balsan.

Learning that Boy was returning to Paris next day, she
impulsively packed a suitcase and went to the railway station
to wait for him, having already left a note for Balsan: 'I am
leaving with Boy Capel. Forgive me, but I love him.' She'd
burned her boats and waiting for Boy to show up at the
station stretched her nerves to anguish. He stepped onto the
platform, saw her and 'opened his arms to me'.

For Balsan, Coco's defection was followed by another setback.
Émilienne left him rather publicly for a very small but famous
jockey she had picked up at the races. The rearrangement
caused merriment, but if Balsan was stung he did not show
it. Infidelity was the recreation of the period, and the demi-
monde his playground since ever.

   In Paris, Coco lived openly with Boy in his apartment
on Avenue Gabriel. She was snubbed by smart society, seen
as a fortune-hunting adventuress who'd nabbed him; she
deserved to be scorned. Besides, she was a milliner; one did
not invite such people. Yet Boy himself was not quite what
he seemed, for his wealth was self-made. In London he was
regarded as a 'Johnny come lately', an upstart, while in France
he passed as the English patrician he appeared. He was rich,
if not *that* rich, but not idle as so many of his peer group.
Work was essential to him. He wanted to *do* something, as
did Coco, not fritter away his life in self-indulgence like the
rest. 'We were made for each other,' Coco says. She would
have many liaisons in her life with men and, occasionally,
women, but Boy was her one true match of body and soul.

Coco had ambitions to design and sell clothes, not just hats. She asked Boy to stake her for a shop in rue Cambon in the most fashionable area of Paris; the premises lay just behind the Ritz. He did so happily, but she insisted the money should be a loan with interest. 'I'll know that I love you when I don't need you anymore,' she told him. Independence was vital to her.

Clients at the rue Cambon shop came from a wider social world than the wives and mistresses of the racing fraternity who were already her customers. At the start it was still only hats she sold, but the demand was greater than she could execute alone. She was creative but wholly untrained in the *business* of millinery or couture. Shrewdly, she chose the experienced Lucienne Rabaté to be her shop manager, poaching her plus two assistants from the established Maison Lewis in rue de la Paix. Next Coco added sportswear to her range: shirts, sweaters and blazers modelled on what Boy wore to polo, at Royallieu and at Deauville, which had come into fashion as a classy resort reached easily from both Paris and London. Sport in the form of tennis, golf and sailing was increasingly being taken up by young women too energetic to be satisfied by croquet and stately promenades with parasol aloft. The tone was about to change and Coco alert in anticipation of what was to come.

At the boutique she worked in a state of frenzy, hypermanic. Soon, young women in her sportswear were to be spotted in the best places; in England the look caused a stir on the lawns at Cowes Week at the peak of the Season. Chanel had become a signature label. Aged thirty, in thrall to no one, she was her own woman and in command of a thriving fashion house whose name was on the lips of the right crowd – the players and consumers of modernity.

This was before invention of the production line made

possible the manufacture of clothing and goods in bulk. Clothes were expensive, their cloth cut by hand and stitched on a manual sewing machine. If a woman wanted a dress, she ran it up herself or went to a dressmaker. The names of some of these designers, Paquin, Lanvin and Worth, had by now emerged to become…what? The word 'brand' came to define the novel concept.

Coco's target market lay in the emergent young of a specific demographic. These girls in their late teens or early twenties still lived at home and did not work, but were active on the social circuit in Paris and Deauville. The resort had become *the* place to be and, after paying off the loan from Boy, she opened a boutique here, selling sportswear and 'casual' clothes – a new concept. Requiring neither stays nor corsets, these were designed to lounge in at a picnic, in a deck chair or when bicycling, the new craze. A girl in Chanel added to the racy tone on a yacht's slanted deck. Suddenly, dignity was perceived as ageing. Chanel was the first to install pockets in women's clothes so they no longer needed a purse. The new woman looked sleek, unencumbered and walked free. Costumed by Chanel, she strolled into being in the last flowering of the Belle Époque before the hurricane. To the stakeholders in that luxuriant garden this was the best in the best of all possible worlds, and it seemed as though the show could go on forever. But things had been too good for too few for too long, and the era had to end. In the Balkans, in a distant country of which people knew little, in a town no one had heard of, an archduke was about to be assassinated by a pistol shot whose resonance would shatter the civilised world.

At the start of the Great War, Boy Capel enlisted in the British Army and was assigned to the headquarters staff of

Sir John French. The frontline lay to the east of France and wealthy Parisians, fearful of German occupation of the capital, fled with considerable luggage to Deauville or other Channel resorts from where, if the worst happened, they could escape by boat to England or America. There was an air of unreality, a frantic gaiety only just this side of hysteria, a sense of *après moi le déluge*. Sport, partying and shopping served to distract them from very real anxiety.

Haute couture is hardly the most essential of industries and the fact that it could thrive in Deauville and Paris concurrent with mass slaughter only miles from the capital is surreal. Yet it was so, fashion thrived. Others were now copying Coco's designs in the informal looseness of the dresses; she changed not only fashion but the shape of those who wore it. Obesity in women, so highly prized for centuries, was suddenly out of style. 'I came up with a new silhouette. To get into it, and with the war's connivance, all my clients lost weight to "become skinny like Coco".'

On leave from the army, Boy took her for a holiday in Biarritz, whose white wedding-cake architecture remained unscarred by war. Its role as a retirement home for redundant royalty had expanded to embrace a tribe of well-heeled refugees from all over Europe, together with their families. The town had been a winter resort, as were Cannes, Nice and Monte Carlo. The concept of 'summer' – sand, sea, swimming and a tan – had not yet appeared, but it was about to. Prescient as ever, Coco decided to open a boutique here.

When the Armistice was declared in 1918 the boutiques in Biarritz, Deauville and Paris were all thriving and Coco employed a staff of over 300 people in manufacture and sales. She'd become the acknowledged leader of fashion in France.

She had spent most of the war at Deauville, only occasionally joined by Boy who was obliged to pass many of his short leaves in England because of his business. She was well aware he had other women. All the men she'd known were promiscuously unfaithful, but she believed what she shared with Boy was special, unique for both of them. She trusted him.

With the return of peace she rented a large house in the Paris suburb of St Cloud, but lived mostly in a suite at the Ritz, which served as her atelier. She worked and lived hard; she ate little, drank little, smoked heavily and used cocaine. Her social radius now extended to the avant-garde, an unruly clique stirring up a revolution in the arts. Its ranks included Diaghilev and Nijinsky, Stravinsky, Braque, Modigliani, Gide and Cocteau. Coco had been recruited into this rarefied milieu by Misia Sert.

Misia (forty-six), eleven years older than Coco, was already a legend – not that she had ever *done* anything in her life. The writer Marcel Proust – just now sequestered behind drawn curtains in his cork-lined bedroom only a few blocks from the Ritz – uses her for one of his characters in *À la Recherche de Temps Perdu*, the relentlessly upwardly mobile, meddlesome and 'in' Madame Verdurin.

Born Polish into a landed aristocracy, who had not yet lost everything, Misia at twenty inherited a family fortune and married Thadée Natanson, a writer. The couple moved to Paris, where he launched an influential magazine, *La Revue Blanche*, which published Proust, Gide and Zola, and was illustrated by Renoir, Bonnard and Toulouse-Lautrec.

Misia was ambitious and outrageous in equal measure, and had the cash to flag their presence in the capital. Soon the pair's flagrantly bohemian lifestyle, scandalous soirées and drug use, plus Misia's ostentatious sucking up to the latest talent, made them notorious. After a sensational divorce in which their unusual relationship received considerable exposure, she married Alfred Edwards, a grossly rich newspaper tycoon with a reputation for coprophilia. Soon he left her for bisexual actress Geneviève Lantelme, who had made her debut aged fourteen in her mother's brothel. After two exacting years with Edwards, she either fell or more likely was pushed off his yacht and drowned in the Rhine.

At the date Coco was snapped up into this louche coterie Misia was the wife of painter José Maria Sert, famous for huge overblown murals in billowing pastiche of the nine-teenth-century manner, defacing a number of public buildings in France and his native Spain. Family rich, he owned an exquisite miniature castle where he and Misia staged disreputable house parties of imported guests.

Fashionable and notoriously fast-living, the pair became the power couple of the Parisian avant-garde. Misia had a consuming desire to be part of the latest trend. She was a forerunner to that breed of society women to whom the arts provide a gratifying role as benefactor/enabler of charity dinners, together with a place at the top table and the right sort of mention in the press.

Coco was guest at a dinner party thrown by the actress Cécile Sorel at her house on the Quai Voltaire when she first met Misia, who recalls the encounter:

> At table I was drawn to a very dark-haired young woman. Despite the fact she did not say a word, she radiated a charm I found irresistible…therefore I arranged to sit next to her after dinner… She seemed to me gifted with infinite grace and when, as we were saying goodnight, I admired her ravishing fur-trimmed, red velvet coat, she took it off at once and put it on my shoulders, saying with charming spontaneity that she would be only too happy to give it to me…her gesture had been so pretty that I found her completely bewitching and thought of nothing but her. Sert was scandalised by the astonishing infatuation I felt for my new friend.

Coco in turn was intrigued by Misia and further allured by the collection of talented individuals to whom she was patron, entrepreneur, publicist and closest friend. She found it pleasing to be introduced as the latest initiate to the club. Also challenging. At Royallieu, where she had learned the rules of society, her role had been that of attentive listener, ready to pounce into the conversation with a sardonic comment or witty line, but never attempting to hold the table. In this new milieu the bar was set high, and Misia herself outrageous and witty. The sparkling circle could have been intimidating, but Coco rose to it with the agile grace that informed her every move. Emboldened by the odd sniff, she found she could more than hold her own. Soon she became notorious. Misia's biographers, Arthur Gold and Robert Fizdale, said it best: 'Her genius, her generosity, her madness combined with her lethal wit, her sarcasm and her maniacal destructiveness intrigued and appalled everyone.'

Till the end of Coco's life, she and Misia were 'best friends', locked in a volatile relationship that followed a cycle of love, fall-out, bad-mouthing, reconciliation…and resumed demanding love.

Physically the two were ill-matched. Coco looked ten years younger than her age, with the slim athletic figure of an adolescent boy. Misia was burly, even stout, dressed by Paquin and Worth, never in Chanel clothes, in which she would have looked ridiculous. Yet Misia's reputation was as a 'beauty'. In youth she modelled for Renoir, Bonnard and Toulouse-Lautrec. The perfect face would not be redefined until the cinema close-up in the 1920s. Until that seminal event a woman's looks were specified by features sufficiently prominent to impact upon a theatre's audience in the most distant seats. Perception changes, as does beauty itself, and here it is for the reader to judge.

Misia by Renoir.

Misia 'took up' Coco, in the phrase of the day. Instant bonding – and she was fortunately at hand when Coco suffered the worst humiliation of her life.

Boy Capel had enjoyed a 'good war'. He ended it with a CBE as Political Secretary to the Supreme War Council, negotiating the terms of the Treaty of Versailles. Unannounced to Coco, in 1918 he married the Honourable Diana Wyndham, daughter of Lord Ribblesdale, a beautiful 25-year-old war widow from one of the country's leading families. Boy had married into the English aristocracy. Self-made, he'd bounded the last hurdle and finally made it to the top.

Coco was prostrated by the news. It was a betrayal – not sexually, that meant nothing, but of the intimacy they'd shared. She'd trusted him, she'd allowed herself to become vulnerable. Never would she make the same mistake again. Worse followed. Boy was killed in a car crash when a tyre burst on his Rolls-Royce while driving to the South of France. His loss crippled her. She withdrew into solitude in her suite, a dark void of despair. 'There is nothing worse than solitude. Solitude can make a man realise himself but it destroys a woman,' she says.

Information at the Ritz's reception desk that Mademoiselle Chanel was receiving no one discouraged Misia not at all; in full sail she was impervious to rebuff. She forced Coco's lair, bearing sympathy and drugs. Morphine helped to numb the pain. Coco had shot up infrequently before. Her taste was cocaine, which worked well for her. But in this extremity of grief morphine soothed and blunted the sharp edges of the world. It cocooned her, and from now on she would increasingly resort to the drug.

Misia says, 'She felt [the loss of Boy] so deeply that she sank into a neurasthenic state... Sert and I took her to Venice the following summer...' The resort was fashionable among the European ultra-rich, many of whom had snapped up decaying palaces on the Grand Canal, which they restored to sumptuous grandeur, each with its own flotilla of gondolas and costumed gondoliers. Misia and Sert threw a lavish party to introduce her. 'I invited Princess de Poix, Count and Countess Volpi, the Prince of Greece, in short, the smartest people I could find. Thanks to her unaffected charm she had a great success, and after that Italian season it was out of the question, once back in Paris, that anyone would dream of not inviting her!'

In Venice she rose to the challenge and delivered a performance. With Misia's help and the occasional sniff of coke she recovered the will to live. On return to Paris, her first act was to have her long hair sheared off. She had a 'bob' – among the first to sport the signature cut of the new era.

'A woman who cuts her hair is about to change her life,' Coco remarks. Through the Serts, she gained entry to the *gratin*, that old-style French aristocracy, still presiding over the grandest salons. She didn't give a fig for the rules obtaining in these decorous snake pits and in no way adapted her caustic manner to conform. 'I don't care what you think about me. I don't think about you at all.'

She had glimpsed the *gratin* at Royallieu, though she was sent to eat in the kitchen when they came to dine. Now she was no longer a below-stairs novice but a star, and rejoiced in the role: 'How many cares one loses when one decides not to do something but to be someone.'

Coco had become a personality, and she was rich. She already owned a property in Biarritz, now she gave up the house in St Cloud to buy a villa in the Parisian suburb of Garches, which she decorated in the Art Deco style.

Misia says, 'For the wealthy woman she imposed an expensive simplicity…and made millions doing it.' She invented chic – 'A woman can be overdressed but never over elegant' – and it was she who created the 'flapper'. A flapper wore a skirt with a hemline nine inches from the ground (it would rise to the knee) and a dropped waistline (so concealing of the larger derrière), though the ideal flapper was unencumbered by bottom and breasts. Not all approved. 'Women no longer exist,' a critic complained, 'all that's left are boys created by Chanel.'

She introduced not just a look but a tone. Moving among the *gens bien*, she loved to shock, to unsettle their complacency. She was intolerant of bores. Her brittle manner and snappy delivery soon was evident in other women's speech, and spread to become a marker of the Twenties. When movie comedies gained sound in mid-decade this was how its sassy bob-haired heroines spoke. By then the manner had gained a name, 'to crack wise'.

★　★　★

Coco was a distinctive figure in the overlapping circles of the beau monde and avant-garde. Trendsetter to the daughters of the former, she now became a patron of the latter – and a rival to Misia in the role.

Among the émigrés who had fled the Russian Revolution to Paris – many with only what they could carry – was Sergei Diaghilev with the entire ensemble of the Ballets Russes. All were penniless, though famous from their pre-war triumph in the capital. They subsisted in penury except for the obese Diaghilev (forty-eight) – his plump fingers embedded with jewelled rings and tie pinned by a giant black pearl – who, despite massive debts, put up at the Hotel Castiglione, a stone's throw from the Ritz, where he lived expansively on room service charged to a mounting bill the hotel knew to be uncollectible if they evicted him. He had announced the imminent opening of *The Rite of Spring*, with music by Stravinsky and sets by Picasso. On learning that he had appealed to both Nancy Cunard and the American-born Princess de Polignac, explaining that without an immediate $5,000 the curtain could not go up that night, Coco called on him at his hotel. She knew the Princess had coughed up 75,000 francs but explained, 'She's a grand American lady, I'm only a French seamstress. Here's 200,000 francs.'

In an equally munificent gesture, on hearing that Stravinsky (another Russian refugee) was homeless, she offered him her house in Garches. It was fully staffed and he, wife and two children moved in to live for free. Meanwhile she started an affair with the composer, who was ardent though ill at ease due to his wife's presence in the house – which troubled Coco not at all.

The first birth control clinic had opened in Brooklyn in 1916, the Dutch cap came on sale two years later. Among the early perceptions of the emergent flapper was that love and sex are not indivisible. Cynical and disillusioned by her experience with Boy, Coco had become the predator; *she* chose her lovers, not they. These included the poet Pierre Reverdy, Picasso ('a nasty man but he fascinated me') and others she encountered at le Boeuf sur le Toit, the in-joint of the period frequented by Max Jacob, Juan Gris, Braque, Modigliani, plus anyone who was anyone in the avant-garde. Jean Cocteau called her a rapacious 'pederast' in her attitude to sex.

In Biarritz, which she visited regularly, she ran into a crop-haired lookalike, the singer and actress Marthe Davelli, who had taken up a new diversion: sunbathing. There was as yet nothing to sunbathe *in*, so Coco designed for her a prototype bathing suit, run up at the boutique. Made of black taffeta reaching from neck to near knee, it was worn over a body stocking. Many young women followed Davelli and copied the look. Sunbathing was seen as both healthy and daring. The actress stood at the height of her career. She lived as befits a diva, flaunting a Rolls-Royce, extensive wardrobe, showy jewellery and a lover of worldwide notoriety.

Russian Grand Dukes were a dime a dozen in Paris at the time, all of them skint, but Dmitry Pavlovich was altogether special. Good-looking, rich, spoilt, he'd been banished from his homeland by the Czar only months before the Revolution, consequently retaining a small fortune in family jewellery though short on ready cash. The cause of his exile was a scandalous murder, for which – had justice been done, which was not usual in Czarist Russia – he should have been shot along with his partners in the killing. When aged twenty-one, Dmitri had fallen in love with another officer in the Guards, the cross–dressing bisexual Prince Felix Yusupov. His passion was reciprocated in full; however, their liaison was complicated by the fact that Yusupov was married to the Czar's niece. Yet the two beautiful young men shared a *folie à deux* in a belief that they were superior beings who inhabited a sphere above the commonplace. Enrolling three accomplices, they conspired to murder the Czarina's lover, the monk Rasputin, in order to save the country from revolution.

Had the murder been discreetly effected it would have been perfectly acceptable, but they spectacularly botched the job. Dmitri dangled before the goatish Rasputin the prospect of an encounter with Yusupov's young and fragrant wife. Lured to Yusupov's home, Rasputin found a party in progress. The pastries and wine were laced with enough arsenic to kill a dozen men, yet one hour later he seemed unaffected by the poison. Exasperated, Yusupov took out a revolver and shot him in the back. Rasputin fell to the floor, apparently dead. Dmitri and Yusupov then ritually castrated him, before leaving his body where it lay and moving upstairs to party.

Some while later, the celebrants returned downstairs where Yusupov checked Rasputin's pulse, finding none, then shook the body vigorously for any sign of life. The corpse opened its eyes, described as 'the green eyes of a viper'. In the moment of frozen shock that followed, Rasputin half-rose to his feet and scrambled to escape. The five chased him into the yard, shooting him twice more before beating him with a club. Bundling his body in a blanket, they dumped it in the Neva River. The police investigation was cursory. The autopsy report listed hypothermia as the cause of death, indicating that Rasputin was still alive when flung into the freezing water. It revealed that he had been shot in the head, but made no mention of poisoning or castration.

As noted earlier, Dmitry was exiled for his part in the murder and, only months later, the Romanov dynasty collapsed in the Revolution of 1917. The Czar, his wife and entire family were murdered by Bolsheviks – but by then Dmitry was already in Paris with a wardrobe of uniforms and fashionable clothes, embarked upon a career exploiting rich women who saw him as a catch.

When Marthe Davelli introduced her lover to Coco in Biarritz she told her, 'If you're interested you can have him, he really is a little expensive for me.'

Why do fabulous women go for bastards?* So many are drawn to scoundrels who cheat them, steal their money, even beat them up. Knowing the reputation of those they take up, why do they deliberately choose such shits?

Because they can afford to is probably the short answer. In Coco's case it was possibly to cock a snook at the respectable and dull, to startle 'society'. Dmitry – alcoholic, a drug user, bisexual gigolo and convicted murderer – was a statement accessory.

Coco's affair with him coincided with her 'Slavic Period'. Her new lover prompted a collection of authentic Russian clothes, adapted to female elegance rather than display. An ethnic workforce lay to hand. Grand Dukes worked as doormen at the best hotels, Paris taxis were driven by Russian noblemen. Now their wives and daughters were recruited by Dmitry from their shabby lodgings. Raised at home in homely skills, these women were expert in needlework, embroidery, beadwork, and not unfamiliar with furs. The younger, slimmer,

---

* The question is explored at book length in *The Irresistible Mr Wrong* (Robson Press, 2012) by your current author Jeremy Scott.

prettier of them served in a dual role as models – a novel concept. Clothes had always been displayed on store dummies, but Coco launched her collections as catwalk shows to such acclaim that society debutantes were soon competing to join the cast. Coco's Slavic line proved a must for winter, and she could afford to be generous with Dmitry for his inspiration. He was more used to receiving than bestowing gifts, but he did present Coco with jewellery he'd inherited from his mother. This included a collection of pearl necklaces that Coco restrung into a single rope, yards in length, which she wore in long loops around her neck, some reaching to the waist, creating a style soon imitated widely. Other pieces of ancestral jewellery she broke up to reset their gems along with coloured glass in wide bracelets. The trashy/precious look perfectly reflected the ambivalent values of the age.

While he lasted, Dmitry – wilful, faithless and undependable – suited Coco rather well. She was repelled by possessiveness and jealousy in a man. He represented notable arm-candy and, when he felt like it, stimulating company, for he was imaginatively alert to the zeitgeist as herself. Quite possibly it was he, not she, who came up with the concept that would generate her enormous fortune and secure her heritage.

Among the Russian émigrés he introduced to Coco was Ernest Beaux – son of the parfumier to the Czar – who was now running a laboratory in Grasse, home of the scent industry. She asked him to create a new perfume for her, which must *not* smell of flowers or herbs as all others did. Something unique.

Through mixing natural with chemical ingredients including benzyl acetate, extracted from coal tar – which contributed its own essence as well as 'fixing' the scent so it did not fade – he came up with several samples. The one eventually chosen by Coco she took to Théophile Bader, owner of the thriving chain of department stores Galeries Lafayette, who guaranteed her a large bulk order. He put her in touch with the Jewish Wertheimer brothers, owners of Parfumeries Bourjois, the largest manufacturer of its kind in France, who provided the necessary funding, production and distribution. They retained 70 per cent of the new company, Bader was given 20 per cent, Coco got 10 per cent for fronting the brand. She was president and publicist, at which she was expert. 'A woman who doesn't wear perfume has no future,' she announced. When asked by a young flapper where she should wear the scent, she told her, 'Wherever one wants to be kissed.'

She named the scent simply Chanel No. 5, her lucky number. And she created its crystal bottle in the then-revolutionary design in which it is still prized today. Misia

Sert, who had insisted in meddling in every stage of the enterprise, reports, 'The success was unlike anything we could have imagined. It was like a winning lottery ticket.'

With the rapid triumph of Chanel No. 5 Coco upped her style of living by acquiring a large apartment in rue du Faubourg Saint-Honoré, and dispensed with Dmitry, passing him on to Audrey Ewing, an American paint heiress who married him, shipping him home to Cleveland, where his opportunities for transgression were limited, and he settled down with the ready adaptability of his class as a Republican donor and prized member of the country club.

As Coco noted, 'There are people who have money and people who are rich.'

Prime example of the rich was the Duke of Westminster, 'Bendor'. He was named after a horse, his grandfather's Derby winner. Devoted to hunting, shooting and fishing, he remained close to both horses and dogs throughout his life. His wealth was incalculable. He owned much of Mayfair, most of Belgravia, most of Pimlico. His town residence was Grosvenor House in Park Lane, his country seat Eaton Hall in Cheshire. He possessed hunting lodges in Scotland, Norway, France, Austria and the Balkans, all fully staffed and awaiting his unannounced arrival together with a dozen guests at any moment.

Bendor was coming up to fifty, tiring of his second wife – there would be a further two Duchesses – and still without a male heir when he spotted Coco in Monte Carlo. He bribed a friend of hers to introduce them. The next night she dined aboard his four-masted sailing yacht, the *Flying Cloud,* with a crew of forty, moored opposite the casino. He had hired a gypsy band to play for his guests while they ate formally on deck. The costumed musicians did so exuberantly, conversation proved difficult and a crowd of spectators gathered on the quay above them to commentate loudly on the show, sometimes to applaud.

Did Coco find the scene corny? Even comic? Perhaps, but she tells Morand 'unlimited wealth is not vulgar. That kind of affluence is beyond envy.' She calls it 'a catastrophe. It had turned Westminster into the last product of a disappearing civilisation, a paleontological curiosity.' She regarded him as a fossil. In her eyes wealth – as opposed to money – was no longer fashionable. It was said of her clothes that 'they made rich women look poor'. Poor was the new chic.

Bendor had never been turned down because he was retro and too rich. He pursued her for months. With invitations, letters, flowers, with dead salmon, grouse and pheasants he'd killed and dedicated to her. His messengers delivered exotic blooms and unseasonable fruit from his garden hothouse, and on one occasion a large crate of fresh vegetables with an uncut emerald nestling at the bottom in the straw.

Coco was unmoved. She was busy, working on a ballet… on an ad campaign…in Hollywood designing wardrobe for a movie…she had a collection to bring out. She was rarely available. 'When I had to choose between the man…and dresses,' she told her friend Lady Abdy, 'I always chose the dresses. I have always been stronger than my desires.'

Yet this was the man she would remain 'with' for a decade. 'I loved him or I thought I loved him, which amounts to the same thing.' A couple of years after their encounter, Winston Churchill wrote to his wife from Mimizan, Bendor's estate in France, where he was hunting boar, 'The famous Coco turned up and I took a great fancy to her – a most capable and agreeable woman – much the strongest personality Benny has yet been up against. She hunted vigorously all day, motored to Paris after dinner, and is today engaged in…improving dresses on endless streams of mannequins…'

There was a certain inevitability in the pairing of the richest man in England with the most famous fashionista in Europe. Coco said to Morand, 'I'm sure it was Boy who sent Westminster to me. He liked me because I was French. English women are possessive and cold. Men get bored with them.'

Intermittences punctuated their relationship, with asides for both. Hers were discreet, his less so. Though not jealous, she felt slighted by his carelessness, and if it became obvious not just to her but to others she responded with style. At a party aboard the *Flying Cloud* in Nice, Bendor had paid undue attention to a female guest. When he came back on board next morning he was carrying a jewel case, which he

presented to Coco on deck. She opened it to find a pearl
necklace. She examined it without expression, then let it
slide heedlessly between her fingers into the sea, turned her
back and strolled away.

Still, the two remained a recognised item. She visited him
regularly at Eaton Hall, which had fifty-six bedrooms,
swarmed with staff and maintained seventeen Rolls-Royces
and chauffeurs on stand-by should anyone want to go
anywhere. But Coco did not warm to English country house
life. 'The rain...everyone for ever doing needlepoint, looking
at rose gardens, changing their clothes, boiling in front of a
fire, and freezing away from it.'

Nor were her attempts to introduce Bendor to her artistic
circle in Paris any more successful. He attended rehearsals
for Cocteau's ballet *Le Train Bleu*; she'd designed the costumes
and Picasso the sets. He sat bemused. At parties he appeared
bewildered by the tribe of seditionaries, foreigners, show-offs,
drug addicts, Jews and homosexuals he encountered. 'My
friends bored him,' Coco told Morand. 'He couldn't understand them at all. He was appalled by Sert, who sawed off
swans' beaks so they would die of hunger, and who pushed
dogs into the Grand Canal in Venice' in his notion of surre-
alist fun.

Bendor made efforts to fit in. He witnessed Misia,
Winnaretta Polignac and Coco sponsoring ballets and exhibitions, and blundered toward literary patronage himself,
suggesting to Cocteau that if he found himself a bit short
on cash he might like to write a group biography of his
(Bendor's) numerous dogs.

In 1930 he married his third Duchess, Loelia, daughter
of Sir Frederick Ponsonby, Treasurer to the King. Seeking
an heir, he chose blue blood to breed from. For Coco it
was a repeat of her experience with Boy Capel. Was she

humiliated, jealous? No, she had already turned down
Bendor's proposal of marriage only months before, 'Because
of my work, I suppose. The two men I loved never understood that. They…didn't understand that a woman, even a
rich woman, might want to work. I could never have given
up the House of Chanel. It was my child.' She said to
Westminster, 'Why should we marry? We're together…people
accept it. I never wanted to weigh more heavily upon a man
than a bird.'

The Wall Street Crash and Great Depression hit hard on the
fashion business, though on Chanel less so than others. Her
'Poor Look' in plain cotton was in tune with the times. The
Depression she largely escaped by working in Hollywood
for Sam Goldwyn, but she was back in Paris at the start of
the Second World War.

Masses fled the city before the German army's advance,
jamming all roads south. Not Coco; she closed up her business and moved into the Ritz. When they occupied the city,
so did the German High Command, who had already made
reservations at its best hotel.

Coco viewed the war with disdain. Living off morphine
and room service, she considered it as a rude interruption
to civilised life and chose to ignore it. Neither did the war
greatly inconvenience her circle in the arts. The Occupation
prompted a theatrical revival in the city that saw 400 new
productions, including plays by Camus, Sartre, Jean Anouilh
and Cocteau. The German officer class proved greedy for
culture and entertainment. French cinema – largely funded
from Berlin through the Thirties – also thrived. Now
Germany was winning the war and *les Boches* looked to be
here for ever. The City of Lights welcomed and assimilated

these new consumers; Parisians are the most pragmatic tribe on earth.

Coco took a lover for the duration of the hostilities. Baron Hans Günther von Dincklage (forty-four) was charming, educated, fluent in French and English and an officer in Military Intelligence. The liaison gained her a powerful protector and a car with driver and petrol coupons, while guaranteeing her suite in the Ritz, the plushy home-from-home of the Nazi Reich.

When Paris was liberated by the Allies, Coco was arrested by the Forces Françaises de l'intérieur, the revenge squad. She faced punishment and, worse, humiliation. Women who had slept with the enemy were tortured or shot, hundreds were shaved bareheaded, stripped, fed paraffin oil and paraded in column through the streets before a baying mob of spectators. To escape such a fate, Coco contacted Winston Churchill, who had a word with General de Gaulle, who fixed things. She went to join her lover Dincklage in Switzerland, where revenue from Chanel No. 5 provided a comfortable exile for the following ten years.

She was rich, famous, secure, but... In time she found life dull. The expat company available comprised the rich and mostly old. Propriety and complacency set the tone of their entertaining, which was restricted to people of their own sort. Dincklage was a dependable escort but enforced leisure had turned him into part of the furniture; his spark had gone. Coco's own retirement from the fray weighed increasingly upon her spirits. Without work her life had no point.

After a facelift she made a comeback in 1954, when the Wertheimer brothers bought her fashion business outright together with her several properties, while guaranteeing

tenure until she had no more need of earthly residence. A
win–win deal for all.

Her first show received considerable publicity. The press
pounced – but only to applaud. *Vogue* lauded the collection
for displaying 'an uncanny timeless Chanel personality' and
Life reported, 'She is already influencing everything. At
seventy-one Gabrielle Chanel is creating more than a fashion:
a revolution.' But it was in America that her couture enjoyed
its greatest success, for the designs were soon copied by
department stores. Pirated – not that Coco minded, she took
it as a compliment. The editor of *Women's Wear Daily* named
her 'the Eighth Wonder of the World…the greatest designer
in history…whose name was a household word throughout
the world'.

On 22 November 1963 another two shots rang around the
globe. Fired in Dallas, Texas, their target was President Jack
Kennedy, riding in the back of an open limo with his wife
Jackie; he died cradled in her arms. Less than two hours
later, and still dressed in the same clothes, she was on board
Air Force One as Lyndon Johnson took the oath of office as
President. Mrs Johnson described her, 'hair falling in her face
but very composed…Mrs Kennedy's dress was stained with
blood. One leg was almost entirely covered with it and her
right glove…her husband's blood. Somehow that was one
of the most poignant sights – that immaculate woman,
exquisitely dressed and caked in blood.'

The little pink suit by Chanel that Jackie was wearing
has never been cleaned. The icon remains venerated in its
niche in the National Archives in Washington: the Brand
anointed by the Presidential blood.

On the day of her own death on 9 January 1971, Coco sat in her suite in the Ritz working on her summer collection, although it was a Sunday, her least favourite day. Around eight that evening, she lay down on her bed fully dressed. Her maid Céline heard her cry out. Coco said she couldn't breathe, asking her to open the windows wide. She was struggling to give herself an injection, but couldn't snap the phial of morphine. Céline took it from her fingers, loaded the syringe and passed it back. Grasping it, Coco smacked the needle through her skirt into her right thigh.

'You see,' she said to her maid, 'This is how one dies.'

9

THE SCENT OF A WOMAN

When Coco refused Bendor's – rather delayed – proposal of marriage, she turned him down with a legendary response, 'Everyone marries the Duke of Westminster. There are a lot of duchesses but only one Coco Chanel.' Bendor's friend Winston Churchill earlier had spoken of him as 'extremely happy to be mated to an equal – her ability matches his power'. He describes her as 'a really great and strong being, fit to rule a man or an Empire'.

She did run an empire of course, and one that endures successfully to this day. At the dawn of our modern era, Coco created the 'look' of a New Woman – ascribing to that figure her own attitudes on life. She gave shape to a brand. It is made up of independence, courage, chutzpah, style and wit. Plus Factor X: Charisma. Trace elements of these qualities are to be found in all the women in this book.

Victoria Woodhull didn't make it to become President of the United States. But had she done so, she and her irrepressible sister Tennie would surely have trumped Trump in the joyous spectacle of their governance. Mary Wollstonecraft – who abhorred flamboyance, and would have felt uncomfortable during even one hour passed in the rowdy Woodhull household – sought no political role, yet what she accomplished was historic. She wrote the gospel for her gender. She articulated what before had been an inchoate female consciousness, and issued the first women's manifesto…whose demands have yet to be fully satisfied.

Some have, however, though none without struggle. Among them, an ordained ministry in the Church. Prior to Aimee McPherson, God was exclusively men's business. Then, emerging from nowhere, she stepped up onto a chair in Main Street America to say, 'Follow me…' and they did in their thousands to form a worldwide church. Along with the spirit that made that possible, she displayed a preternatural foresight: in the creation of the modern world in the 1920s she understood new media before media understood itself; she set the pace.

Through her deeds Aimee achieved sainthood in her own lifetime, as did Edwina Mountbatten. In her case secular. Before her epiphany during the Blitz, her existence had been wholly selfish. Afterward, her efforts saved or succoured the lives of millions of men, women and children. She devoted herself to caring for the most undesirable people on earth, homeless refugees. In her boldness and quasi-royal authority, it is even possible she believed the problem soluble.

But how did the appalling Margaret Argyll achieve a place in English history? Because she was what she was at a seminal moment. Indeed her notorious trial flagged that moment, cued its nativity and set its tone: the Sixties. The bonfire of traditions. Deference and respect for individuals – and all institutions excepting jurisprudence and medicine – was torched by exposure and ridicule. To be replaced by cynicism beyond scepticism, the obtaining climate of today.

And Coco? Let her give voice to the dominant brand. She was ever smart and scripted her own copy:

The most courageous act is still to think for yourself.
Aloud…there is not time for cut-and-dried monotony.
There is time for work and time for love. That leaves
no other time.

As long as you know men are like children, you
know everything… I don't know why women want
any of the things men have when one of the things
women have is men… Passion goes, boredom
remains… Sin can be forgiven, but stupid is forever.
Fashion changes but style endures… A girl should
be two things: who and what she wants… You can
be gorgeous at thirty, charming at forty, and irresistible for the rest of your life.

Alone among these controversial heroines Coco left a tangible
heritage, a scent. Not every woman wants to smell like a
summer meadow or a hillside in Provence – or not *always*.
There is more to full being than fragrant wholesomeness.
Coco chose a dash of coal tar to vivify the potion that is
Chanel No. 5. Many have tried to describe the perfume,
which remains indefinable. Coco called it simply, 'the scent
of a woman'.

NOTES ON SOURCES

MRS SATAN: PRESIDENTIAL CANDIDATE and MONOGAMY IS UNACCEPTABLE BEHAVIOUR

Brooks, Van Wyck *New England, Indian Summer* (New York: E.P. Dutton, 1940).

Broon, Heywood and Leech, Margaret, *Roundsman of the Lord* (New York: A. C. Boni, 1927).

Hibben, Paxton, *Henry Ward Beecher: An American Portrait* (New York: George Doran & Co., 1927).

Irving, Wallace, *The Square Pegs* (New York: Knopf, 1957).

Irving, Wallace, *The Nympho and Other Maniacs* (New York: Simon & Schuster, 1971).

Johnston, Johanna, *Mrs Satan: The Incredible Saga of Victoria C. Woodhull* (New York: Macmillan, 1967).

Sachs, Emanie, *The Terrible Siren: Victoria Woodhull* (New York: Harper, 1928).

Stowe, Harriet Beecher, *My Wife and I* (New York: Ford & Co., 1872).

Tilton, Theodore, *Tempest Tossed* (New York: Sheldon & Co., 1874).

Tilton, Theodore, *Victoria Woodhull: A Biographical Sketch* (New Delhi: Isha Books, 2013).

Whitton, Mary Ormiston, *These Were the Women* (New York: Hastings House, 1954).

LIBERTY, EQUALITY, AND... *WHAT*?

I am most indebted to Lucy Moore for her account of the Women's March on Versailles in her book *Liberty* (London: Harper Press, 2006). Also:

Cameron, Kenneth N. (ed.), *Shelley and His Circle, 1773–1822* (Cambridge, Mass: Harvard University Press, 1970).

Flexner, Eleanor *Mary Wollstonecraft: A Biography* (New York: Coward, McCann & Geoghegan, 1972).

Godechot, Jacques, *The Taking of the Bastille, July 14th 1789* (London: Faber, 1970).

Holmes, Richard (ed) *Godwin on Wollstonecraft: Memoirs of the Author of 'The Rights of Woman'* (New York: Harper Perennial, 2005).

Knowles, John, *Life and Writings of Henry Fuseli* (London: Henry Colburn and Richard Bentley, 1831).

Levy, Darline Gay, Applewhite, Harriet and Johnson, Mary Durham (eds), *Women in Revolutionary Paris 1789–1795* (Chicago: University of Illinois Press, 1979).

Linford, Madeline, *Mary Wollstonecraft* (London: Leonard Parsons, 1924).

Rousseau, Jean-Jacques, *The Confessions* (Paris: François Grasset, 1793).

Schama, Simon, *Citizens: A Chronicle of The French Revolution* (London: Penguin, 1989).

Wollstonecraft, Mary, *Thoughts on the Education of Daughters* (London: Joseph Johnson, 1787).

Wollstonecraft, Mary, *A Vindication of the Rights of Women* (London: Joseph Johnson, 1792).

Wollstonecraft, Mary, *Letters Written During a Short Residence in Sweden, Norfolk and Denmark* (London: Johnson, 1796).

Wollstonecraft, Mary, *Letters to Imlay* (London: Kegan Paul, 1879).

HOLY-ROLLING IN CARMEL LOVE NEST

Adamic, Louis, Campbell, Edward, Schindler, Mike and Mason, Robert B., *The Truth about Aimee Semple McPherson* (Girard, Kans.: Haldeman-Julius, 1927).

Blumhofer, Edith, *Aimee Semple McPherson: Everybody's Sister* (Michigan: William B. Eerdmans Publishing, 1993).

Epstein, Daniel Mark, *Sister Aimee: The Life of Aimee Semple McPherson* (New York: Harcourt Brace & Co, 1993).

McPherson, Aimee Semple, *This is That* (Los Angeles: Bridal Call Publishing, 1919).

McPherson, Aimee Semple, *Aimee: Life Story of Aimee Semple McPherson* (Los Angeles: Foursquare Publications, 1979).

McPherson, Aimee Semple, *In the Service of the King* (Los Angeles: Foursquare Publications, 1988).

McPherson, Aimee Semple, *The Personal Testimony of Aimee Semple McPherson* (Los Angeles: Foursquare Publications, 1998).

McWilliams, Carey, *Southern California: An Island in the Land* (Salt Lake City: Gibbs Smith, 1946).

Rudd, Douglas H., *Aimee Semple McPherson* (Ontario: Essence, 2006).

Sutton, Matthew Avery, *Aimee Semple McPherson: Resurrection of Christian America* (Cambridge, Mass. Harvard University Press, 2007).

'SOCIETY SHAKEN BY TERRIBLE SCANDAL'

Breese, Charlotte, *Hutch* (London: Bloomsbury, 1999).

Cooper, Diana, *The Light of Common Day* (London: Rupert Hart-Davis, 1959).

Cooper, Duff, *Old Men Forget* (London: Rupert Hart-Davis, 1953).

Hough, Richard, *Mountbatten: Hero of Our Time* (London: Weidenfeld & Nicolson, 1980).

Hough, Richard, *Edwina, Countess Mountbatten of Burma* (New York: William Morrow & Co., 1984).

Holman, Dennis, *Lady Louis: Life of the Countess Mountbatten of Burma* (London: Odhams Press, 1952).

Masson, Madeleine, *Edwina* (London: White Lion Publishing, 1975).

Morgan, Janet, *Edwina Mountbatten: A Life of her Own* (London: Fontana, 1992).

Murphy, Ray, *The Last Viceroy* (London: Jarrolds, 1948).

Ziegler, Phillip, *Mountbatten: The Official Biography* (London: Orion, 2001).

THE MESSALINA COMPLEX

de Beauvoir, Simone, *The Second Sex* (London: Vintage, 1997).

Graves, Robert, *The Twelve Caesars* (London: Penguin, 1957).

Groneman, Carol, *Nymphomania: A History* (London: W. W. Norton, 2001).

Holland, Jack, *Misogyny: The World's Oldest Prejudice* (London: Robinson, 2006).

'I AM NEWS JUST BECAUSE IT'S ME'

Argyll, Margaret, *Forget Not* (London: W. H. Allen, 1975).

Castle, Charles, *The Duchess Who Dared* (London: Sidgwick & Jackson, 1994).

Furnasse, J.C., *Stormy Weather: Crosslights on the Nineteen Thirties* (New York: Putnam, 1977).

Horst, *Salute to the Thirties* (New York: Viking Press, 1971).

Leighton, Isabelle (ed.), *The Aspirin Age: 1919–1941* (New York: Simon & Schuster, 1949).

Maxwell, Elsa, *I Married the World* (London: Heinemann, 1955).
Maxwell, Elsa, *Celebrity Circus* (London: W. H. Allen, 1964).

THE BRAND BECOMES HER

Baillen, Claude, *Chanel Solitaire* (Paris: Gallimard, 1971).
de Castellane, Boni, *L'Art d'Etre Pauvre* (Paris: Crès, 1925).
Cosgrave, Bronwyn, *Vogue on Coco Chanel* (London: Quadrille Publishing, 2012).
Crowder, Henry, *As Wonderful as All That?* (California: Wild Free Press, 1987).
Edmonde, Charles-Roux, *Chanel* (London: Jonathan Cape, 1976).
Field, Leslie, *Bendor, The Golden Duke of Westminster* (London: Weidenfeld & Nicolson, 1983).
Gide, André, *Journal* (Paris: Gallimard, 1948).
Gold, Arthur and Fizdale, Robert, *Misia: The Life of Misia Sert* (New York: Knopf, 1980).
Hugo, Jean, *Avant d'Oublier* (Paris: Fayard, 1976).
Kessler, Count Harry, *The Diaries of a Cosmopolitan* (London: Weidenfeld & Nicolson, 1971).
Madsen, Axel, *Coco Chanel: A Biography* (London: Bloomsbury, 1990).
Picardie, Justine, *Coco Chanel: The Legend and the Life* (London: Harper Collins, 2010).
Sert, Misia, *Misia par Misia* (Paris: Gallimard, 1952).
Steegmuller, Francis, *Cocteau: A Biography* (New York: Little, Brown, 1970).
Vaughan, Hal, *Sleeping with the Enemy: Coco Chanel's Secret War* (London: Chatto, 2011).

ACKNOWLEDGEMENTS

I'd like to thank Sam Carter, the best of editors, who has published my last four titles. Also Jonathan Bentley-Smith, Georgia Summers and Jacqui Lewis, who contributed much to this book.

INDEX

ABOUT THE AUTHOR

Jeremy Scott became a full-time writer following a colourful career in advertising, as described in his acclaimed memoir *Fast and Louche*. He is the author of *Dancing on Ice, Show Me a Hero, The Irresistible Mr Wrong* and *Coke: The Biography*. He lives in Chelsea, London.